S0-BRO-825

Seeing Spots

Recent Titles in the Praeger Series in Political Communication
Robert E. Denton, Jr., *General Editor*

Communication Consultants in Political Campaigns: Ballot Box Warriors
Robert V. Friedenberg

Manipulation of the American Voter: Political Campaign Commercials
Karen S. Johnson-Cartee and Gary A. Copeland

Presidential Crisis Rhetoric and the Press in the Post–Cold War World
Jim A. Kuypers

The 1996 Presidential Campaign: A Communication Perspective
Robert E. Denton, Jr., editor

Reconciling Free Trade, Fair Trade, and Interdependence: The Rhetoric of
Presidential Economic Leadership
Delia B. Conti

Politics and Politicians in American Film
Phillip L. Gianos

Electronic Whistle-Stops: The Impact of the Internet on American Politics
Gary W. Selnow

Newspapers of Record in a Digital Age: From Hot Type to Hot Link
Shannon E. Martin and Kathleen A. Hansen

Campaign '96: A Functional Analysis of Acclaiming, Attacking, and Defending
William L. Benoit, Joseph R. Blaney, and P. M. Pier

Political Communication in America, Third Edition
Robert E. Denton, Jr., editor

Reelpolitik: Political Ideologies in '30s and '40s Films
*Beverly Merrill Kelley, with John J. Pitney, Jr., Craig R. Smith, and
Herbert E. Gooch III*

World Opinion and the Emerging International Order
*Frank Louis Rusciano, with Roberta Fiske-Rusciano, Bosah Ebo, Sigfredo Hernandez,
and John Crothers Pollock*

Seeing Spots

A Functional Analysis of Presidential Television Advertisements, 1952–1996

William L. Benoit

Praeger Series in Political Communication

PRAEGER

Westport, Connecticut
London

Library of Congress Cataloging-in-Publication Data

Benoit, William L.
  Seeing spots : a functional analysis of presidential television
advertisements, 1952–1996 / William L. Benoit.
    p. cm.—(Praeger series in political communication, ISSN
1062–5623)
  Includes bibliographical references.
  ISBN 0–275–96645–3 (alk. paper)
    1. Presidents—United States—Election.   2. Advertising,
Political—United States.   3. Television in politics—United States.
I. Title.   II. Series.
JK524.B46   1999
324.7'3'097309045—dc21   98–56624

British Library Cataloguing in Publication Data is available.

Copyright © 1999 by William L. Benoit

All rights reserved. No portion of this book may be
reproduced, by any process or technique, without the
express written consent of the publisher.

Library of Congress Catalog Card Number: 98–56624
ISBN: 0–275–96645–3
ISSN: 1062–5623

First published in 1999

Praeger Publishers, 88 Post Road West, Westport, CT 06881
An imprint of Greenwood Publishing Group, Inc.
www.praeger.com

Printed in the United States of America

The paper used in this book complies with the
Permanent Paper Standard issued by the National
Information Standards Organization (Z39.48–1984).

10 9 8 7 6 5 4 3 2 1

Contents

Series Foreword

Those of us from the discipline of communication studies have long believed that communication is prior to all other fields of inquiry. In several
other forums I have argued that the essence of politics is "talk" or human
interaction.[1] Such interaction may be formal or informal, verbal or non-
verbal, public or private, but it is always persuasive, forcing us con-
sciously or subconsciously to interpret, to evaluate, and to act.
Communication is the vehicle for human action.

From this perspective, it is not surprising that Aristotle recognized the
natural kinship of politics and communication in his writings *Politics* and
Rhetoric. In the former, he established that humans are "political beings
[who] alone of the animals [are] furnished with the faculty of language."[2]
In the latter, he began his systematic analysis of discourse by proclaiming
that "rhetorical study, in its strict sense, is concerned with the modes of
persuasion."[3] Thus, it was recognized over twenty-three hundred years
ago that politics and communication go hand in hand because they are
essential parts of human nature.

In 1981, Dan Nimmo and Keith Sanders proclaimed that political communication was an emerging field.[4] Although its origin, as noted, dates
back centuries, a "self-consciously cross-disciplinary" focus began in the
late 1950s. Thousands of books and articles later, colleges and universi-
ties offer a variety of graduate and undergraduate coursework in the
area in such diverse departments as communication, mass communication, journalism, political science, and sociology.[5] In Nimmo and Sanders's early assessment, the "key areas of inquiry" included rhetorical
analysis, propaganda analysis, attitude change studies, voting studies,
government and the news media, functional and systems analyses, tech-

nological changes, media technologies, campaign techniques, and re-search techniques.[6] In a survey of the state of the field in 1983, the same authors and Lynda Kaid found additional, more specific areas of con-cerns such as the presidency, political polls, public opinion, debates, and advertising.[7] Since the first study, they have also noted a shift away from the rather strict behavioral approach.

A decade later, Dan Nimmo and David Swanson argued that "political communication has developed some identity as a more or less distinct domain of scholarly work."[8] The scope and concerns of the area have further expanded to include critical theories and cultural studies. Al-though there is no precise definition, method, or disciplinary home of the area of inquiry, its primary domain comprises the role, processes, and effects of communication within the context of politics broadly de-fined.

In 1985, the editors of *Political Communication Yearbook: 1984* noted that "more things are happening in the study, teaching, and practice of po-litical communication than can be captured within the space limitations of the relatively few publications available."[9] In addition, they argued that the backgrounds of "those involved in the field [are] so varied and pluralist in outlook and approach, . . . it [is] a mistake to adhere slavishly to any set format in shaping the content."[10] More recently, Swanson and Nimmo have called for "ways of overcoming the unhappy consequences of fragmentation within a framework that respects, encourages, and ben-efits from diverse scholarly commitments, agendas, and approaches."[11]

In agreement with these assessments of the area and with gentle en-couragement, in 1988 Praeger established the series entitled "Praeger Se-ries in Political Communication." The series is open to all qualitative and quantitative methodologies as well as contemporary and historical stud-ies. The key to characterizing the studies in the series is the focus on communication variables or activities within a political context or di-mension. As of this writing, over 70 volumes have been published and numerous impressive works are forthcoming. Scholars from the disci-plines of communication, history, journalism, political science, and so-ciology have participated in the series.

I am, without shame or modesty, a fan of the series. The joy of serving as its editor is in participating in the dialogue of the field of political communication and in reading the contributors' works. I invite you to join me.

Robert E. Denton, Jr.

NOTES

1. See Robert E. Denton, Jr., *The Symbolic Dimensions of the American Presidency* (Prospect Heights, IL: Waveland Press, 1982); Robert E. Denton, Jr., and Gary

Woodward, *Political Communication in America* (New York: Praeger, 1985; 2d ed., 1990); Robert E. Denton, Jr., and Dan Hahn, *Presidential Communication* (New York: Praeger, 1986); and Robert E. Denton, Jr., *The Primetime Presidency of Ronald Reagan* (New York: Praeger, 1988).

2. Aristotle, *The Politics of Aristotle*, trans. Ernest Barker (New York: Oxford University Press, 1970), p. 5.

3. Aristotle, *Rhetoric*, trans. W. Rhys Roberts (New York: The Modern Library, 1954), p. 22.

4. Dan D. Nimmo and Keith R. Sanders, "Introduction: The Emergence of Political Communication as a Field," in *Handbook of Political Communication*, ed. Dan D. Nimmo and Keith R. Sanders (Beverly Hills, CA: Sage, 1981), pp. 11–36.

5. Ibid., p. 15.

6. Ibid., pp. 17–27.

7. Keith Sanders, Lynda Kaid, and Dan Nimmo, eds., *Political Communication Yearbook: 1984* (Carbondale: Southern Illinois University, 1985), pp. 283–308.

8. Dan Nimmo and David Swanson, "The Field of Political Communication: Beyond the Voter Persuasion Paradigm," in *New Directions in Political Communication*, ed. David Swanson and Dan Nimmo (Beverly Hills, CA: Sage, 1990), p. 8.

9. Sanders, Kaid, and Nimmo, *Political Communication Yearbook: 1984*, p. xiv.

10. Ibid.

11. Nimmo and Swanson, "The Field of Political Communication," p. 11.

Preface

This book is a continuation of a research program that began when Bill Wells asked me to direct a research practicum (all Ph.D. students in the Department of Communication at the University of Missouri are required to conduct research with a faculty mentor) on the 1992 presidential debates. That project extended my past work on persuasive defense (image repair) (Benoit, 1995a) by investigating persuasive attack and defense in those debates (Benoit & Wells, 1996). Subsequently, Joe Blaney, Penni Pier, and Bill Wells worked with me to extend this approach to include acclaiming (self-praise, a concept developed by P. J. Benoit, 1997) along with attacking and defending. We analyzed nominating convention acceptance addresses from 1960 to 1996 (Benoit, Wells, Pier, & Blaney, in press), keynote speeches from 1960 to 1996 (Benoit, Blaney & Pier, 1996), television spots from 1980 to 1996 (Benoit, Pier, & Blaney, 1997), and the 1996 presidential campaign (Benoit, Blaney, & Pier, 1998). I also analyzed the 1960 presidential debates with Allison Harthcock (Benoit & Harthcock, 1998). Bill Wells' dissertation is extending our work on presidential debates by analyzing acclaims, attacks, and defenses in the 1976, 1980, and 1984 debates (in progress). I wanted to extend our initial study of presidential television spots (Benoit, Pier, & Blaney, 1997) in four ways, and that is the subject of this study.

First, I wanted to go back to the very beginning, studying every presidential campaign that used television spots. Other research (e.g., Kaid & Johnston, 1991; West, 1997) used samples that were limited (as I discuss in detail in the Appendix). Second, I wanted to include both primary and general spots in the same study. When one of the major party candidates is weak (e.g., presidents Ford in 1976, Carter in 1980, or Bush in

1992), the outcome of the primary contest may essentially determine who will become president. Third, I wanted to include some spots by third-party candidates. Although these candidates are occasionally mentioned in reviews of a given election campaign, there seems to be no study that focuses on third-party television spots. Finally, I wanted to increase the number of spots in our study of advertisements from 1980 to 1996. This book, therefore, is designed to investigate the use of acclaiming, attacking, and defending in presidential television spots from 1952 to 1996.

I would like to express my appreciation to the Central States Communication Association for the Federation Prize, which enabled me to purchase videotapes of hundreds of the spots I analyzed. The Loren Reid Fund, the Department of Communication, and the College of Arts and Science also helped purchase videotapes of spots. I also appreciate receipt of a University of Missouri Big Twelve Fellowship, which allowed me to spend two weeks at the University of Oklahoma Political Communication Archive, where I transcribed hundreds of additional spots. I want to thank Lynda Lee Kaid, Charles E. Rand, and Marie Mathos, at the Archive, for assistance and access to those spots. The George Bush Presidential Library sent me videotapes of Bush's television spots without charge. Other presidential libraries sold me tapes, and many spots were obtained courtesy of the Dwight D. Eisenhower, John F. Kennedy, Lyndon Baines Johnson, Jimmy Carter, Ronald Reagan, and Gerald R. Ford presidential libraries. I also want to thank Joseph R. Blaney, who graciously coded spots for this study. Unfortunately, I cannot offer thanks to the Nixon Presidential Library, which outsources videotape duplication, making their cost far too high for my limited resources. I especially regret not having more primary spots from President Nixon for this study.

I would also like to thank the co-authors with whom I've worked on other projects: K. Kerby Anderson, Julie Berman, Joe Blaney, Susan Brinson, Anne Czerwinski, Mike D'Agostine, Bruce Dorries, Shirley Drew, Paul Gullifor, Robert Hanczor, Allison Harthcock, Diane Hirson, Kim Kennedy, Andrew Klyukowski, Jim Lindsey, Dawn Nill, Dan Panici, Penni Pier, Bill Wells, and Jim Wilkie. I would also like to thank the students in my Political Campaign Communication course (Comm 373), who listened to me work out some of these ideas in class.

Most importantly, I want to acknowledge the support of my family. Pam, my wife, developed the theory of acclaims on which I rely so heavily. My daughter, Jennifer, is a constant source of delight. I will miss her greatly when she goes to college in 1999. More importantly, Pam and Jennifer support me in tangible and intangible ways too numerous to mention.

Part I

Preliminaries

Chapter 1

Introduction:
Presidential Television Spots

This chapter provides background on presidential television advertising. First, I will argue that political spots are an important form of campaign message that we need to understand. Second, I will review past research on presidential television advertising. Finally, I will describe my purpose in conducting this research.

THE IMPORTANCE OF PRESIDENTIAL TELEVISION SPOTS

Television spots are an extremely important component of modern presidential campaigns. Several arguments support this contention. First, candidates expend huge amounts of money on producing and broadcasting television advertising. Ansolabehere and Iyengar (1995) observed that "The amounts of money spent on political advertising are staggering: Hundreds of millions of dollars are poured into what has become the main means of political communication in the United States" (p. 3). For example, Devlin (1993) reported that in 1992, Bush, Clinton, and Perot together devoted $133 million (three-quarters of their budgets) to television spots. In 1996, Dole, Clinton, and Perot lavished even more money, about $200 million, on television advertising (Devlin, 1997). The enormous amount of money candidates devote to television spots is a clear indication of the significance of this kind of political message form. It is also an indication of how many presidential television commercials are broadcast, with many advertisements being shown over and over. A vast audience is purchased with this money, and it is exposed repeatedly to these campaign messages. As Jamieson (1996) recognizes, "The spot ad is the most used and most viewed of all available forms of advertising" (p. 517).

A second reason that political advertising merits scholarly attention is the fact that voters obtain substantial amounts of information on the candidates and their policy positions from them. For example, West (1993) analyzed data from eighteen campaigns, concluding that political advertisements affected candidates' images, likability, electability, and assessment of policy positions. In fact, empirical research on both the 1972 (Patterson & McClure, 1976) and the 1984 (Kern, 1989) campaigns concluded that "by a ratio of 4 to 1, Americans received the majority of their information about candidate positions on the issues from ads rather than the news" (Kern, 1989, p. 47). This latter finding, that the electorate obtains more information about the issues in campaigns from commercials than from the news, may seem surprising. However, a closer look at the news media can explain why this is the case.

Three different factors are at work here. One reason that voters obtain more information from presidential spots than news is simply that campaign news is only one story topic among many. The nightly network news enjoys a 30-minute time slot, but after we subtract commercials and stories on non-campaign topics, relatively little time remains for campaign news. Furthermore, the number of campaign stories covered in the news decreased 20% from 1968 to 1988 (Steele & Barnhurst, 1996). Exacerbating these trends is the fact that the average length of a political news story decreased by about 20% (Hallin, 1992). Thus, the nightly news devotes precious little time to providing coverage of presidential campaigns.

Second, when the campaign does make the news, this coverage of presidential campaigns has a tendency to focus on the "horse race" elements of the presidential campaign. Patterson (1980) explained that "In its coverage of a presidential campaign, the press concentrates on the strategic game played by the candidates in their pursuit of the presidency, thereby de-emphasizing the questions of national policy and leadership" (p. 21). News stories are likely to report on such questions as: Who is ahead in the polls? Who are the candidates' campaign managers? What campaign strategies are in play for each candidate? What is the status of fund-raising efforts? Which states are being actively contested by the candidates? Who will be included in presidential debates? The answers to these questions are clearly news, but they don't really provide advice to the electorate about who would make a better president. In fact, Patterson's (1980) investigation of the 1976 campaign concluded that "The election's substance . . . received only half as much coverage as was accorded the game" (p. 24). Thus, "horse race" coverage of the presidential campaign overwhelms coverage of the substance of the campaign.

Finally, when the news media do cover the issues in a campaign, in recent years they have devoted less and less coverage to the candidates themselves. The news is increasingly likely to offer short sound bites from candidates instead of extended quotations that provide thoughtful consideration of the issues in the campaign. Hallin (1992) reported that the average quotation from presidential candidates included in the news had dropped from 43 seconds in 1968 to a mere nine seconds in 1988. While the length of statements from journalists has also diminished, they spoke in campaign stories almost twice as often in 1988 as in 1968: "Journalists inserted their voices more often, by an increment of .17 times per report per year" (Steele & Barnhurst, 1996, p. 191). Thus, the stories tend to be fewer in number and shorter in length, they spend far less time quoting the candidates, and they feature the opinions and commentary of journalists (instead of candidates) more frequently. It is easy to understand why the electorate obtains more information about the issues in the presidential campaign from televised spots than from the news.

A third reason that campaign spots deserve scholarly attention is that considerable research conducted on the effects of televised political spots shows that such ads can affect viewers. Mulder (1979) found that advertising in a Chicago mayoral campaign correlated positively with attitudes toward the candidates. Studies have established a positive relationship between election outcomes and advertising expenditures (Joslyn, 1981; Palda, 1973). Wanat (1974) found that, for candidates who won elections, broadcast expenditures correlated highly (.56) with voting outcomes. McClure and Patterson (1974) reported that in the 1972 presidential campaign, "Exposure to political advertising was consistently related to voter belief change" (p. 16; see also Atkin & Heald, 1976). Therefore, empirical research documents the fact that political campaign advertising can influence voters and voting (studies have also examined the effects of political advertising on trust, involvement, and participation: Ansolabehere & Iyengar, 1995; Garramone, Atkin, Pinkleton, & Cole, 1990; Martinez & Delegal, 1990).

Furthermore, experimental research employing advertisements actually used by candidates (Atkin, 1977; Basil, Schooler, & Reeves, 1991; Christ, Thorson, & Caywood, 1994; Faber & Storey, 1984; Faber, Tims, & Schmitt, 1993; Garramone, 1984, 1985; Garramone & Smith, 1984; Geiger & Reeves, 1991; Hitchon & Chang, 1995; D. D. Johnston, 1989; Just, Crigler, & Wallach, 1990; Kaid, 1997; Kaid & Boydston, 1987; Kaid, Leland, & Whitney, 1992; Kaid & Sanders, 1978; Lang, 1991; McClure & Patterson, 1974; Merritt, 1984; Newhagen & Reeves, 1991) as well as commercials developed by researchers (Becker & Doolittle, 1975; Cundy, 1986; Donohue, 1973; Garramone, Atkin, Pinkleton, & Cole, 1990; Hill, 1989; Meadow & Sigelman, 1982; Roddy & Garramone, 1988; Rudd, 1989; Thorson, Christ, & Caywood, 1991) demonstrate that televised political advertisements have a variety of effects (recall, attitudes toward candidates, voting intention) on viewers. Therefore, televised political spots are an important form of messages in political campaigns, messages that merit scholarly attention.

Of course, it is true that other factors—like political party affiliation, the state of the economy (and other domestic affairs), or significant foreign policy events—can influence voting intention. I would not dispute, for example, the contention that political advertising rarely alters the voting intentions of committed partisans. However, the role political party affiliation plays in elections does not mean campaigns and the messages in those campaigns (like television spots) are unimportant.

First, party affiliation cannot determine (or explain) the outcome of *primary campaigns*, because the candidates who contend with one another for their party's nomination are by definition members of the same party. In 1996, for instance, party affiliation could not help voters choose between Lamar Alexander, Pat Buchanan, Bob Dole, Steve Forbes, and Phil Gramm, because they are all Republicans. Second, the growth in the number of independent voters means that neither political party can win the *general campaign* without persuading other, non-party members to vote for their candidate. In fact, the number of independent voters has increased from 22.6% in 1952 to 38.0% in 1992 (Weisberg & Kimball, 1993). Furthermore, Nie, Verba, and Petrocik (1979) observed that voting defections have increased over time: "Even among those who have a partisan identity, the proportion voting for the opposition party has grown" (p. 164). Thus, party affiliation is a significant impact on the voting behavior of many citizens, but it cannot account for the behavior of all voters and it does not determine (alone) the outcome of elections. Indeed, the simple fact that we have had five Republicans (Eisenhower, Nixon, Ford, Reagan, Bush) and four Democrats (Kennedy, Johnson, Carter, Clinton) in the White House since 1952 is good evidence that political party does not determine election outcomes. Finally, Iyengar and Kinder's (1988) research on agenda-setting indicates that on some issues (although not all) the *actual economic figures* had little or no impact on the perceived importance of an issue; but *presidential speeches* did have a substantial impact on viewers' attitudes. This study did not focus on campaigns or on television spots, but it does demonstrate that politicians can influence people's attitudes on the issues addressed in their messages (and that what they *say* in their messages can have more impact on attitudes than the *actual economic figures* themselves).

Furthermore, there are other important forms of campaign messages in addition to television advertisements. Presidential debates, for example, typically attract relatively vast audiences (see Benoit & Wells, 1996), and provide viewers with an hour or more of the candidates side-by-side, answering (more or less) the same questions. However, this study is limited to television advertisements.

For these reasons, television spots are an extremely important component of the modern presidential campaign and merit scholarly attention. This work is designed to provide a comprehensive analysis of the functions of presidential TV spots. It investigates spots from the first presidential campaign to use television spots—the 1952 contest between Dwight Eisenhower and Adlai Stevenson—through the most recent battle between Bill Clinton and Robert Dole. These are analyzed into spots from Republicans and Democrats, incumbents and challengers, and winners and losers. This study also contrasts general campaign spots with commercials from primary contests. Primary spots are analyzed by party as well as by winners (the nominees) and losers and primary ads are compared with general spots. This study also examines advertisements from several third-party candidates. These spots are compared with general campaign spots from the two major political parties. No study has ever included all three kinds of spots (the Appendix provides more detail on the sample).

This study applies the functional perspective on political campaigns, analyzing the utterances in spots into acclaims (self-praise or positive remarks), attacks (negative remarks), and defenses (see Benoit, Blaney, & Pier, 1998; Benoit, Pier, & Blaney, 1997; or Benoit, Wells, Pier, & Blaney, in press). Chapter 2 elaborates this functional approach. The candidates' statements are divided into those that address policy and those that concern character. Policy comments are further divided into those that address past deeds, future plans, and general goals, while character remarks are divided into personal qualities, leadership ability, and ideals. Defenses are divided into the strategies for image repair (Benoit, 1995a, 1997b). Together, these analyses will provide the most comprehensive analysis of presidential television advertisements available.

PAST RESEARCH ON PRESIDENTIAL TELEVISION SPOTS

A great deal of research has been conducted on televised spots (see, e.g., Aden, 1989; Kaid, Nimmo, & Sanders, 1986; Louden, 1989). For a history of the spot, see Devlin (1977, 1982, 1987b, 1989, 1993, 1997), Diamond and Bates (1992), or Jamieson (1996); for a discussion of negative advertisements in particular, see James and Hensel (1991) or Johnson-Cartee and Copeland (1993). There are also a number of studies of nonpresidential spots (Johnston & White, 1994; Latimer, 1984, 1989; Nowlan & Moutray, 1984; Payne & Baukus, 1988; Prisuta, 1972; Rose & Fuchs,

1968; Tinkham & Weaver-Lariscy, 1995; Tucker, 1959; or Weaver-Lariscy & Tinkham, 1987). There have also been a number of studies that compare political advertising in the United States with spots from other countries (Foote, 1991; Griffin & Kagan, 1996; Holtz-Bacha & Kaid, 1995; Holtz-Bacha, Kaid, & Johnston, 1994; A. Johnston, 1991; Kaid, 1991; or Kaid & Holtz-Bacha, 1995a, 1995b). A few studies discuss agenda-setting and political advertising (Ghorpade, 1986; Roberts & McCombs, 1994; Schleuder, McCombs, & Wanta, 1991). Several studies adopt more of a rhetorically oriented approach to political advertising (Cronkhite, Liska, & Schrader, 1991; Descutner, Burnier, Mickunas, & Letteri, 1991; Gronbeck, 1992; Jamieson, 1989; Larson, 1982; Shyles, 1991; or Smith & Johnston, 1991). This next section reviews the literature on the two primary dimensions of televised political spots: negative (attack) versus positive (acclaim) ads and image versus issue ads.

Here, I focus on research designed to analyze the nature of political television commercials (as opposed to experimental studies of the effects of political spots). Most studies tend to discuss two dimensions: negative versus positive spots, and issue versus image ads.

Functions: Positive versus Negative Ads

Kaid and Davidson's (1986) analysis of 1982 Senate ads found that incumbents used more positive (90%) than negative ads (10%); challengers used a more balanced approach (positive: 54%; negative: 46%). Benoit, Pier, and Blaney (1997), using the same approach employed in this study, found that 50% of the utterances in presidential television spots from 1980 to 1996 were attacks (negative), 49% were acclaims (positive), and 1% were defenses. They reported that Republicans (55%) and challengers (54%) used more attacks, while Democrats (45%) and incumbents (53%) used more acclaims. West (1997) studied 379 spots from 1952 to 1996, reporting that 46% of the ads were positive and that Democratic ads were more positive than Republican ones. Kaid and Johnston (1991) found that 71% of the ads from 1960 to 1988 were positive and 29% negative. However, the number of negative ads varied over time: negative spots spiked at 40% in 1964, dropped to 22–28% in the 1970s, and increased to 35–37% in the 1980s. Kaid and Johnston (1991) did not find that challengers use more negative ads than incumbents, or that Republicans use significantly more negative ads than Democrats. See also Geer (1998).

Devlin (1989) reported that in 1988 Bush produced 37 ads, 14 of which were negative (38%), while Dukakis had 47 ads, 23 of which were negative (49%). In 1992, 63% of Clinton's 30 ads were negative, while 56% of Bush's 24 ads were negative (Devlin, 1993). Kaid (1994) reported that 17% of the ads in the 1992 primary were negative. In the general election

Bush employed 44% positive and 56% negative ads; Clinton 31% positive and 69% negative, and Perot had only positive ads. These studies of 1992 suggest that Clinton, the challenger, used more negative ads than Bush, but still more than half of both Bush's and Clinton's ads were negative. In 1996, Clinton and Dole both produced about 40 spots for the general campaign. About 10% of Clinton's spots were negative, and about 40% were comparative (Devlin, 1997). Two-thirds of Dole's spots were negative (and two spots were comparative). Thus, with few exceptions (e.g., Perot), political ads take both positive and negative approaches.

Topics: Policy versus Character Ads

Most research on televised political spots has reported a heavier emphasis on issues than on image. Patterson and McClure (1976) found that 42% of the television commercials in 1972 focused on issues, and another 28% included issue information. Hofstetter and Zukin (1979) reported that 85% of the ads by Nixon and McGovern addressed issues. Joslyn (1980) found that while 77% of the ads discussed issues, only 47% focused on images. Kern's study of 1984 ads indicated that "issues were mentioned in 84 percent of such [30-second] spots" (1989, p. 51). Benoit, Pier, and Blaney (1997) found that 67% of the utterances in spots from 1980 to 1996 concerned policy, while 33% addressed character. West (1997), studying 379 spots from 1952 to 1996, reported that 61% mentioned issues.

The most extensive of this type of study was conducted by Kaid and Johnston (1991), who examined 830 television spots from 1960 to 1988. They reported that 67% of the positive ads and 79% of the negative ads provide issue information, and that 65% of the positive spots and 64% of the negative spots include image information. In the 1992 campaign, Kaid (1994) found that 59% of primary television ads addressed image, 24% issues, and 17% were negative ads. In the general election, Bush's ads were divided evenly between issue and image; Clinton used two-thirds issue and one-third image, while Perot used about 60% issue and 40% image.

Three studies provide more specifics on issues and image in political advertising. Johnson-Cartee and Copeland (1989) generated a list of topics found in negative political ads, grouped them into ten categories, and asked respondents to rate them as fair or unfair. The topics clustered into two groups, labeled "Political Issues" (political record, stands on issues, criminal record, and voting record) and "Personal Characteristics" (personal life, marriage, family, religion, medical history, and sex life). At least 83% rated each political issue as a fair topic for an attack; no more than 36% rated any of the personal characteristics as an acceptable topic for political attack. This reveals that there was general, albeit not universal, agreement on which topics are fair for an attack. It also suggests that respondents did not condemn political attacks wholesale, but believed that attacks on some topics were more suitable than others. Joslyn's (1986) study of 506 political ads from 1960 to 1984 reported that 37% of the ads reveal future policy plans, 60% evaluate past governmental policy, 57% mention candidate qualities (compassion, empathy, integrity, strength, activity, and knowledge). Shyles (1986) analyzed 140 political ads from 1980. He divided his results into issue and image, reporting mentions of these topics: Carter's record, domestic, economy, energy, federalism, foreign policy, government management, national security, and national well-being (issue); altruism, competence, expertise, honesty, leadership, personal, strength, and other qualities (image). It is clear that political advertising addresses both issues and images (see also Benze & Declercq, 1985).

Of course these two approaches to political ads are not as discrete as one might assume. Benoit and Wells (1996), in their analysis of the 1992 presidential debates, argue that a candidate's stance on issues shapes that candidate's image, and that a candidate's image probably influences perceptions about his or her issue stances. This relationship between issues and image should hold true in advertising as well. Furthermore, as Devlin (1977) noted in his analysis of advertising in the 1976 presidential campaign, Carter's campaign "used issues or themes as a vehicle for Carter to achieve an image as a legitimate candidate" (p. 244; see also Rudd, 1986; Kern, 1989). Thus, issues and image are interrelated concepts.

Finally, although the distinction between "issues" and "image" is very well established in the literature, I prefer an alternate terminology. Confusion can arise because the term "issue" has two meanings. Generally, it refers to points or topics of conflict in a discussion or conflict. In the context of political discourse, "issue" also is used as a synonym for policy considerations. However, the candidates' character, or qualifications for office (e.g., their experience, their integrity) are certainly legitimate grounds for discussion and dispute during a campaign (whether aspects of a candidate's private life are acceptable topics is another question). This means that "image" is an "issue"—not an issue in the second sense of a policy disagreement, but in the first sense as a point of dissention. To try to avoid this possible confusion, I propose an alternative terminology, contrasting *policy* stands with the *character* of the candidates.

PURPOSE OF THIS STUDY

It is clear that these scholars have provided important insights into the nature of political advertising. The purpose of this study is to extend this important work in several ways. First, I offer a theoretical framework for understanding the fundamental functions of political advertising—acclaiming, attacking, and defending—articulated in the next section.

Second, unlike many of these studies, I analyze presidential spots on both dimensions used in the literature: functions (acclaim, attack, defend) and topic (policy, character). Other research does not always do so. For example, Kaid (1994) divided 1992 primary ads into image ads, issue ads, and negative ads, a category system that implies that image and issue ads were distinct from negative spots. Surely negative ads can address issues and image, but this classification system does not make that point clear.

Third, most research relies on binary classification of television spots, coding the entire advertisement as enacting *either* one category *or* another (either positive or negative; either policy or character). In contrast, my procedure identifies each of the appeals (themes) in a given spot. To illustrate the nature of this problem, consider the following Clinton spot from 1996:

Ten million new jobs. Family income up $1,600 (since 1993). President Clinton cut the deficit 60%. Signed welfare reform—requiring work, time limits. Taxes cut for 15 million families. Balancing the budget. America's moving forward with an economic plan that works. Bob Dole: $900 billion in higher taxes. Republicans call him tax collector for the welfare state. His risky tax scheme would raise taxes on nine million families. Bob Dole. Wrong in the past. Wrong for our future.

The italicized portion of this ad is positive, praising Bill Clinton's accomplishments and suggesting future benefits if he is re-elected. The underlined portion, however, attacks Bob Dole's past deeds and his proposed tax cut. A coding system that classifies this spot as *either* positive *or* negative clearly ignores or misclassifies half of this message. Incidentally, some research acknowledges this limitation by adding a third category, comparative ads. However, this move doesn't really resolve this problem, because ads exist on a continuum from all positive to completely negative. Only if all of the ads that contained both negative and positive appeals had equal amounts of each would addition of a third category, "comparative," solve this problem. Coding each theme in a spot as positive or negative (and as concerning policy or character) will provide a more accurate description of the content of TV spots.

Furthermore, some research (especially on policy and character, or issue and image) tends to count the number of advertisements that "mention" issues. However, this gives us no idea of how much time was devoted to issues in an ad. Was the entire spot devoted to issues, or was an issue simply mentioned in passing? More information would be gleaned from counting the number of policy (issue) and character (image) utterances that were contained in a spot.

Fourth, although positive and negative ads may well predominate, some political television spots are defenses, or explicit responses to prior attacks from opponents (Trent & Friedenberg, 1995, acknowledge that such spots exist, but do not study them). Benoit, Pier, and Blaney (1997) found defenses in the presidential spots they analyzed. While defenses do not seem to be nearly as common in television spots as acclaims and attacks, they are an option in campaign discourse that should not be ignored by critics and analysts.

Fifth, the sample of spots gathered for this study includes multiple commercials from both major party candidates in every presidential campaign that employed television spots, from 1952 to 1996. This will permit an unparalleled description of presidential television spots. The Appendix contrasts the sample in this study with the samples used by the other two most extensive studies of television spots: Kaid and Johnston (1991), who studied virtually the same number of spots (albeit fewer campaigns), and West (1997), who studied as many campaigns (but far fewer spots). It also contrasts my sample of primary spots with those used by Kaid and Ballotti (1991) and West (1997).

Finally, I propose to study three different kinds of campaigns. Most of this investigation concerns general campaign television spots from candidates representing the two major political parties. However, I will devote a chapter each to primary spots and third-party spots. Then I will compare each with general spots from Republicans and Democrats.

In this study I will address several topics. Chapters 3–8 will present the results of my analysis of general election campaign spots, considered two campaigns at a time (I discuss two campaigns in each chapter as a compromise: I did not want to devote a chapter to each of the twelve campaigns, but I also didn't want to lump together all general spots in a single chapter). In these chapters I begin with a little background about the situation, the candidates, and their spots. I reproduce the transcripts of several spots from these campaigns to try to give a flavor for each contest. In each of these chapters I take up four topics. First, I describe the functions of presidential television spots (acclaims, attacks, defenses). Second, I consider these spots' treatment of policy and character topics. Third, I will discuss the subdivisions of policy (past deeds, future plans, general goals) and of character (personal qualities, leadership ability, ideals) as delineated in Chapter 2. Fourth, I analyze statements made by the candidate (the candidate sponsoring the ad) with statements made by others (e.g., "ordinary people," celebrity endorsers, anonymous announcers) to see who is the source of the utterances in each spot. Then I offer two chapters on other kinds of advertisements—spots from primaries and from third-party candidates—discussing the same basic ideas.

This analysis is followed by a comparative chapter. Chapter 11 discusses trends in general television spots, compares primary with general campaigns, major party (Republican and Democratic) spots with ads from third-party candidates, incumbents versus challengers, commercials by Republicans and those from Democrats, the advertisements of winners and losers, and, finally, the source of utterances in spots. Chapter 12 offers a discussion of implications and conclusions derived from this study. As mentioned earlier, the Appendix describes my sample in some detail.

Chapter 2

The Functional Approach
to Political Advertising

This chapter begins by explicating the functional theory of campaign discourse (Benoit, Blaney, & Pier, 1998; Benoit, Pier, & Blaney, 1997; Benoit, Wells, Pier, & Blaney, in press), which provides the theoretical underpinnings of this investigation. Then I describe the method used to analyze the television spots in this study. Finally, I will discuss my approach in the analytical chapters that follow.

THE FUNCTIONAL THEORY OF CAMPAIGN DISCOURSE

Political television spots have three basic functions, each contributing to the ultimate goal of accumulating sufficient votes to win the election. Elections are inherently comparative: A voter chooses among two or more candidates, and the candidate who appears most suitable (on whatever criteria are most important to a given voter) will receive that person's vote. A candidate does not need to win all votes to win the election; nor must a candidate appear perfect to voters. All that is necessary is for a candidate to appear *preferable* to other candidates for the office for enough voters. Popkin writes that "each campaign tries hard to make its side look better and the other side worse" (1994, p. 232). Therefore, political television spots have three basic functions: (1) to enhance their own credentials as a desirable office-holder (positive utterances or acclaims), (2) to downgrade their opponent's credentials as an undesirable office-holder (negative utterances or attacks), and, if their opponent attacks them, (3) to respond to those attacks (rebuttals or defenses). Each of these functions may occur on policy (issue) or character (image) grounds.

Scholars have offered other lists of functions. For example, Gronbeck (1978) discusses a number of instrumental and consummatory functions of presidential campaigning. Some of these sound much like uses and gratifications for the audience. Of course, it is important to know how auditors make use of campaign discourse. However, those sorts of functions supplement, rather than compete with, this analysis of campaign functions because I explicitly privilege the viewpoint of the candidate's purposes in this analysis.

Similarly, Devlin (1986; 1987a) discusses several functions of political ads. However, these three functions (acclaims, attacks, defenses) are more basic. For example, one of the functions Devlin lists is raising money. A candidate must tout his or her desirable qualities (and/or attack his or her opponent) in order to convince donors to contribute. Another function identified by Devlin is reinforcing a candidate's supporters. Supporters are reinforced by stressing the good qualities of the candidate (and, quite possibly, the negative qualities of the opponent). Thus, these three activities—attacking, acclaiming, and defending—are the three *fundamental* functions of political advertising.

Of course, candidates may not necessarily use all three options in a given campaign. While it is difficult to imagine a candidate who refuses to proclaim his or her desirable traits, it is possible that some candidates may be reluctant to attack or defend. A candidate may believe that attacks appear unpresidential. Some research (e.g., Stewart, 1975; Merritt, 1984) has shown that many voters say they do not like negative campaigns or mudslinging, and candidates may eschew attacks for that reason (although that does *not* necessarily mean such tactics are ineffectual). It is possible that some candidates may be concerned that issuing an ad that defends against an attack would make them appear to be on the defensive, an undesirable impression. They may decide not to "dignify" an attack with a defense. However, former presidential candidate Michael Dukakis implied that he believed defense could be important, explaining that "he was glad President Clinton was responding quickly to attacks, something Mr. Dukakis said he failed to do in his 1988 campaign" (Clines, 1996, p. A12). Regardless of whether, or how often, each candidate uses these strategies, they are the three basic functions of televised political ads, available to all candidates and capable (if used appropriately) of convincing voters that one candidate is a better choice than another: attacking, acclaiming, and defending.

Acclaiming

Pamela Benoit offers the first analysis of the speech act of acclaiming, or self-praise, in the communication literature (1997; see also Schlenker, 1980). This kind of utterance is intended to enhance the reputation of the speaker. Benoit defines acclaims as positive self-presentation, and argues that it has two components: "increased responsibility and the positive evaluation of an act" (p. 16). She analyzed self-presentational discourse in three settings: Nobel Prize acceptance addresses; statements by athletes who had broken a record, won an award, or won a game/championship; utterances at Mary Kay success meetings. I focus more on *topoi* for acclaiming in the specific context of a political campaign: what kinds of claims can televised spots make about candidates and their suitability for office? Next, I will describe potential topics for acclaiming.

Topics for Acclaims. The functional theory of political campaign discourse argues that televised political spots may acclaim (positive spots) by crediting candidates with desirable policy stands and by attributing positive character traits to candidates (e.g., honesty, integrity, experience). Policy acclaims may take the form of lauding past accomplishments (reducing taxes, increasing jobs) or promising future benefits (reducing the federal deficit, making health care more affordable) if elected (or re-elected). It is important that the qualities praised, and benefits touted or promised, be viewed as good by voters (desirability), and that the candidate be seen by voters as possessing those qualities or likely to accomplish policy benefits (responsibility). See Table 2.1.

Acclaims in televised political advertisements may address policy considerations. In 1988, George Bush touted *past deeds*: "Over the past six years, eighteen million jobs were created, interest rates were cut in half. Today, inflation is down, taxes are down, and the economy is strong." Michael Dukakis stressed his *future plans*: "Mike Dukakis wants to help. His college opportunities plan says that if a kid like Jimmy has the grades for college, America should find a way to send him." George Bush stressed his *goals*: "I will not allow this country to be made weak again. I will keep America moving forward, always forward, for an endless enduring dream and a thousand points of light." So, some spots acclaim on policy grounds.

Candidate advertisements also acclaim on the basis of their character traits. In this ad in 1988, George Bush is characterized as an experienced *leader*: "Perhaps no one in this century is better prepared to be President of the United States" than Bush. In 1992, Bill Clinton mentioned one of his positive *personal qualities*: "I care so much about people." Michael Dukakis stressed his *ideals* in the 1988 campaign, suggesting that he would be "a president who fights for you," the common people. Thus, acclaims can address the character traits of the candidates.

Attacking

Some research has investigated persuasive attack (Fisher, 1970, on subversion; Ryan, 1982, on *kategoria*; see also Pfau & Kenski, 1990; Jamieson,

Table 2.1

Examples of Acclaiming and Attacking on Each Form of Policy and Character

Policy

Past Deeds: Acclaim

Reagan (1984): Today, inflation is down, interest rates are down. We've created six and a half million new jobs. Americans are working again, and so is America.

Past Deeds: Attack

Eisenhower (1952): Man: General, the Democrats are telling me I never had it so good.

Eisenhower: Can that be true when America is billions in debt, when prices have doubled, when taxes break our backs, and we are still fighting in Korea?

Future Plans: Acclaim

Ford (1976): Under my proposal to increase the personal exemption, you would get an additional exemption of $1,250. Now that would make a sizeable increase in your weekly take-home pay.

Future Plans: Attack

Johnson (1964): The other candidate wants to go on testing more atomic bombs. If he's elected, they might start testing all over again.

General Goals: Acclaim

Reagan (1980): We must act to put American back to work. We must balance the budget. We must slow the growth of government. We must cut tax rates.

General Goals: Attack

Forbes (1996 Primary): The politicians can keep on raising your taxes and wasting your money.

Character

Personal Qualities: Acclaim

Humphrey (1968): Humphrey is without question a man that I feel everyone in this country can trust.

Personal Qualities: Attack

Dukakis (1988): The other side has pursued a campaign of distortion and distraction, of fear and of smear.

Leadership Ability: Acclaim

Nixon (1960): Above everything else, the American people want leaders who will keep the peace without surrender for America and the world. Henry Cabot Lodge and I have had the opportunity of serving with President Eisenhower in this cause for the last seven and a half years. We both know Mr. Krushchev. We have sat opposite the conference table with him.

Table 2.1 (continued)

Leadership Ability: Attack

Kennedy (1960): [Republicans want you to believe Mr. Nixon has experience in the White House.] A reporter recently asked President Eisenhower for an example of a major idea of Nixon's that Eisenhower had adopted. [Eisenhower]: If you give me a week, I might think of one. I don't remember.

Ideals: Acclaim

Humphrey (1968): [Woman] Humphrey is a man who has a very strong liberal background.

Ideals: Attack

Johnson (1964): Senator Goldwater said on Oct. 12, 1960, in Jacksonville, FL, the child has no right to an education. In most cases the child can get along just as well without it.

1992a). However, this work is not designed to offer a set of *topoi* for persuasive attack (negative spots).

Topics for Attacks. The functional theory of political campaign discourse argues that, like acclaims, persuasive attacks in political advertising may address issues, or policy considerations, or the image, or character of the candidate (see Table 2.1). I illustrate these possibilities from ads in the 1988 and 1992 campaigns.

First, persuasive political attack may concern policy considerations. In 1988, a Bush/Quayle ad discussed Michael Dukakis's *past deeds*:

As Governor, Michael Dukakis vetoed mandatory sentences for drug dealers. He vetoed the death penalty. His revolving door prison policy gave weekend furloughs to first degree murderers not eligible for parole. While out, many committed other crimes like kidnaping and rape.

Michael Dukakis warned against George Bush's *future plans*: "George Bush wants to give the wealthiest 1% of the people in the country a tax break worth $30,000 a year." Finally, Dukakis also criticized Bush's *goals*: "Mr. Bush does not object to the wave of merger and of speculation that has put our companies and our country itself on the auction block." So, televised political ads attack candidates on policy matters.

Some political spots focus on the character of the candidates. In 1988, Michael Dukakis's ad featured actors pretending to be Bush/Quayle campaign advisors. One simulated reluctant testimony, reflecting unfavorably on the vice-presidential candidate's *leadership* potential: "Suddenly, the words 'President Quayle' even make me nervous." After being the target of negative ads by George Bush (especially on crime and the

Massachusetts furlough program), a Dukakis ad characterized Mr. Bush in the process: "The real story about furloughs is that George Bush has taken a furlough from the truth." In other words, Dukakis is suggesting that one of Bush's *personal qualities* is that he is a liar. Dukakis also characterized his opponent's *ideals* in a political spot: George Bush is a man who "fights for the privileged few." These kinds of ads attack the character of the candidates.

Defending

Of the three functions of discourse discussed here, most research by far has examined self-defense, *apologia*, accounts, or image repair. Several approaches have been developed for explaining verbal self-defense, some developed in communication and rhetoric and some in sociology (Burke, 1970; Ware & Linkugel, 1973; Scott & Lyman, 1968), but each theory includes options neglected by the others (see also Jamieson [1992a] or Gold [1978] for discussions of defense in politics specifically). Benoit (1995a) developed a typology of image repair strategies that is more complete than those currently available in the rhetorical literature. Because they are explicated in several places (Benoit, 1995a, 1995b, 1997a, 1997b, 1998; Benoit & Anderson, 1996; Benoit & Brinson, 1994, in press; Benoit & Czerwinski, 1997; Benoit, Gullifor, & Panici, 1991; Benoit & Hanczor, 1994; Benoit & Nill, 1998, in press ; Benoit & Wells, 1998; Blaney & Benoit, 1997; Brinson & Benoit, 1996, in press; Kennedy & Benoit, 1997), I do not repeat that discussion here.

METHOD

The analytic procedure consisted of four steps (campaign year, party, and incumbency information was also recorded). First, advertisements were unitized into themes, or parts of the ad that addressed a coherent idea. Because these utterances are enthymematic, themes vary in length from a phrase to several sentences. Themes were then classified as acclaims, attacks, or defenses according to these rules:

- Themes that portrayed the sponsoring candidate or the candidate's political party in a favorable light were *acclaims*.
- Themes that portrayed the opposing candidate or opposing candidate's political party in an unfavorable light were *attacks*.
- Themes that explicitly responded to a prior attack on the candidate or the candidate's political party were *defenses*.

Other utterances were not analyzed. For example, some ads discussed current or past events without attributing credit to their own party or candidate, or blame to the opposing party or its candidate. Such utterances were excluded from the analysis.

Second, a judgment was made about whether the theme primarily concerned a policy consideration or a character trait, according to these rules:

- Utterances that concern governmental action (past, current, or future) and problems amenable to governmental action were considered *policy* themes.
- Utterances that address characteristics, traits, abilities, or attributes of the candidates (or their parties) were considered *character* themes.

Third, policy themes were further analyzed into past deeds, future plans, and general goals, while character themes were subdivided into personal qualities, leadership ability, and ideals (see Table 2.1). Finally, the source of each theme was identified as the candidate or other (including people "in the street" and anonymous announcers). I will illustrate these steps to show how they were analyzed in four of the advertisements studied.

In 1992, a Clinton/Gore ad reported that Clinton had moved 17,000 people from welfare to work. This is an *acclaim* (because voters presumably believe it is good to move welfare recipients to jobs) that focused on a *policy consideration* (welfare) generally and *past deeds* in particular. This theme was also attributed to an "other" source.

A second Clinton/Gore spot reported that President Bush wanted a $108,000 tax break for the rich. This was considered an *attack* (because most voters oppose tax breaks for the rich), one that concerned *policy considerations* (taxation) generally and a future plan specifically. Again, the source was not the candidate but an "other" person.

In 1992, the Bush/Quayle campaign used an ad that asserted that America needs a leader who understands the world. This utterance was an *acclaim* of the president, the kind of leader America needs. This acclaim concerns a *character trait* of the candidate *leadership ability*. Bush was filmed speaking these words, so the source was the candidate.

Another 1992 Bush/Quayle advertisement featured voters commenting on the last debate. One declared that he did not trust Clinton. This utterance functions as an *attack* (Clinton was untrustworthy) that focused on a *character trait* of the candidate, one of his *personal qualities* (trustworthiness). Voters were considered "other" sources.

This study analyzed 1,656 televised presidential campaign advertisements from 1952 to 1996, over 19 and one-half hours of political spots. Two coders content-analyzed these television spots. To check for intercoder reliability, both coders analyzed a subset of 20% of the sample. Cohen's *kappa* for coding themes as acclaims, attacks, and defenses was

.98; for classifying themes as policy or character, it was .71; for classifying policy themes as past deeds, future plans, or general goals, *kappa* was .84; and *kappa* for coding character themes as personal qualities, leadership ability, or ideals was .72. Fleiss (1981) indicates that "values [of kappa] greater than .75 or so may be taken to represent excellent agreement beyond chance, values below .40 or so may be taken to represent poor agreement beyond chance, and values between .40 and .75 may be taken to represent fair to good agreement beyond chance" (p. 218). Thus, these figures all indicate good or excellent reliability in the coding of these television spots.

ANALYTICAL CHAPTERS

The next section of the book (Part II) presents my analysis of general election campaigns. The third section (Part III) offers results of my analysis of primary and third-party candidates. I will begin each chapter by giving examples of several advertisements. I "cite" these by giving the candidate, year, and title of the spot (not all spots have clear titles, so I created some). Material placed inside square brackets ("[" "]") are descriptions of visual images or sounds in the commercial. In these chapters, I discuss the functions (attacks, acclaims, and defense), the topic (policy versus character), forms of policy utterances (past deeds, future plans, general goals) and of character comments (personal qualities, leadership ability, ideals), and the source of utterance (candidate versus other). To illustrate the results of my analysis, I also provide excerpts from spots, without specific citations. Chapter 11 discusses several contrasts and Chapter 12 addresses conclusions and implications of the study.

Part II

General Campaigns

Chapter 3

In the Beginning: 1952, 1956

The campaigns of 1952 and 1956 are unique for at least two reasons. First, and most importantly, these are the earliest presidential campaigns to employ television spots. This form of message was novel: Especially in 1952, the candidates could not look to the trials and errors of previous contests as guides. Television was a relatively new medium and people were understandably fascinated by it; the campaigns wanted to try to harness this new tool for their own purposes. Of course, this is not to say there were no reservations about the use of television. Jamieson (1996) reports that the Republicans were willing to devote over ten times as much as the Democrats to broadcast their advertisements, $800,000 to $77,000.

Second, these are the only campaigns to feature the same presidential candidates: Republican Dwight D. Eisenhower and Democrat Adlai E. Stevenson. Of course, several other candidates ran in two elections: Jimmy Carter, Ronald Reagan, George Bush (who also ran for vice president twice with Reagan), and Bill Clinton. Richard Nixon ran three times for president (and twice for vice president with Eisenhower). However, the only difference in the tickets in the 1950s was Stevenson's running mates: John Sparkman in 1952 and Estes Kefauver in 1956. This raises the question of whether they would make changes in their television advertising strategies after one candidate won and the other lost in the first confrontation.

One aspect of the 1952 campaign that is especially noteworthy is Eisenhower's series of 20-second spots entitled "Eisenhower Answers America." Thus, the very first presidential campaign with television spots produced a series of spots with a common theme. These began with their title and a still photo of Eisenhower. Then citizens asked questions which were answered, of course, by Eisenhower. Twenty-nine different commercials in this format survive today. These questions ranged from inflation and taxes ("food prices, clothing prices, income taxes, won't they ever go down?"), to governmental waste ("Recently, just one government bureau actually lost $400 million. And not even the FBI can find it"), to inadequate benefits ("I can't live on my social security. Nobody can"), to corruption in Washington ("What's wrong down in Washington? Graft, scandal, headlines?"), to military preparedness ("We won't spend hundreds of billions and still not have enough tanks and planes for Korea"). Here are two examples of this series of spots:

Man: General, the Democrats are telling me I never had it so good.

Eisenhower: Can that be true when America is billions in debt, when prices have doubled, when taxes break our backs, and we are still fighting in Korea? It's tragic and it's time for a change. (Eisenhower, 1952, "Never Had it So Good")

Woman: You know what things cost today. High prices are just driving me crazy.

Eisenhower: Yes, my Mamie gets after me about the high cost of living. It's another reason why I say, it's time for a change. Time to get back to an honest dollar and an honest dollar's work. (Eisenhower, "Honest Dollar")

Notice that the concept of "Eisenhower answers America" subtly suggests two points: first, that Americans have many important questions about the current (Democratic) administration, and, second, that Eisenhower is the one who has the answers. Commercials using citizens and asking (and answering) questions became staples of the political television commercial. Other candidates have also adopted the idea of developing a series of spots on a common theme. Eisenhower also developed "The Man from Abilene," a biographical spot, in the 1952 campaign.

One-third of Stevenson's spots in 1952 were songs, and two were mini–soap operas (which included songs at the end). In the following advertisement, a woman sang this song:

Vote Stevenson, vote Stevenson
A man you can believe in son.
From Illinois whence Lincoln came,
His leadership has won him fame.
A soldier man is always bound
To think in terms of battlegrounds.
But Stevenson, a civilian son,
Will lead us 'till the peace is won. (Stevenson, 1952, "Vote Stevenson")

Here, Stevenson attempts to point out the risks of putting a man from the military (General Eisenhower) into the White House. It also touts (vaguely) his leadership experience as governor of Illinois. Two of Stevenson's ads ("Ike & Bob" 1 and 2) used cartoons and suggested that Eisenhower would be controlled by Republican Robert Taft:

Ike. Bob. Ike. Bob [slowly, in soft voices like lovers, with two hearts labeled Ike and Bob].
We must lower taxes Bob.
Yes Ike, we must lower taxes.
But we have to spend more for defense, Bob.
You see Ike, we agree perfectly.
Bob. Ike. Bob. Ike.
Announcer: Will Bob give Ike the additional money for defense after Ike cuts taxes? Stay tuned for a musical interlude.
Song: Rueben, Rueben, I've been thinkin', 'bout the Gen'ral and his mob. If you're voting for the Gen'ral, you really are electing Bob.
Let's vote for Adlai—and John. (Stevenson, 1952, "Ike & Bob" 1)

While they occasionally occur in subsequent campaigns, the concepts of songs and mini–soap operas were far less popular than the concepts introduced by Eisenhower in his 1952 spots.

As mentioned above, in 1952 one of Eisenhower's spots was partly biographical and called "The Man from Abilene." In the 1956 rematch, Stevenson produced three longer "Man from Libertyville" spots. These were "informal chats" designed to help us get to know the candidate, his family, and his running mate Estes Kefauver. He also attacked his opponent, as this passage from a 1956 spot illustrates:

Eisenhower said that there would be tax relief. And there has been, to some degree, but it was for the benefit of the well-to-do and for the big corporations. The Republicans gave the lion's share of it to them. Out of every dollar of tax cut savings, ninety-one cents went to the higher income families and to the big corporations. And for the rest of Americans, eighty percent of all American families, got only nine cents out of each tax cut dollar. Now for older people, for you people who live on pensions, on fixed incomes, for the younger people just getting started, this is a serious matter. (Stevenson, 1956, "Man from Libertyville 2" [excerpt])

This advertisement attacks Eisenhower for giving most of the tax cut he promised to the rich. Several of Stevenson's spots in his second run for the presidency focused on the broken promise argument at work in this advertisement. To further illustrate this kind of spot, consider "How's That Again General?"

Announcer: How's that again, General? During the 1952 campaign, General Eisenhower promised a great crusade:

Eisenhower: Too many politicians have sold their ideals of honesty down the Potomac. We must bring integrity and thrift back to Washington.

Announcer: How's that again, General?

Eisenhower: Too many politicians have sold their ideals of honesty down the Potomac. We must bring back integrity and thrift back to Washington.

Kefauver: This is Estes Kefauver. Let's see what happened to that promise. Wesley Roberts, a Republican National Chairman, sold Kansas a building it already owned for eleven thousand dollars. He got a silver tree from Mr. Eisenhower. Hal Talbott pressured defense plants to employ a firm which paid him a hundred and thirty thousand dollars while he was Air Force Secretary. He received the General's warm wishes and an official welcome. And there are many others, like Strobel, the Public Buildings Administrator; Mansure, the General Services Administrator. (Stevenson, 1952, "How's That Again, General?")

The argument of broken campaign promises, and the tactic of employing the opponent's own words in the indictment, have proved quite durable over time. Eisenhower had health problems, including a heart attack, in 1955 and Stevenson also produced spots suggesting that voters should be "nervous" about the prospect of President Nixon. However, Jamieson (1996) reports that these commercials never aired.

   In their second clash Eisenhower eschewed 20-second ads (this sample includes only one 20-second advertisement from 1956), but used several five-minute spots. These featured ordinary citizens, "people on the street," to praise the candidate and his first-term record. For example, in these two excerpts, the first passage praises Eisenhower's accomplishments while the second acclaims his character and experience:

Man: I want to see President Eisenhower reelected. He's brought honesty and integrity to the White House, and peace and prosperity to the country. That's good enough for me.

Woman: Eisenhower strikes me as a fundamentally peaceful man. And I think he knows enough about war that he would keep us out of it. (Eisenhower, 1956, "People in the Street" [excerpts])

Tributes from ordinary citizens have become another common device in political advertising.

   Thus, these candidates inaugurated presidential television advertising. They developed several different formats for political spots that subsequently functioned as models for subsequent campaigns. Each of these candidates had two opportunities at defeating the other and securing the White House. But what about the content of the advertisements?

Table 3.1
Functions of the 1952 and 1956 Campaigns

Year	Candidate	Acclaims	Attacks
1952	Eisenhower	22 (31%)	**48 (69%)**
	Stevenson	**30 (64%)**	17 (36%)
1956	Eisenhower	**78 (98%)**	2 (2%)
	Stevenson	41 (62%)	**25 (38%)**
Total		**171 (65%)**	92 (35%)

FUNCTIONS OF TELEVISION SPOTS

These campaigns stressed acclaiming: 65% of their utterances were instances of self-praise. For example, a 1952 Stevenson ad explained that "The farmer, the businessman, the veteran, and the working man, to each in turn he has said that he will represent not their interests alone, but the interests of all of us. That's why I am excited about Governor Stevenson. He will be a President for all the people." This utterance praises Stevenson for caring about all Americans rather than just for some special interest groups. Eisenhower declared in 1952 that "I stand for expanded social security and more real benefits. Believe me sir: If I am President, I'll give you older folks action, not just sympathy." While this passage ends with a swipe at Democrats for providing sympathy rather than action, the main point is that Eisenhower promises to improve social security for older Americans. Thus, both candidates repeatedly acclaimed in their advertisements (see Table 3.1).

Both candidates also relied on attacks in their television spots: 35% of their remarks were negative. For instance, in 1952 Eisenhower posed questions that functioned to attack the Democratic status quo: "Today across the nation, Americans everywhere are burdened with a multitude of problems. What to do about skyrocketing prices? What to do about backbreaking taxes? What to do about the staggering national debt? And, close to our hearts, when will we have an end to war in Korea?" Stevenson also attacked his opponent. Several of his 1952 advertisements featured songs. Here, he questioned whether Eisenhower or Robert Taft would really be in charge if Eisenhower won the election: "Rueben, Rueben, I've been thinking 'bout the Gen'ral and his mob. If you're voting for the Gen'ral, you really are electing Bob." These data are displayed in Table 3.1. Neither candidate used defense in any of the television spots examined here.

Table 3.2
Policy versus Character in the 1952 and 1956 Campaigns

Year	Candidate	Policy	Character
1952	Eisenhower	**60 (86%)**	10 (14%)
	Stevenson	23 (49%)	**24 (51%)**
1956	Eisenhower	35 (44%)	**45 (56%)**
	Stevenson	**37 (56%)**	29 (44%)
Total		**155 (59%)**	108 (41%)

POLICY VERSUS CHARACTER

In these two contests the candidates devoted 59% of their utterances to policy matters, discussing character in 41% of their comments. For example, in 1956 Eisenhower acclaimed his past deeds accomplished in his first term, explaining to voters that:

You will hear your Secretary of Treasury, George Humphrey, tell how his department has checked the galloping inflation, cut taxes, balanced the budget, and reduced the debt. You will hear your Secretary of Defense, Charles E. Wilson, tell how we have saved billions of dollars on the Armed Forces, reduced our manpower requirements, and still provided a more secure defense. You will hear your Secretary of Labor, James Mitchell, tell how employment, wages, and income have reached the highest levels in history. You will hear your Attorney General, the Secretary of our new Department of Health, Education, and Welfare, and other Cabinet officers tell what we have done to combat monopoly, to extend Social Security for seventy million Americans, and other accomplishments of this Republican administration.

However, Eisenhower addressed his goals for the future as well: "We in the Republican party pledge ourselves to continue our program of peace, security, and prosperity, that has made our party the party of the future" (see Table 3.2).

These candidates discussed character as well in their television spots. This Stevenson spot from 1952 discusses his leadership ability, referring to his experience as governor of Illinois. Notice that he criticizes Eisenhower's lack of governmental experience at the same time: "I sure think that this is no time for an amateur in the White House. We need a man who knows civilian government. I switched to Stevenson." Eisenhower combines an attack on the establishment with praise of his personal qualities in this passage from 1952: "Too many politicians have sold their ideals of honesty down the Potomac. We must bring back integrity and thrift back to Washington. This we are determined to do." So, Eisenhower and Stevenson offered character as well as policy appeals in these campaign advertisements.

FORMS OF POLICY AND CHARACTER

The form of policy utterance which was used most often in the 1950s was past deeds. Overall, 66% of Eisenhower's and Stevenson's policy utterances employed past deeds. An Eisenhower spot from 1956 observed that "Eisenhower promised he'd get us veteran servicemen out of the war there and he did." In 1956, Stevenson lamented Eisenhower's first-term performance: "Small business profits are down 52%. . . . Farm income is down 25%. . . . Your schools like this one need a third of a million more classrooms." Past deeds were used to acclaim and attack in these campaigns (see Table 3.3).

Future plans were virtually non-existent in these campaigns (a single instance by Stevenson in 1952). However, general goals accounted for one-third of their policy comments. In 1952, Eisenhower promised that "We will put the lid on government spending." In the second campaign, Stevenson revealed his goal of achieving peace: "I'm Adlai Stevenson, and this is what I believe—that there is only one sound formula for peace: a sturdy defense, cooperation with our friends, and intelligent action to win the hearts and minds of the uncommitted peoples." Goals were a fairly common topic in these commercials.

When Eisenhower and Stevenson discussed character, they discussed personal qualities (46%), leadership ability (31%), and ideals (22%). In 1952, one of Stevenson's advertisements noted that he has the courage to stand up for his beliefs. In 1956, one of Eisenhower's commercials praised his leadership ability: "That's why we all depend on Ike so much. He can stand up to Krushchev and those fellows. He's a big man who's used to handling big problems." A 1952 Stevenson spot reported on the Democratic candidate's ideals: "In the South, he has made a strong statement for civil liberties and full equality." Character was a substantial component of these television ads.

SOURCE OF UTTERANCE

The acclaims in these spots were more often spoken by others (59%) than by the candidates themselves (41%). This situation was almost exactly reversed for attacks: More attacks came from the candidates themselves (58%) than from other speakers (42%). For example, when answering a question about waste in Washington, Eisenhower declared that it was so bad that "Recently, just one government bureau actually

Table 3.3
Forms of Policy and Character in the 1952 and 1956 Campaigns

Year	Candidate	Policy			Character		
		Past Deeds	Future Plans	General Goals	Personal Qualities	Leadership Ability	Ideals
1952	Eisenhower	45 (75%)	0	15 (25%)	5 (50%)	3 (30%)	2 (20%)
	Stevenson	13 (57%)	1 (4%)	9 (39%)	13 (54%)	6 (25%)	5 (21%)
1956	Eisenhower	21 (60%)	0	14 (40%)	26 (58%)	16 (36%)	3 (7%)
	Stevenson	24 (65%)	0	13 (35%)	6 (21%)	9 (31%)	14 (48%)
Total		103 (66%)	1 (1%)	51 (33%)	50 (46%)	34 (31%)	24 (22%)

Table 3.4
Source of Utterance in the 1952 and 1956 Campaigns

Year	Candidate	Acclaims		Attacks	
		Candidate	Other	Candidate	Other
1952	Eisenhower	15 (68%)	7 (32%)	36 (75%)	12 (25%)
	Stevenson	0	30 (100%)	0	17 (100%)
1956	Eisenhower	8 (10%)	70 (90%)	0	2 (100%)
	Stevenson	27 (66%)	14 (44%)	20 (80%)	5 (20%)
Total		50 (41%)	121 (59%)	56 (58%)	36 (42%)

lost $400 million. And not even the FBI can find it." In another, he was the source of an acclaim, promising that "we will put the lid on government spending." Thus, both candidates and others were sources for the utterances in their spots (see Table 3.4).

The contrasts between the two candidates' appearances in their spots (use of sources), however, were sharp. Stevenson did not appear in any of these spots in 1952 (as Jamieson [1996] observes, Stevenson relied most heavily on the broadcast speech, which "hobbled the 1952 Stevenson campaign," p. 60). In contrast, Eisenhower spoke in over half of the acclaims (68%) and of the attacks (75%) in his advertisements. However, in 1956 the situation was almost reversed: Stevenson was the source of most acclaims (66%) and attacks (80%). Eisenhower himself made none of the attacks in his 1956 spots and only one out of ten of the acclaims.

CONCLUSION

Although both candidates invented types of spots that would be used in subsequent campaigns, Eisenhower's use of spots was better than Stevenson's. He adapted his use of acclaims and attacks appropriately, using more attacks as a challenger and more acclaims as an incumbent. Stevenson's use of these two functions was roughly the same in both campaigns. Eisenhower also had more important innovations: a series of thematically related spots, use of endorsements by ordinary citizens, biographical spots, and question and answer formats. Both candidates used songs and cartoons. In the second campaign, Stevenson used reluctant testimony to argue that Eisenhower had failed to fulfill his campaign promise. Finally, especially in the "Eisenhower Answers America" series, Eisenhower addressed a variety of topics, making it likely that his spots touched on topics important to most voters (while still maintaining a campaign theme). It should come as no surprise that Eisenhower won both campaigns.

Chapter 4

The Democrats Ascend: 1960, 1964

In 1960, Republican Vice President Richard M. Nixon ran against Democratic Senator John F. Kennedy. Nixon ran heavily on the administration's record, arguing that he was partly responsible for its successes and had the experience, as vice president, to continue that record. Nixon pledged to campaign in all 50 states, a commitment he fulfilled with difficulty (a symbolic gesture that flies in the face of the strategy of devoting time, energy, and money in the states that are most likely to tip the balance in the candidate's favor). This campaign also featured the first general election presidential debates.

Nixon's television spots addressed a relatively limited number of themes. The topic of national defense—including peace and the Communist threat—is illustrated in advertisements like this one in 1960:

Announcer: Mr. Nixon, what is the truth about our defenses? How strong should they be?

Nixon: Well, they must be strong enough to keep us out of war, powerful enough to make the Communists in the Soviet Union and Red China understand that America will not tolerate being pushed around, that we can if necessary retaliate with such speed and devastation to make the risk too great for the Communists to start a war any place in the world. We have this kind of strength now, and we are getting stronger every day. We must never let the Communists think we are weak. This is both foolish and dangerous. And so I say, let's not tear America down. Let us speak up for America.

Announcer: Vote for Nixon and Lodge November 8. They understand what peace demands [Vote for Nixon and Lodge: They understand what peace demands]. (Nixon, 1960, "Defense Truth")

This topic alone accounted for almost half of the Nixon commercials in this sample.

This spot also illustrates a series of at least seven advertisements that imitate Eisenhower's "Eisenhower Answers America" commercials of 1952. Here, an announcer asks a question, prefaced by "Mr. Nixon, what is the truth about . . .". As in Eisenhower's spots, this format enacts the theme that Nixon is the one with answers. In fact, he did not simply have answers, but he had "the truth." These ads may also have, like Eisenhower's spots, created the impression that citizens had questions that needed answering. In Eisenhower's advertisements (produced when the Republicans were challenging the Democratic White House), this impression helped him challenge the party in control. In Nixon's spots, this factor might have inadvertently undermined confidence in the Eisenhower/Nixon administration.

A second theme concerned the qualifications of the candidates, Vice President Nixon and Ambassador Henry Cabot Lodge, for office.

Announcer: Yes, our nation needs Nixon [our nation needs Nixon]. Experience counts.

Myler: I'm Mrs. Robert Myler Jr., and I think Nixon and Lodge are the best-trained to win the cold war and to keep the peace. I also like Nixon because he's a native Californian and knows our problem [Nixon-Lodge]. (Nixon, 1960, "Experience Counts")

This spot echoes, in brief form, Eisenhower's 1956 commercials of ordinary citizens endorsing his candidacy.

Nixon also discussed jobs and the economy quite frequently. He denied weakness in the economy (a defense) and acclaimed its strength:

Announcer: Mr. Nixon, what is the truth? Is America lagging behind in economic growth?

Nixon: Certainly not. The fact is that Americans are earning more, investing more, saving more, living better than ever before. More Americans than ever before are bringing home the weekly paycheck. Sixty-eight million people are employed today. Now this is growth. The kind that ensures our strength at home, and it exceeds the economic growth in Russia today. Ours is a growth based on paying our bills, too. Not a system of reckless borrowing that will burden our children tomorrow. This is the kind of economic growth we must continue to have, in order to continue to help us keep the peace.

Announcer: Vote for Nixon and Lodge Nov. 8. They understand what peace demands [Vote for Nixon and Lodge. They understand what peace demands]. (Nixon, 1960, "Truth Economy")

Thus, Nixon acclaimed the economic record of the incumbent (Republican) administration in which he served as vice president. Nixon also argued that Democratic spending proposals would necessitate either more taxes or deficit spending, both of which were undesirable:

Announcer: Ladies and Gentlemen, the Vice President of the United States, Richard M. Nixon.

Nixon: I would like to talk to you for a moment about dollars and sense. Your dollars and sense. Now my opponents want to increase federal expenditures as much as eighteen billion dollars a year. How will they pay for it? There are only two ways. One is to raise your taxes: That hurts everyone. The other is to increase our national debt and that means raising your prices, robbing you of your savings, cutting into the value of your insurance, hurting your pocketbook everyday at the drug store, the grocery store, the gas station. Is that what you want for America? I say no. I say that's a false doctrine. I say that we can remain the strongest nation on earth only by continuing our program of responsible government.

Announcer: Nixon and Lodge: They understand what peace demands [Nixon and Lodge: They understand what peace demands]. (Nixon, 1960, "Dollars and Sense")

The spot began with Nixon announcing his status as vice president. Nixon discussed the issues of hunger and civil rights in his political television advertisements.

Kennedy addressed far more topics in his 1960 commercials than Nixon discussed. His television spots addressed such topics as education, leadership, defense and Communism, civil rights, social welfare (including Medicare and Social Security), jobs and the economy, the environment, and urban affairs. This spot illustrates his treatment of several issues:

Kennedy: I believe if we're moving ahead here, we'll move ahead around the world. We are opposing those in this election who wish to stand still. Those who in their legislative careers, and the Republican party, have stood still. Those who opposed all that we've tried to do during the past years to strengthen our country and strengthen our economy, and protect our farmers, and protect small businessmen, build homes, provide better educational facilities for our children. Provide medical care for our older citizens under social security. This is the unfinished business of our generation. And I come now to ask your help in this campaign. And I can assure you that if we are successful, we will give leadership to this country through the Democratic party, and we'll start America moving again.

Announcer: Help elect John F. Kennedy for President [Citizens for Kennedy/Johnson]. (Kennedy, 1960, "Moving Ahead")

He discussed strengthening the economy, protecting farmers and small businesses, providing housing, education, and medical care for the aged. Similarly, the next advertisement discussed several topics related to urban affairs:

Kennedy: Hello, my name is John Kennedy. I live in one of the oldest cities in the United States, and I believe that these problems that our cities face really one of the most important if undiscussed problems that now face our great country. Most of our people live in cities. Many of those cities are old. The housing is old. The schools are crowded. The teachers are inadequately compensated. The streets are narrow and can't stand the great transportation mass which we now have in the center of our cities at the rush hour. If our cities are going to maintain their vitality, they're going to remain a good place to live, if our property taxes are going to remain in reason, then we're going to have to go to work: the community, the state, the national government. I believe we should create a Department of Urban Affairs for housing, transportation, and all the rest and begin to move our cities forward again.

Announcer: Vote for John F. Kennedy for President [Vote for John F. Kennedy for President]. (Kennedy, 1960, "Urban Affairs")

He pointed to many problems that need work: housing, schools, transportation, and property taxes. In these ads he doesn't discuss specific plans to solve them, but he does lay out an ambitious agenda (while suggesting that the present administration has not done much to help these problem areas).

However, Kennedy also offered a strong stand about the role of the United States in world affairs in this commercial:

Announcer: This historic moment is brought to you by Citizens for Kennedy [scene from Nixon-Kennedy debates].

Kennedy: As I said at the beginning, the question before us all, that faces all Republicans and all Democrats, is can freedom in the next generation conquer, or are the Communists going to be successful? That's the great issue. And if we meet our responsibilities I think freedom will conquer. If we fail, if we fail to move ahead, if we fail to develop sufficient military, and economic, and social strength here in this country, then I think that the tide could begin to run against us. And I don't want historians ten years from now to say these were the years when the tide ran out for the United States. I want them to say these were the years when the tide came in. These were the years when the United States started to move again. That's the question before the American people and only you can decide what you want, what you want this country to be. What you want to do with the future. I think we're ready to move. And it is to that great task, if we are successful, that we will address ourselves. (Kennedy, 1960, "High Tide")

Thus, while concentrating on domestic issues, Kennedy also stressed the importance of a strong defense against Communist aggression.

The Kennedy campaign also produced a memorable song, with still photos and cartoon signs:

> Kennedy, Kennedy, Kennedy, Kennedy, Kennedy, Kennedy, Kennedy, Ken-Ken, Kennedy for me. Kennedy, Kennedy, Kennedy.
> Do you want a man for president who's seasoned through and through?
> But not so doggoned seasoned that he won't try something new.
> A man who's old enough to know and young enough to do.
> It's up to you, it's up to you, it's simply up to you.
> Do you like a man who answers straight, a man who's always fair?
> We'll measure him against the others and when you compare,
> You'll cast your vote for Kennedy and the change that's overdue.
> So it's up to you, it's up to you, it's simply up to you.
> Kennedy, Kennedy, Kennedy, Kennedy, Kennedy, Kennedy, Kennedy for me.
> Kennedy, Kennedy, Kennedy, Kennedy, Kennedy, Kennedy, Kennedy, Kennedy, Kennedy. (Kennedy, 1960, "Jingle")

Thus, Kennedy's spots addressed a much wider range of topics than did Nixon's advertisements. While he does address national defense and Communism, he devoted far more attention than Nixon to domestic affairs. Unlike Nixon, Kennedy did not use an easily recognizable series of commercials.

Vice President Lyndon B. Johnson took office after Kennedy was assassinated in 1963, and as a sitting president (albeit one elected as vice-president) he was the Democratic nominee in 1964. Senator Hubert Humphrey was selected as the vice-presidential nominee. Johnson was challenged by Senator Barry M. Goldwater and his running mate, Representative William Miller. The Gulf of Tonkin Resolution was passed in August of 1964, initiating the Vietnam conflict. The Democrats believed Nixon was wrong to have agreed to debate when he was ahead in 1960, and did not want to make the same mistake in 1964 (Democrats in the Senate prevented suspension of the equal time television rule, effectively prohibiting debates [Splaine, 1995]).

Several of Johnson's spots worked from the idea that Goldwater was a warmonger. The "Daisy" spot is the most famous of these:

Girl [small girl picking petals from a daisy]: One, two, three, four, five, seven, six, six, eight, nine, nine.

Technician: Ten, nine, eight, seven, six, five, four, three, two, one, zero. [zoom to girl's eye, revealing mushroom cloud. Sound of blast.]

Johnson: These are the stakes: to make a world in which all God's children can live, or go into the dark. We must either love each other or we must die.

Announcer: Vote for President Johnson on November 3 [Vote for President Johnson on November 3]. The stakes are too high for you to stay home. (Johnson, 1964, "Daisy")

This spot employed very powerful images to evoke its message: an innocent little child with a flower and the mushroom cloud of an atomic bomb. Johnson provided an equally powerful contrast in his words: Love one another or die. Another such advertisement concerned Goldwater's support for nuclear weapons tests. One commercial argued that the red "hot line" telephone must be in responsible hands. These concerns were fueled in part by fears about Russia, Communist China, and the cold war. Goldwater's nomination acceptance address, which declared that "extremism in defense of liberty is no vice," reinforced these worries for some voters. The following spot plays on these fears less directly:

The Constitution does not tell us what kind of man the President must be. It says he must be 35 years old and a natural born citizen. It leaves the rest to the wisdom of the voters. Our Presidents have been reasonable men. They have listened. They have thought clearly, and spoken carefully. They have cared about people, for the pieces of paper on which they sign their names change people's lives. Most of all, in the final loneliness of this room, they have been prudent. They have known that the decisions they make here can change the course of history. Or end history altogether. In crisis and tragedy, we have found men worthy of this office. We have been fortunate. Vote for President Johnson on November 3 [Vote for President Johnson on November 3]. The stakes are too high for you to stay home. (Johnson, 1964, "Our President")

This spot adopts a low-key, deliberative approach. The implication is that Goldwater is an impulsive warmonger, while Johnson is a calm but strong peace lover.

The Johnson campaign attempted to portray Goldwater as an extremist on other issues besides defense. This spot argues that he would threaten social security:

Announcer [Social Security card on table]: On at least seven different occasions, Barry Goldwater has said that he would drastically change the present Social Security system. In the *Chattanooga Tennessee Times* [newspaper put on card], in a "Face the Nation" interview [film can on newspaper], in the *New York Times Magazine* [put on top], in a "Continental Classroom" television interview [television reel on top], in the *New York Journal American* [paper on top], in a speech he made only last January in Concord, New Hampshire [speech manuscript on top], and in the *Congressional Record* [journal on top]. Even his running mate William Miller [hands tear Social Security card in two] admits that Barry Goldwater's voluntary plan would wreck your Social Security.

Johnson: Too many have worked too long, and too hard, to see this threatened now by policies which threaten to undo all that we have done together over all these years [whole Social Security card].

Announcer: For over thirty years, President Johnson has worked to strengthen Social Security. Vote for him on November 3 [Vote for President Johnson on November 3]. The stakes are too high for you to stay home. (Johnson, 1964, "Social Security")

Many people were concerned about having enough money to survive in retirement, and this ad suggested that Goldwater could be a threat to domestic as well as foreign policy. Another creative Johnson spot suggested that Goldwater, who was a senator from Arizona, would not be equally concerned about the fate of the entire country.

Announcer: [sounds of sawing and water lapping]: In a *Saturday Evening Post* article dated August 31, 1963, Barry Goldwater said: "Sometimes I think this country would be better off if we could just saw off the eastern seaboard and let it float out to sea" [saw goes through wooden map; eastern seaboard floats off]. Can a man who makes statements like this be expected to serve all the people justly and fairly? Vote for President Johnson on November 3. The stakes are too high for you to stay home [Vote for President Johnson on November 3]. (Johnson, 1964, "Eastern Seaboard")

Clearly, voters want a president who will represent the entire country, not just one geographical region. Another spot reinforced this premise, suggesting that Goldwater opposed spending federal funds on dams unless they were built in Arizona, his home state.

The Johnson campaign also addressed character issues. This commercial mentions several issues to make the argument that the Republican candidate is inconsistent:

When somebody tells you he's for Barry Goldwater, you ask him which Barry Goldwater he's for? [Goldwater faces on both sides of screen; pans from side to side]. Is he for the one who said, we must make the fullest possible use of the United Nations, or is he for the one who said the United States no longer has a place in the United Nations? Is he for the Barry who said, I've never advocated the use of nuclear weapons anywhere in the world, or is he for the one who said I'd drop a low yield atomic bomb on the Chinese supply lines in North Vietnam? Is he for the Barry who said, I seek the support of no extremist, or is he for the one who said extremism in the defense of liberty is no vice? And how is a Republican supposed to indicate on his ballot which Barry he's voting for? There's only one Lyndon Johnson. Vote for him on November 3 [Vote for President Johnson on November 3]. The stakes are too high for you to stay home. (Johnson, 1964, "Which Barry Goldwater?")

While revisiting the charges of extremism, this spot charges Goldwater with being inconsistent and, presumably, untrustworthy. Voters who decide on character will want their president to be consistent, and voters who decide on policy want to be able to accurately predict what their president will do after the election.

These Democratic attacks (and perhaps his remark in his acceptance address as well) forced Goldwater to defend in several of his spots. Here is one of his defenses against the accusation that he is rash:

Announcer: Mr. Goldwater, what's this about your being called imprudent and impulsive?

Goldwater: Well, you know, it seems to me that the really impulsive and imprudent president is the one who is so indecisive that he has no policy at all, with the result that potential aggressors are tempted to move because they think that we lack the will to defend freedom. Now there was nothing impulsive or imprudent about Dwight Eisenhower when he moved with firmness and clear purpose in Lebanon and the Formosa Straits. Compare these Eisenhower policies with the appalling actions of this administration—in Laos and the Bay of Pigs, in Berlin and the Congo. We need a clear and resolute policy, one which is based on peace through strength. Only when we have such a policy will we reclaim our rightful role as the leader of the free world.

Announcer: In your heart, you know he's right. Vote for Barry Goldwater [Vote for Barry Goldwater]. (Goldwater, 1964, "Impulsive")

This advertisement is designed to clearly deny the accusations and reassure voters that Goldwater was not a warmonger. It also attacked the Kennedy/Johnson administration for foreign policy failures like the Bay of Pigs fiasco. Another spot used Ronald Reagan to dispute attacks on Goldwater.

Goldwater revisited a favorite Republican approach in 1964, question and answer. Several of his spots began with the statement: "The people ask Barry Goldwater." This was followed by a question from a citizen, and then Goldwater's response.

Announcer: The people ask Barry Goldwater.

Woman: I have a question for Mr. Goldwater. I'm Cynthia Port. We keep hearing about hot wars, cold wars, and brushfire wars. I have an older brother and many of my former classmates who are now serving in the armed forces. I'd like to know what Mr. Goldwater will do to keep us out of war.

Goldwater: Well, let me assure you here and now, and I've said this in every corner of the land throughout this campaign and I'll continue to say it, that a Goldwater-Miller administration will mean once more the proven policy of peace through strength that was the hallmark of the Eisenhower years. The Eisenhower approach to foreign affairs is our approach. It served the cause of freedom and avoided war during the last Republican Administration. It will do so again. We are the party of preparedness and the party of peace.

Announcer: In your heart you know he's right. Vote for Barry Goldwater [Vote for Barry Goldwater]. (Goldwater, 1964, "Out of War")

He also made several other spots that did not begin with the phrase "The people ask Barry Goldwater," but which did start with a question posed by a citizen and a response from the candidate (a similar idea to the Nixon "What is the truth about" ads). As with Eisenhower's "Eisenhower Answers America" series of commercials, these spots suggested that the candidate with answers was Goldwater. However, unlike Eisenhower's more successful spots, many of Goldwater's questions did not concern problems of the current administration. Some were defenses (what will he do about Social Security) and others were simply springboards for Goldwater to explain his viewpoint.

Goldwater also attacked what he saw as the widespread moral decay in the Johnson administration.

[Bobby Baker] *Announcer*: Graft [Graft]. [Billy Sol Estes]. Swindles [Swindles]. Juvenile delinquency [Juvenile delinquency]. Crime [Crime]. Riots [Riots]. [video for each topic]

Hear what Barry Goldwater has to say about our lack of moral leadership.

Goldwater: The leadership of this nation has a clear and immediate challenge to go to work effectively and go to work immediately to restore proper respect for law and order in this land, and not just prior to election day either. America's greatness is the greatness of her people. And let this generation then make a new mark for that greatness. Let this generation set a standard of responsibility that will inspire the world.

Announcer: In your heart you know he's right. Vote for Barry Goldwater [Vote for Barry Goldwater].

This spot listed several examples (Bobby Baker, Billie Sol Estes) of corruption in the current administration. Then Goldwater takes the high moral ground, declaring the need for America's president to take responsibility for our actions as the leader of the free world.

FUNCTIONS OF TELEVISION SPOTS

These four candidates devoted 70% of their comments in television spots to acclaims. For example, Nixon boasted that "the record shows there's been more progress in civil rights in the past eight years than in the preceding eighty years, because this administration has insisted on making progress. And I want to continue and speed up that progress." In 1964, a Johnson spot declared that "America is stronger and more prosperous than ever before—and we're at peace. Vote for President Johnson on November 3" (see Table 4.1).

Table 4.1
Functions of the 1960 and 1964 Campaigns

Year	Candidate	Acclaims	Attacks	Defenses
1960	Nixon	**140 (85%)**	14 (9%)	10 (6%)
	Kennedy	**105 (73%)**	38 (27%)	0
1964	Goldwater	**98 (60%)**	55 (34%)	11 (7%)
	Johnson	**59 (58%)**	42 (42%)	0
Total		**402 (70%)**	149 (26%)	21 (4%)

About a quarter (26%) of the utterances in these spots were attacks. One of Kennedy's attacking ads noted that "Every Republicans politician wants you to believe that he [Nixon] has actually been making decisions in the White House—but listen to the man who knows best." This was followed by video from an Eisenhower press conference, in which he was asked for "an example of a major idea of his [Nixon's] that you had adopted." Eisenhower paused and answered, "If you give me a week, I might think of one. I don't remember." Eisenhower's answer was shown twice. A spot by Goldwater showed video of anti-American protests around the world. Goldwater then asked, "Is this what President Johnson means when he says we are 'much beloved'? Well, I don't like to see our flag torn down and trampled anywhere in the world.... I don't like to see American citizens pushed around, and there's no good reason for letting it happen. All this results from weak, vacillating leadership." Thus, these candidates relied heavily on acclaims and attacks.

Defenses, which did not appear in the 1950s spots, were used for the first time in television advertisements in 1960 and 1964. However, they were far less common than acclaims and attacks, accounting for 4% of the utterances (and only used by Republicans in these campaigns). For instance, one Nixon spot in 1960 began by announcing that "President Eisenhower answers the Kennedy-Johnson charges that America has accomplished nothing in the last eight years." Then, Eisenhower reported that "I am proud of you, proud of what you have done. And proud of what has been done by America. And let no one diminish your pride and confidence in yourselves or belittle these accomplishments. My friends, never have Americans achieved so much in so short a time." While rambling and vague, this spot is clearly meant as a defense. Similarly, Goldwater noted in one of his spots that "Our opponents are referring to us as warmongers," and Eisenhower replied, "Well, Barry, in

Table 4.2
Policy versus Character in the 1960 and 1964 Campaigns

Year	Candidate	Policy	Character
1960	Nixon	56 (36%)	**98 (64%)**
	Kennedy	71 (50%)	**72 (50%)**
1964	Goldwater	73 (48%)	**80 (52%)**
	Johnson	**66 (65%)**	35 (35%)
Total		266 (48%)	**285 (52%)**

my mind, this is actual tommyrot," explicitly denying the accusation. Thus, these spots made use of defense.

POLICY VERSUS CHARACTER

These campaigns had a slight tendency to prefer character (52%) over policy (48%). In 1960, Nixon discussed the economy, arguing that "We must keep growing to stay strong and free. Only by staying strong can we keep peace." This statement acclaims Nixon's ideals. Kennedy revealed one of his ideals in this commercial:

We need the best-educated citizens in the world. The schools in your own state may be good and the teachers may be well compensated. And they may be in my own state of Massachusetts. But we are our brother's keeper. This is not fifty separate states, this is a national problem to make sure that whatever talent or ability any young man or woman may have, that they have a chance to develop it in good schools, with competent and well-compensated teachers.

Goldwater attacked his opponent's leadership ability in 1964: "Our country has lacked leadership that treats public office as a public trust." A Johnson spot, in contrast, praised his leadership with a spot about the "hot line" telephone linking Washington with Moscow: "This particular phone only rings in a serious crisis. Leave it in the hands of a man who has proven himself responsible. Vote for President Johnson on November 3." Thus, character served as a ground for both acclaims and attacks in these advertisements (see Table 4.2).

Policy was also used frequently in these commercials. A spot for Kennedy acclaimed his goals in 1960:

The Democratic party, and our standard-bearer, Senator John F. Kennedy, is determined to see to it that agricultural income goes up. We believe that our food abundance is a blessing and not a problem. We believe in putting food to work at home and abroad to help humanity. We believe in the family farm as the best system of agriculture and we seek an economic program for agriculture that will protect it.

Nixon acclaimed the Eisenhower/Nixon administration's record on civil rights: "The last eight years have seen more progress toward equal rights and equal opportunity for all Americans than the previous twenty years. We must continue that progress." He ends with a statement of goals on this issue. A Johnson spot featured a little girl eating an ice cream cone discussing the nuclear test-ban treaty, attacking Goldwater's past deeds and future plans:

They got together and signed a nuclear test-ban treaty and then the radioactive poison started to go away. But now, there's a man who wants to be President of the United States, and he doesn't like this treaty. He fought against it. He even voted against it. He wants to go on testing more bombs. His name is Barry Goldwater. And if he's elected, they might start testing all over again.

An announcer in a Goldwater spot explained that "Here is Barry Goldwater, who calls him [Johnson] to account for this Administration's colossal bungling on Cuba and Castro." Then Goldwater declared "The same bearded dictator is still ninety miles off, thumbing his nose at us. And the Bay of Pigs has left us not a monument to freedom, but a dark blot on our national pride." Thus, policy was used in both acclaims and attacks in these spots.

FORMS OF POLICY AND CHARACTER

These spots tended to emphasize past deeds (45%) and general goals (45%) when they discussed policy, and leadership ability (41%) and personal qualities (37%) when they addressed character. In 1964, for example, a Johnson spot acclaimed his accomplishments while attacking Goldwater's past deeds: "President Johnson has signed over a dozen laws for the improvement of education. Laws about education for handicapped children, people displaced by automation, medical schools, graduate schools, training programs, and others. Senator Goldwater voted against all of them." In response to a question about how to "keep the Communists from taking over in Africa," Nixon acclaimed his goals: "Well, I believe we can if we keep on working through the United Nations." In the realm of character, Adlai Stevenson praised Kennedy's leadership ability: "The great majority of the world's nations wait eagerly for America to assume again the leadership for freedom and for peace. I believe Senator Kennedy offers us the vigorous, principled direction which will answer Krushchev's bluster." There is also an implied attack on the current lack of leadership. A Goldwater commercial in 1964 stressed his personal qualities: "Put a man of honesty, integrity, and strength in the White House. Vote for Barry Goldwater." While future plans and ideals occurred at times, these topics were relatively less common in these campaigns (see Table 4.3).

SOURCE OF UTTERANCE

These commercials relied most heavily on the candidates for acclaims (53%) and defenses (62%) and on other speakers for attacks (58%) (see Table 4.4). Kennedy explicitly announces his goals when he discusses the problem of medical costs for the elderly in this spot: "I believe that the way to meet this problem is the way Franklin Roosevelt met it in the Social Security Act of 1935. I believe that people during their working years would want to contribute, so that when they retired, when they reach the age of 65 for men or 62 for women, then they can receive assistance in paying their bills." In 1964, Goldwater announced his goals for foreign aid (with an indication of his ideals): "I'm for giving foreign aid only to countries who really want to be self-supporting and who are willing to support American policy in our search for peace and freedom." Thus, acclaims frequently were spoken by the candidates themselves.

Attacks are more often stated by sources other than the candidates. One Goldwater spot used Senator John Tower to attack the Democratic vice-presidential candidate, Hubert Humphrey:

The Democratic national convention nominated as its choice for the Vice President a man who is one of the founders of the left-wing Americans for Democratic Action, one of the most socialistically minded organizations in this country today. Mr. Hubert Horatio Humphrey was not only one of the founders of ADA; he was one of its principal officers. The ADA advocates such things as the recognition of Red China, admission of Red China to the United Nations, a soft line toward Castro, the surrender of much of America's national sovereignty, unilateral disarmament in the face of continued communist aggression, and a thoroughly managed society. Do you want to vote for an administration where a man who subscribes to this line will be next in line for the presidency?

This spot uses guilt by association to question Humphrey's ideals, and to suggest inappropriate policy choices that he might support. However, Goldwater is not (explicitly) the source of these attacks. An anonymous announcer made this series of attacks on Goldwater on behalf of Johnson, with a visual aid of a flipping poster of Goldwater:

Table 4.3
Forms of Policy and Character in the 1960 and 1964 Campaigns

Year	Candidate	Policy			Character		
		Past Deeds	Future Plans	General Goals	Personal Qualities	Leadership Ability	Ideals
1960	Nixon	13 (23%)	9 (16%)	34 **(61%)**	17 (17%)	67 **(68%)**	14 (14%)
	Kennedy	27 (38%)	2 (3%)	42 **(59%)**	28 (39%)	31 **(43%)**	13 (18%)
1964	Goldwater	40 **(55%)**	2 (3%)	31 (42%)	46 **(58%)**	7 (9%)	27 (34%)
	Johnson	39 **(59%)**	14 (21%)	13 (20%)	15 **(43%)**	12 (34%)	8 (23%)
Total		119 **(45%)**	27 (10%)	120 **(45%)**	106 (37%)	117 **(41%)**	62 (22%)

48

Table 4.4
Source of Utterances in the 1960 and 1964 Campaigns

Year	Candidate	Acclaims		Attacks		Defenses	
		Candidate	Other	Candidate	Other	Candidate	Other
1960	Nixon	66 (47%)	**74 (53%)**	**9 (64%)**	5 (36%)	**7 (70%)**	3 (30%)
	Kennedy	**59 (56%)**	46 (44%)	**25 (66%)**	13 (34%)	0	0
1964	Goldwater	**56 (57%)**	42 (43%)	17 (31%)	**38 (69%)**	**6 (55%)**	5 (45%)
	Johnson	**33 (56%)**	26 (44%)	12 (29%)	**30 (71%)**	0	0
Total		**214 (53%)**	188 (47%)	63 (42%)	**86 (58%)**	**13 (62%)**	8 (38%)

49

It's a funny thing about Barry Goldwater. Six different times he told the world he wants to make Social Security voluntary. Then he turns around and says he never said that. Five times he's been quoted as saying we ought to get out of the UN. But now he turns around and says he never said that either. He voted against the tax cut. Then he turns around and says he wants to cut taxes. He made a big speech and said extremism in the defense of liberty is no vice. Then he turns around and says "I seek the support of no extremist." He suggested using nuclear weapons in Laos and in Vietnam. Then he turns around and says "I have never advocated the use of nuclear arms anywhere in the world." There's only one Lyndon Johnson.

These examples are clearly designed to attack Goldwater's personal qualities (his consistency and integrity), and are not directly attributed to Johnson.

Defenses were also frequently uttered by the candidates themselves. For instance, Nixon provided "the truth about the charge that America is not growing in economic strength," declaring that "The best answer is look at your own paycheck. More Americans are working at better jobs than ever before. Americans are earning more and saving more than ever before." Similarly, in 1964 Goldwater responded to charges that he doesn't support the United Nations: "I support the United Nations. I want to see it come closer to its original purpose, and I want to make full use of it as a forum in which the voice of freedom is always heard." Thus, defenses were usually presented by the candidates themselves.

CONCLUSION

In 1960, Kennedy defeated Nixon. The Republican candidate would have to wait eight more years before ascending to the presidency. Although Eisenhower did appear on Nixon's behalf in a few of his advertisements, Eisenhower's lack of enthusiastic support (as showcased prominently in the Kennedy "Ike's Press Conference" spots) surely hurt Nixon's campaign. There are, of course, numerous factors at work in this campaign (Nixon's ill-considered pledge to campaign in all 50 states; Kennedy's strong performance in the presidential debates), but Kennedy's advertising campaign was well conceived. He addressed more issues than did the Republican nominee. Nixon, on the other hand, appeared to be somewhat on the defensive. Nixon's "What is the Truth . . ." spots were not nearly as effective as Eisenhower's "Eisenhower Answers America" advertisements.

Johnson won the next election, defeating Goldwater. Among other themes, the Democratic president secured election on his own in part by playing on many voters' fears that Goldwater could be too militarily aggressive. The "Daisy" spot, while only once aired in a paid broadcast (but seen on the news), neatly encapsulated these concerns. Johnson's television spots were generally well developed. As mentioned earlier, some of Goldwater's own statements may have worked against him here. Goldwater's spots attacked Johnson, but not as effectively as Eisenhower had attacked the incumbent Democratic administration in 1952. Goldwater was also on the defensive in many of his commercials (even if he wasn't always explicitly responding to charges, he spent much time attempting to explain away voters' fears). His "The People Ask Barry Goldwater" advertisements again fall short of the standard established in "Eisenhower Answers America." Thus, Johnson's spots were more effectively developed than Goldwater's advertisements.

Chapter 5

Nixon's Return: 1968, 1972

In 1968, President Johnson had decided not to seek another term in office. His vice president, Hubert Humphrey, was selected as the Democratic nominee. Senator Edmund Muskie was chosen to be his running mate. Richard Nixon, who had lost the presidential campaign to Kennedy in 1960 and the 1962 gubernatorial campaign to Edmund Brown, was nominated to lead the Republican Party. Governor Spiro Agnew was selected as his running mate. (Governor George Wallace and General Curtis LeMay ran on the American Independent Party ticket, winning some electoral votes [see Splain, 1995].) The Vietnam War was very controversial and Martin Luther King was assassinated in October of 1968.

Nixon's spots attacked the status quo, arguing that the Johnson/Humphrey administration had been inept, and that Nixon would improve matters. Several of these spots discussed foreign affairs:

Never has so much military, economic, and diplomatic power been used as ineffectively as in Vietnam. And if after all of this time and all of this sacrifice and all of this support there is still no end in sight, then I say the time has come for the American people to turn to new leadership not tied to the policies and mistakes of the past. I pledge to you: we will have an honorable end to the war in Vietnam [This time, Nixon. This time, Republican all the way]. (Nixon, 1968, "Vietnam")

Other spots lamented the state of domestic affairs and pledged improvements at home if we elect Nixon to be president:

In recent years crime in this country has grown nine times as fast as the population. At the current rate, the crimes of violence in America will double by 1972.

We cannot accept that kind of future. We owe it to the decent and law-abiding citizens of America to take the offensive against the criminal forces that threaten their peace and security, and to rebuild respect for law across this country. I pledge to you that the wave of crime is not going to be the wave of the future in America [This time vote like your whole world depended on it. Nixon]. (Nixon, 1968, "Crime")

These spots functioned both to attack the past deeds of the incumbent party and to acclaim the general goals of Nixon's alternative approach.

A large number of Nixon's television advertisements consisted of endorsements from established politicians. This spot featured five different endorsers:

Announcer: Five distinguished Americans talk about Richard Nixon.

Goldwater [Senator Barry Goldwater]: There has never been a man in American history so thoroughly trained for the Presidency as Richard Nixon.

Reagan [Governor Ronald Reagan of California]: The Republican Party united behind Richard Nixon offers a chance, a return to individual freedom. A return to efforts on the part of communities and of the private sector and private groups; not just always under government domination.

Tower [Senator John Tower of Texas]: I think you have to start by putting your own house in order at home and I think Dick Nixon would do this by restoring respect for law and order in this country.

Baker [Senator Howard Baker of Tennessee]: We're tired of the tired old theories of the thirties and we want answers that are relevant to the sixties and the seventies and Dick Nixon has them to offer.

Dirksen [Senator Everett Dirksen of Illinois]: Putting it all together, it runs in my mind that Dick Nixon would not be a good President; he would be a great President of the United States [This time vote like your whole world depended on it. Nixon]. (Nixon, 1968, "Distinguished")

Other commercials featured senators (George Murphy, Hiram Fong, Jacob Javits, Charles Percy, Mark Hatfield, Hugh Scott, and Edward Brock), another governor (George Romney), and at least one congressman (George Bush). Another spot featured an endorsement from entertainer Pat Boone.

Humphrey used some of his spots in the 1968 presidential contest to highlight his past accomplishments:

Announcer: When he fought for civil rights twenty years ago, a lot of people said he was ahead of his time. He was. He was ahead of his time when he outlined health insurance for the aged, sixteen years before Medicare. He was ahead of his time when he urged a nuclear test ban treaty ten years before it was signed. He was ahead of his time when he proposed job training for unemployed young people, seven years before the job corps. He was ahead of his time when he defined food for peace five years before the program saw life. And he was ahead of his time when he dreamed up the Peace Corps, four years before Congress adopted it. Hubert Humphrey has been ahead of his time for the last twenty years, that's why he's the man we need for the future. Don't just vote for the right ideas, vote for the man who thought of them. With Hubert Humphrey, it's not just talk. He gets it done [zoom in on Humphrey picture; HHH]. (Humphrey, 1968, "Ahead of his Time")

The argument that he has been ahead of his time flows smoothly into the claim that he would be good for the future. He is portrayed here as a man of action, not just of words. His advertisements also employed quotations from ordinary citizens to acclaim Humphrey's leadership ability:

Announcer: These are critical times. Who do you want to be the next President?

Man: As things stand right now, I definitely feel Mr. Humphrey would be the best, best possible candidate for the Presidency.

Man: This is a man who has had a very strong liberal background.

Woman: He's not only a man of new ideas, he's a man who's ahead of the times.

Man: I think he's a man who's ready for the job. He can handle it because he's very familiar with the problems involved, the issues.

Man: He was very active and very much acquainted with the problems of the cities many years ago when we talked about civil rights and the poor people.

Man: Vice President Humphrey is without question a man that I feel that everyone in this country can trust.

Man: I think Mr. Humphrey is a leader. He's one who can unite all the people behind him. He's just the best man for the job right now.

Announcer: People believe in Humphrey. The country needs him [Humphrey]. (Humphrey, 1968, "Critical Times")

This commercial briefly mentions policy (civil rights), but it focuses primarily on Humphrey's character. The Democratic campaign also had a few endorsements for its candidate. This spot used Senator Ted Kennedy to acclaim Humphrey's leadership ability:

Announcer: Senator Ted Kennedy.

Kennedy: Because he has the experience, the ability, and the heart to measure up to what we need, because he is a man of character, I support Hubert Humphrey for the Presidency of the United States [Humphrey-Muskie: There is no alternative]. (Humphrey, 1968 "Kennedy 20")

Thus, these commercials used a variety of approaches to acclaiming the Democratic candidate in 1968.

Humphrey also attacked his opponents in his television advertisements. Notice how this spot intersperses acclaims with attacks as a voter muses on the question of what Nixon has done for America:

Announcer: What has Richard Nixon ever done for you?

Man: What has Richard Nixon ever done for me? Ah, Medicare. No, that was Humphrey's idea. Nixon, Nixon, oh the bomb, the bomb. No, that was Humphrey's idea to stop testing the nuclear bomb. Nixon. Well, what has Richard Nixon ever done for me? Ah, let's see. Working people, I'm a worker. Nixon ever do anything—No, Humphrey and the Democrats gave us Social Security. But Nixon. Nothing in education. Nothing in housing. Hasn't done anything there either.

Announcer: The preceding was a political announcement paid for by Citizens for Humphrey-Muskie.

Man: That's funny. There must have been something Nixon's done. (Humphrey, 1968, "What Has Nixon Done?")

This spot manages to praise Humphrey and his party while attacking his Republican opponent. Nixon's running mate, Spiro Agnew, was also the target of attacks in this campaign:

Announcer [heart monitor screen]: Never before in our lives have we been so confronted with this reality [Edmund Muskie, Spiro Agnew]. Who is your choice to be a heartbeat away from the presidency? [Vote Humphrey Muskie November 5th]. (Humphrey, 1968, "Heartbeats")

Humphrey also felt it necessary to attack the third-party candidate, George Wallace. This spot attacks both of Humphrey's opponents:

Announcer [soap bubbles]: Some men will tell you anything. Mr. Nixon pledges he'll end the war in Vietnam [bubble pops], but Spiro Agnew says Nixon has no plan. Mr. Wallace talks about law and order [bubble pops], but under the Wallace administration, Alabama had the highest murder rate [highest murder rate] in the country. Mr. Nixon wants to offer security to older citizens [bubble pops], but Mr. Nixon opposes Medicare [opposes Medicare]. Mr. Wallace says he'll lower taxes for the little man [bubble pops], but Wallace raised the Alabama food sales tax to 6%, highest in the country [Wallace raises taxes]. Mr. Nixon tells us he's ready to meet the challenge of international politics [bubble pops], but at home Nixon will not even meet Hubert Humphrey on TV [Nixon: won't discuss issues]. Some men will tell you anything to get the job, while other men are interested in the truth [Vote Humphrey-Muskie on November 5]. (Humphrey, 1968, "Bubbles")

Not only does this spot attack Humphrey's opponents' past deeds, but it also questions their integrity, suggesting that they will say anything to get elected. These examples give a general idea of the nature of the advertising in the 1968 campaign.

In 1972, Nixon and Agnew were nominated by the Republican Party to run for a second term in office. The Democrats selected Senator George McGovern to run for president and Senator Thomas Eagleton for vice president. When it was revealed that Eagleton had been treated for depression, McGovern initially supported him but later replaced him with Sargent Shriver. The Vietnamese War continued. President Nixon had visited both Communist China and Russia in his first term. The Watergate break-in occurred in June of 1972.

In his campaign for a second term in the office of the president, Nixon acclaimed his first-term accomplishments.

Announcer [slow pans over still photos; "America" playing softly in background]: He has brought home over 500,000 men from the war, and less than 40,000 remain. None engaged in ground combat. He has overhauled the draft laws and made them fair for everyone, black and white, rich and poor. He certified an amendment giving 18-year-olds the right to vote. He has created an economy that is growing faster than at any time in years. The rate of inflation has been cut in half. He created the first governmental agency we have ever had to deal solely with the problems of our environment. He is using the vast resources of government to find a cure for cancer and sickle cell anemia. He's gone to China to talk peace with Mao Tse Tung. He's gone to the Soviet Union to talk peace with Leonid Breshnev. For four years President Nixon has responded to the needs of the people. That's why we need President Nixon, now more than ever [Nixon, now more than ever]. (Nixon, 1972, "Record")

Notice that both domestic and foreign affairs are used to support the argument that Nixon has been successful in his first four years as president. The implication, of course, is that a second term in office would extend his praiseworthy record with clear benefits for voters.

Some of Nixon's 1972 television spots attacked his opponent, Senator George McGovern:

In 1967, Senator George McGovern [photo of McGovern] said he was not an advocate of unilateral withdrawal of our troops from Vietnam. Now of course he is [photo flips from facing left to right]. Last year the Senator suggested regulating marijuana along the same lines as alcohol, which means legalizing it. Now he's against legalizing it and says he always has been [photo flips back]. Last January Senator McGovern suggested a welfare plan that would give a thousand dollar bill to every man, woman, and child in the country [photo flips]. Now he says maybe the thousand dollar figure isn't right [photo flips back]. Last year he proposed to tax inheritances over $500,000 at 100% [photo flips]. This year he suggests 77% [photo flips]. In Florida he was pro-busing [photo flips]. In Oregon he said he would support the anti-busing bill now in Congress [photo flips]. Last year, this year. The question is, what about next year [photo flips around and around rapidly]? [Democrats for Nixon]. (Nixon, 1972, "McGovern Turnaround")

This theme of inconsistency appeared in other Nixon advertisements that year as well. Some of Nixon's spots attacked McGovern's policy proposals. In this commercial, McGovern's welfare plan was attacked:

[worker sitting on girder to eat lunch]: Senator George McGovern recently submitted a welfare bill to the Congress. According to an analysis by the Senate Finance Committee, the McGovern bill would make 47% of the people of the U.S. eligible for welfare—47% [pan to show people walking in the street]. Almost every other person in the country would be on welfare. The Finance Committee estimated the cost of this incredible proposal at $64 billion per year. That's six times what we're spending now. And who's going to pay for this? Well, if you're not the one out of two people [worker looks sad] on welfare, you do [Democrats for Nixon]. (Nixon, 1972, "McGovern Welfare")

Clearly, a proposal that would put almost half of Americans on welfare would be a bad idea. Another spot criticized McGovern's defense plans:

The McGovern defense plan. He would cut the marines by a third [hand sweeps some toy soldiers off table], the Air Force by a third [more toy soldiers swept off table]. He would cut Navy personnel by one-fourth [more toy soldiers swept off]. He would cut interception planes by one-half [hand removes toy planes], the Navy fleet by one-half [hand removes ships], and carriers from sixteen to six [hand removes carriers]. Senator Hubert Humphrey had this to say about the McGovern proposal: "It isn't just cutting into the fat. It isn't just cutting into manpower. It is cutting into the very security of this country" [jumble of toys]. President Nixon doesn't believe we should play games with our national security. He believes in a strong America to negotiate for peace from strength [Nixon on naval ship] [Democrats for Nixon]. (Nixon, 1972, "McGovern Defense Plan")

This spot used reluctant testimony (from fellow Democrat Hubert Humphrey), and its use of toys to vividly illustrate McGovern's plans was innovative.

McGovern attempted to use the Watergate break-in to attack his Republican opponent in this spot:

[all words of ad scroll across screen]: Alfred C. Baldwin, a former FBI agent, has stated this. He was hired by James McCord, security chief for both the Republican National Committee and the Nixon Campaign Committee. Mr. Baldwin was assigned to listen illegally to over two hundred private telephone conversations— calls made by Democratic Chairman Lawrence O'Brien and others from tapped telephones in Democratic headquarters at the Watergate. He sent reports on these conversations to William E. Timmons, assistant to President Nixon for congressional relations, at the White House. In 1968 Mr. Nixon said: "The president's chief function is to lead, not to oversee every detail but to put the right people in charge, provide them with basic guidance, and let them do the job." The question is, do we want the system to continue to work this way for the next four years? [McGovern]. (McGovern, 1972, "Watergate")

The argument here is that the Watergate break-in is evidence that Nixon's concept of presidential leadership has failed. Other McGovern spots used the opinions of ordinary citizens to attack Nixon:

Announcer: Most people have deep feelings about President Nixon.

Woman: He has put a ceiling on wages and done nothing about controlling prices.

Man: The one thing I knew his last four years was that he knew in some way he would have to please me come this election. And what frightens me is that if he gets in again he doesn't have to worry about pleasing me anymore.

Woman: He was caught in the act of spying and stealing. They used to go to jail for these things. He is the president and should set an example.

Woman: There always seems to be some big deal going on with the Nixon people, some wheat deal or something.

Woman: When I think of the White House, I think of it as a syndicate, a crime outfit, as opposed to, you know, a government.

Woman: All I know is that the prices keep going up and he is president.

Man: I think he's smart. I think he's sly. He wants to be the president of the United States so badly he will do *anything*.

Announcer: That's exactly why this is brought to you by the McGovern for President Committee. (McGovern, 1972, "Deep Feelings")

This spot mixes policy (e.g., wages and prices) with character (he is a liar and a thief). Another McGovern advertisement argued that Nixon's first-term record was not as bright as Nixon would have voters believe:

Announcer [all words of scroll across screen]: Four years ago, Richard Nixon said "We are on the road to recovery from the disease of runaway prices." Since Mr. Nixon became President, the cost of whole wheat bread has gone from 31 cents to 45 cents. Since Mr. Nixon became President, the cost of hamburger has gone from 58 cents to 89 cents. Since Mr. Nixon became President, the cost of frozen fish has gone from 69 cents to $1.29. Since Mr. Nixon became President, the cost of living has gone up 19%—and your wages have been frozen. So next time you're in the supermarket, ask yourself: Can you afford four more years of Mr. Nixon? [McGovern]. (McGovern, 1972, "Four More Years?")

This advertisement suggests not only a policy failure (inflation), but also a gap between Nixon's words (campaign promises) and his deeds. It extrapolates from past deeds to the future ("Can you afford four more years of Mr. Nixon?"). Thus, these spots illustrate the campaign in 1972.

Table 5.1
Functions of the 1968 and 1972 Campaigns

Year	Candidate	Acclaims	Attacks	Defenses
1968	Nixon	**71 (71%)**	29 (29%)	0
	Humphrey	**119 (73%)**	36 (23%)	5 (3%)
1972	Nixon	**124 (78%)**	35 (22%)	0
	McGovern	58 (39%)	**90 (60%)**	1 (1%)
Total		**372 (65%)**	190 (33%)	6 (1%)

FUNCTIONS OF TELEVISION SPOTS

Presidential television spots from 1968 and 1972 tended to emphasize acclaims (65%). For example, in 1968 Humphrey praised his general goals: "What this country needs are more decent neighborhoods, more educated people, better homes." His opponent Nixon praised his own ideals: "Dissent is a necessary ingredient of change. But in a system of government that provides for peaceful change there is no cause that justifies resort to violence. There is no cause that justifies rule by mob instead of by reason." Given the riots at the 1968 Democratic National Convention in Chicago, there is an implied criticism of the opposing party as well. In 1972, McGovern identified his goals on drug abuse: "We've got to have a program that's better than the one we have now to deal with drugs if we're gonna get on top of the crime problem." That same year a spot for Nixon acclaimed his past deeds: "Since taking office, President Nixon has brought over 500,000 men from the war and completely ended our involvement in ground combat." These excerpts illustrate how these candidates praised themselves in their television advertisements (see Table 5.1).

Attacks were also fairly common in these commercials, accounting for 33% of the utterances. For example, in 1968 Nixon discussed the need for a new initiative for fighting crime, combining attacks on the Democratic administration with his ideas for solving these problems:

I pledge to you that our new attorney general will be directed by the President of the United States to launch a war against organized crime in this country. I pledge to you that the new attorney general will be an active belligerent against the loan sharks and the numbers racketeers that rob the urban poor in our cities. I pledge to you that the new attorney general will open a new front against the filth peddlers and the narcotics peddlers who are corrupting the lives of the children of this country. Because my friends let this message come through clear from what I say tonight: time is running out for the merchants of crime and corruption in American society. The wave of crime is not going to be the wave of the future in the United States of America [applause].

This commercial both attacks the incumbents for the increase in crime and promises to take action to avert a future crime wave if Nixon is elected. A McGovern spot in 1972 attacked the failures of the first Nixon term:

Since Mr. Nixon became President, the cost of whole wheat bread has gone from 31 cents to 45 cents. Since Mr. Nixon became President, the cost of hamburger has gone from 58 cents to 89 cents. Since Mr. Nixon became President, the cost of frozen fish has gone from 69 cents to $1.29. Since Mr. Nixon became President, the cost of living has gone up 19%—and your wages have been frozen.

The pain of inflation is even worse when wages are stagnant. In the campaign for his second term in office, a Nixon spot questioned McGovern's consistency [a photo of McGovern flipped back and forth during the spot]:

In 1964, Senator McGovern voted in favor of the Gulf of Tonkin Resolution which supported escalation of the war in Vietnam. Now he says he is against the war and always has been. In 1965, McGovern said we should wage war rather than surrender South Vietnam to Communism. Three years later he said it would not be fatal to the United States to have a Communist government in South Vietnam. In 1967, he was against unilateral troop withdrawal. Now of course he favors unilateral withdrawal. Throughout the year he has proposed unconditional amnesty for draft dodgers. But his running mate claims he proposed no such thing. For the war, against the war. For amnesty, against amnesty. The question is, where will he stand next year?

Inconsistency is hardly considered a virtue. This spot clearly suggests that McGovern's inconsistency means we don't know what he would do if elected president. There is also a hint that he is pandering to his audience rather than operating from firm principles.

Defense was uncommon at 1% of the utterances in these spots (Table 5.1), and Nixon (who defended in 6% of his utterances in his 1960 loss) did not defend in either campaign. When it was suggested in 1968 that Humphrey was not sufficiently independent, he replied: "I've been reading that Hubert Humphrey ought to be his own man. That's exactly what I am. . . . Hubert Humphrey as Vice President is a member of a team. Hubert Humphrey as President is captain of a team. There's a lot of difference." In 1972, McGovern dismissed an attack from Nixon: "Richard Nixon goes around talking as if I'm some kind of a radical because I believe in guaranteed jobs for people he's throwing out of work." Note that this is coupled with an attack on Nixon on joblessness. Thus, the candidates in 1968 and 1972 employed acclaiming, attacking, and a little defending in their television commercials.

POLICY VERSUS CHARACTER

These candidates showed a preference for policy (56%) over character (44%) in their television spots (only Humphrey in 1968 had more character utterances than policy). For instance, in 1968 Nixon argued that "In recent years crime in this country has grown nine times as fast as the population. At the current rate, the crimes of violence in America will be doubled by 1972." A Humphrey advertisement acclaimed his accomplishments as a senator: "Let's keep score. The 1964 Civil Rights Act. Medicare. The Job Corps. Project Head Start. Get behind the man behind them all: Hubert H. Humphrey for President." A Nixon commercial in 1972 featured Democrat John Connally attacking the future plans of the Democratic nominee:

Senator McGovern has made proposals to cut an unprecedented thirty-two billion dollars worth of men and weapons out of the United States' defense budget. The McGovern defense budget is the most dangerous document ever seriously put forth by a presidential candidate in this century. It would end the United States' military leadership in the world; it would make us inferior in conventional and strategic weapons to the Soviets. The total United States Armed Forces level would be cut to a point lower than at the time of Pearl Harbor. Dean Rusk, Secretary of State in the administrations of John F. Kennedy and Lyndon Johnson, has termed the McGovern defense, and I quote him, "insane."

McGovern attacked Nixon's economic record in 1972: "Well, I don't know how you can pay twice as much for a tractor, and taxes that are twice as high and interest rates that are at 7–8 percent a year and then make it with corn at a dollar a bushel." Thus, policy was a common topic in these commercials (see Table 5.2).

These ads also took up character issues. A Nixon spot in 1968 touted his leadership ability: "Well I think Richard M. Nixon probably is more qualified in world affairs than anybody I know." The 1968 Humphrey "Weathervane" ad depicted Nixon as a weathervane spinning in the wind, stressing his inconsistency and strongly hinting that he pandered without principles: "Ever noticed what happens to Nixon when the political winds blow? Last year he said, I oppose a federal open housing law. This year he said, I support the 1968 Civil Rights Bill with open housing. Again this year he said, I just supported it to get it out of sight. Which way will he blow next?" Inconsistency is not a positive attribute.

Table 5.2
Policy versus Character in the 1968 and 1972 Campaigns

Year	Candidate	Policy	Character
1968	Nixon	**54 (54%)**	46 (46%)
	Humphrey	67 (43%)	**88 (57%)**
1972	Nixon	**98 (62%)**	61 (38%)
	McGovern	**94 (64%)**	54 (36%)
Total		**313 (56%)**	249 (44%)

In 1972, a Nixon spot proclaimed that "He's a very positive man. He's a leader." That same year a McGovern spot questioned Nixon's integrity:

One of the reasons I'm disturbed about the President's $10 million secret election fund is that it indicates that there's something there that he's afraid to disclose. What are they hiding? I'm perfectly willing to publish the name of every dollar contributed to my campaign. And I don't see what the President is covering up. But it's that kind of thing that puts a kind of a damper on the moral tone of the whole nation.

McGovern also acclaims his own integrity ("I'm perfectly willing to publish the name of every dollar contributed to my campaign") in this spot. Thus, character was the basis of both acclaims and attacks in these campaigns.

FORMS OF POLICY AND CHARACTER

Policy utterances most often appeared in these advertisements as past deeds (56%), with general goals (33%) and future plans (11%) also appearing (only Nixon in 1968 deviated from this pattern, devoting 52% of his policy remarks to goals and 44% to deeds). For example, a 1968 Nixon ad reported that "Crimes of violence in the United States have almost doubled in recent years. Today a violent crime is committed every sixty seconds. A robbery every two-and-a-half minutes. A mugging every six minutes. A murder every forty-three minutes." The implication is that the current (Democratic) administration has failed to adequately deal with crime. A Humphrey commercial that same year attacked third-party candidate George Wallace: "Mr. Wallace talks about law and order, but under the Wallace administration, Alabama had the highest murder rate in the country." In 1972, this McGovern advertisement sympathized with the problems faced by farmers under the Nixon administration: "Well, I don't know how you can pay twice as much for a tractor, and taxes that are twice as high and interest rates that are at seven to eight percent a year and then make it with corn at a dollar a bushel." Thus, attacks on past deeds were quite common in these campaigns (see Table 5.3).

To illustrate their use of general goals, in 1968 a Nixon spot acclaimed his general goals in the area of crime: "I believe that he will back up the efforts of our state and local law enforcement officers through block grants and other means. I think he would appoint to the court judges who are as interested in protecting the law abiding citizen as the criminal. And I believe that he would see that federal laws are vigorously enforced and wage an active campaign against organized crime." Utterances on future plans were less common, but still occurred. This 1972 Nixon spot contrasted the two candidates' proposals:

Seems to me that this election is a lot more than a simple choice between two men or two parties. It's a choice between Senator McGovern's plan to walk out of Vietnam now, or the President's plan to make sure of the release of our prisoners first. It's a choice between the Senator's radical tax and welfare schemes or continuing the economic growth of the past four years. It's a choice between the Senator's plan to cut our military budget to the point that we would become a second class power, or keeping this country as strong as it needs to be.

This ad juxtaposed the two candidates' positions on ending the war in Vietnam, tax and welfare, and the defense budget. These candidates all discussed policy in their television spots.

Character utterances most often occurred as discussions of personal qualities (49%). For instance, in 1968 Senator Fong declared that Nixon could be trusted to follow through with his promises: "I know Richard Nixon: when he says he's going to do a thing, he will do it." This Humphrey commercial used an ordinary person to acclaim the Democratic candidate's integrity: "I believe Mr. Humphrey and I can trust him." In 1972, this Nixon advertisement impugned McGovern's character: "Since the beginning of this thing with McGovern he's been saying one thing and then turning around a week or two or three weeks later and doing something entirely different." Leadership abilities were also common topics of spots (32%; Nixon used this form of character utterance the most in 1968, and just as often as personal qualities in 1972). For instance, in this spot from 1968, Nixon's qualifications for leadership are touted: "Dick Nixon has that kind of resolution, knowledgeability, and purpose which is urgently needed in dealing with the foreign policy of our country today." Ideals were the subject of 19% of the utterances in these campaigns. In 1972, McGovern articulated the principle of fairness in taxation: "Now if you had a president who was working in the other direction on behalf of ordinary taxpayers rather than these big corpo-

Table 5.3
Forms of Policy and Character in the 1968 and 1972 Campaigns

Year	Candidate	Policy			Character		
		Past Deeds	Future Plans	General Goals	Personal Qualities	Leadership Ability	Ideals
1968	Nixon	24 (44%)	2 (4%)	28 **(52%)**	8 (7%)	26 **(57%)**	12 (26%)
	Humphrey	34 **(51%)**	8 (12%)	25 (37%)	44 **(50%)**	28 (32%)	16 (18%)
1972	Nixon	54 **(55%)**	22 (22%)	22 (22%)	23 **(38%)**	23 **(38%)**	15 (25%)
	McGovern	63 **(67%)**	3 (3%)	28 (30%)	47 **(87%)**	2 (4%)	5 (9%)
Total		175 **(56%)**	35 (11%)	103 (33%)	122 **(49%)**	79 (32%)	48 (19%)

rations, we could have a tax system that's fair." These passages illustrate how these campaigns addressed character issues.

SOURCE OF UTTERANCE

In general, these campaign commercials tended to rely more on the utterances of others than on those of the candidate. Most of the acclaims (69%) and most of the attacks (67%) originated with other speakers. Defenses were made only by the candidates themselves, though. There were only two exceptions to this general pattern. In 1972, McGovern made more of the acclaims in his spots (55%) than did other speakers (45%). In 1968, Nixon was the source of more of the attacks (66%) in his advertisements than were others. Interestingly, in his bid for re-election four years later, Nixon dramatically reversed this trend and made none of the attacks personally in his spots (see Table 5.4).

CONCLUSION

Nixon won both of these campaigns. He did seem to shift the proportions of the three functions in his advertising for these campaigns. He curtailed his use of acclaims somewhat (1960: 85%; 1968: 71%; 1972: 78%), increased his attacks noticeably (1960: 9%; 1968: 29%; 1972: 22%) and eschewed defenses altogether (1960: 6%; 1968: none; 1972 none) (Table 5.1). There was also a steady shift away from character to policy (character dropped from 64% in 1960 to 46% in 1968 and 38% in 1972; policy increased from 36% in 1960 to 54% in 1968 and 62% in 1972) (Table 5.2). Although he discussed foreign policy, his second and third campaigns addressed a wider range of topics than in 1960, when he had focused so heavily on Communism.

Table 5.4
Source of Utterances in the 1968 and 1972 Campaigns

Year	Candidate	Acclaims		Attacks		Defenses	
		Candidate	Other	Candidate	Other	Candidate	Other
1968	Nixon	25 (35%)	46 (65%)	19 (66%)	10 (34%)	0	0
	Humphrey	43 (36%)	76 (64%)	15 (42%)	21 (58%)	5 (100%)	0
1972	Nixon	17 (14%)	107 (86%)	0	35 (100%)	0	0
	McGovern	32 (55%)	26 (45%)	28 (31%)	62 (69%)	1 (100%)	0
Total		117 (31%)	255 (69%)	62 (33%)	128 (67%)	6 (100%)	0

Chapter 6

After Watergate: 1976, 1980

Vice President Spiro Agnew resigned during Nixon's second term, in October 1973, after pleading no contest to charges of tax evasion. President Nixon appointed Representative Gerald Ford in his stead. However, in the wake of Watergate, Nixon himself resigned in August of the following year, making Gerald Ford a president who had not been elected as either president or vice president. The Vietnam War was over by 1976, no longer an albatross around the neck of the incumbent party, but Ford's decision to pardon Nixon was widely unpopular. Robert Dole was selected as Ford's running mate. Jimmy Carter, governor of Georgia, was the Democratic nominee. Senator Walter Mondale was selected as Carter's vice-presidential candidate.

In 1976, President Ford attempted to campaign on his first-term record (as did Nixon in 1972), but unfortunately for Ford the economy wasn't doing very well. His spots, accordingly, sandbagged: "He came to the office of the President in troubled times" said one, and another made the excuse that "Two years ago we were mired in the worst economic crisis since the depression." The point here is not that these statements weren't true, but that they sounded defensive to voters. These excuses made it sound more like Ford was apologizing for his record rather than boasting of it. Here is one advertisement that emphasized his record:

He came to the office of the President in troubled times. He began an open administration. Now, quietly and firmly, he is leading us out of the worst recession in years. Rather than loose promises, he has made the hard decisions. Rather than frantic spending he has had the courage to say no. The worst is over. Over two million more Americans are working than at the bottom of the recession.

Inflation is cut almost in half. President Ford is your President. Keep him. (Ford, 1976, "Accomplishment")

Creating two million additional jobs is an important accomplishment, but phrases like "The worst is over" pale in comparison with Nixon's acclaims of his first-term accomplishments, as illustrated in the last chapter. Ford also acclaimed his foreign policy accomplishments:

In just two years, he has strengthened the ties with our allies in Europe, Japan, and Israel [series of relevant still photos]. He has negotiated firmly and fairly with our adversaries, while making sure our military strength is second to none. He has directed the peace efforts in the Middle East, and Africa. And today, there is not a single American soldier fighting anywhere in the world. Let's keep President Ford in charge. (Ford, 1976, "Foreign Policy")

Thus, Ford's campaign attempted to convince voters that his record as president, both in domestic and foreign policy areas, justified keeping him in office.

Another recurrent theme in this campaign was that Ford was a nice person: "He's just a downright decent, honest person, seems to me," and "I trust the man, I think he's an honest man and that's the kind of guy that I want representing me." He also used testimony from ordinary citizens to acclaim Ford and then to attack Carter:

Man: The thing that I like the most about Mr. Ford is that he's steady. He's not erratic; we can count on him to do what's in the best interests of the country.

Man: I think he offers solidarity.

Woman: I think he's a strong person. I think he stands up for what he thinks is right.

Man: I think Ford's been very stable.

Woman: He takes things very gradual, and very carefully. And I don't think he's gonna make any big mistakes. I'm afraid that Carter is too ambiguous.

Man: Carter is not quite sure which direction he goes. He changes his mind on his stand every other day or so.

Man: He contradicts himself from one day to another.

Man: Well, he's changed his opinions from one day to the next.

Woman: He's much too wishy-washy.

Man: He's very, very wishy-washy.

Man: He seems to be a little wishy-washy.

Man: If he'd stand up and say what he was for he'd be a little easier to understand and maybe to believe.

Woman: All the things we've read about Jimmy Carter I think are true: that he is fuzzy on a lot of the issues. I like President Ford, a man who will tell you just exactly where he does stand. (Ford, 1976, "Man in the Street, Stable 3")

This spot managed to acclaim Ford's character as stable while attacking Jimmy Carter on the same grounds.

Ford also attacked Carter's record as the governor of Georgia. This played off of Carter's acclaims of his record (discussed below) and his campaign slogan.

Announcer: What Jimmy Carter did as Governor, he'll do as President [television with Carter still].

Announcer: His ads say that he will do the same as President that he did as Governor of Georgia [pan in on U.S. map to Georgia]. Then you should know that during his one term as Governor, government spending increased by 58% [government spending increased by 58%, on blank outline of state of Georgia]. Government employees went up 25% [Government employees went up 25%]. And the state of Georgia went 100% deeper into debt [Bonded indebtedness up 100%]. Don't let Jimmy Carter give us more big government [More big government]. Keep President Ford. (Ford, 1976, "Carter Record")

This ad argues from his past failures to likely future problems if elected President. Another spot attacked Carter as inconsistent:

When Jimmy Carter was Governor of Georgia, he was for the right to work laws that protect [Right to Work; Carter on left, For; right side blank] the workers of Georgia, and this state. But now that he's running for President, with the support of the big labor unions [Right to Work; Carter on right, Against, left side blank], he is committed to signing the bill which would do away with our right to work laws. Many working people feel that this is not just a flip-flop [photo flips back to left, then to right], but a betrayal of working people. That's another reason for supporting President Ford. (Ford, 1976, "Flip-flop, Generic")

As noted before, voters have an interest in a consistent candidate whether they believe policy or character is most important. An interesting twist was to use newspapers who endorsed Ford's reelection. In this ad, all of the newspapers mentioned are from Carter's home state:

[all words scroll]: Those who know Jimmy Carter best are from Georgia. That's why we thought you ought to know: The Savannah, Georgia NEWS endorses Gerald Ford for President. The Augusta, Georgia HERALD endorses President Ford. The Atlanta, Georgia DAILY WORLD endorses President Ford. The Marietta, Georgia JOURNAL endorses President Ford. The Albany, Georgia HERALD endorses President Ford. The August, Georgia CHRONICLE endorses President Ford. The Savannah, Georgia PRESS endorses [fades out]. (Ford, 1976, "Georgia Papers")

Thus, Ford praised his accomplishments as president and attacked Carter's failures as governor.

As McGovern had attempted to do in 1972, but with more success, Carter attacked the record of the Ford administration in its first term of office:

The Republican television commercials assure us the economy is healthy, inflation's controlled, our leadership is great. But when I look around, I see: every trip to the supermarket a shock, cities collapsing, suburbs scared, policemen cut, welfare skyrocketing. That's reality. The Republicans won't face up to it, but we can change it. (Carter, 1976, "Reality")

Carter's television spots also discussed the principles that should drive government: "competent, well-managed, efficient, economical, purposeful." He elaborates this idea in the following spot:

I believe in tough, competent management. I believe that the best government is the one closest to the people. I believe that people ought to control their own government, and not the other way around. I believe in long-range planning. I believe in balanced budgets. I believe in screening out or eliminating programs that have long past served their usefulness. I believe in an open government, one that people can both understand and control. I believe that when there is a choice to be made between government and private industry, if it's an equal choice, I'd go with the private industry. This is the kind of a concept that is generally considered to be conservative. But at the same time I believe in human beings, in equal opportunity and freedom, in equality of opportunity, and I'll fight for it.

Announcer: If you agree that government should be sensible yet sensitive, vote for Jimmy Carter: A leader, for a change [Jimmy Carter: A leader, for a change]. (Carter, 1976, "List")

This spot lists nine of Carter's beliefs about governing. Besides discussing the principles that will guide his administration, Carter acclaims his accomplishments as governor of Georgia:

Announcer: Jimmy Carter talks about government reorganization [Jimmy Carter on the issue of Government Reorganization].

Carter: When I was elected Governor, I went into office not as a politician, but as an engineer and a farmer and a businessman; a planner. We had 300 agencies and departments in the state government. We abolished 278 of them and set up a very simple economical structure of government. That saved a lot of money, yes, but more importantly, it was so people could understand it for a change and control it. With a new budgeting technique called zero-based budgeting, we eliminated all the old obsolescent programs, put into effect long-range goals and planning and cut administrative costs more than 50%. And shifted that money and that service and that work toward giving better government services to our people.

Announcer [Government Reorganization]: What Jimmy Carter did as Governor he'll do as President. If you agree that government should be reorganized, vote for Jimmy Carter. A leader, for a change [Jimmy Carter. A leader, for a change]. (Carter, 1976, "Reorganization")

Thus, Carter focused on Ford's dismal record as president and his own bright record as governor.

In 1980, Carter and Mondale were nominated by the Democratic Party to seek a second term in office. However, the economy was still not in very good shape. Ronald Reagan, former governor of California (and former actor), was nominated by the Republican Party to challenge Carter, and George Bush was chosen as his running mate. Illinois Representative John Anderson ran as an Independent candidate.

Not surprisingly, Reagan's advertisements in 1980 attacked Carter's first-term record in office:

[Just for the Record, in red]: For the last three and a years, every American has been staggered by the economic record of the Carter administration [bar graphs; each goes up in red as announcer mentions it]. Food prices up over 35%. Auto prices up over 31%. Home prices up over 46%. Clothing up over 20%. Transportation up over 50% [bar goes off screen]. The new Carter economics will give us more of the same. That adds up to less for everyone. The Carter record speaks for itself [The Carter record speaks for itself, in red]. The time is now for Reagan [Reagan]. (Reagan, 1980, "Everything Up")

This spot not only attacks Carter's past failures, but it also predicts future problems if he is re-elected ("more of the same"). While the incumbents' records in office were not the only topics covered in these campaigns, they were very prominent topics in these commercials.

Carter's nomination had been challenged in the primaries by fellow Democrat Senator Edward Kennedy. Reagan, the Republican challenger, made use of this in the general campaign by revisiting Kennedy's primary jibes:

Announcer: Senator Kennedy speaks out on foreign policy [March 1980].

Kennedy: I call this administration's foreign policy the surprise foreign policy, Soviet troops go into Cuba, and the administration is surprised. Soviet troops go into Afghanistan, and this administration is surprised.

Announcer: A reminder, from Democrats for Reagan [Democrats for Reagan]. (Reagan, 1980, "Kennedy Foreign Policy")

Reagan's advertisements also used Carter's statements against him. In 1976, Carter had attacked the Ford administration for economic difficulties. This Reagan spot from 1980 allowed Gerald Ford the chance to attack the man who had ejected him from the White House four years earlier:

Ford: When I left the White House inflation was 4.8%. This year under Carter it's reached 18%. Can any President do anything about inflation? We did. The President must be a leader. Jimmy Carter has had five different economic programs and we still have 13% inflation and sky-high interest rates. We need strong leadership. We need Ron Reagan, our next President.

Announcer: The time is now for strong leadership: Reagan for President [Reagan & Bush]. (Reagan, 1980, "Ford/Inflation")

This spot suggests that Carter has no consistent policy ("five different economic programs") and no effective policy ("still have 13% inflation"). The Reagan campaign also developed advertisements featuring endorsements by President Ford, Mrs. Ford, Senator Eugene McCarthy, Congressman Jack Kemp, Senator Howard Baker, and multiple governors (Thornburgh, Thompson, Rhodes, Milliken, Dreyfuss, Alexander).

Reagan's advertising campaign also used acclaiming. Several spots praised Reagan's record as governor of California:

Announcer: This is a man [Reagan] whose time has come. A strong leader with a proven record. In 1966, answering the call of his party, Ronald Reagan was elected Governor of California—next to President, the biggest job in the nation. What the new Governor inherited was a state of crisis. California was faced with a $194 million deficit, and was spending a million dollars a day more than it was taking in. The state was on the brink of bankruptcy. Governor Reagan became the greatest tax reformer in the state's history. When Governor Reagan left office, the $194 million deficit had been transformed into a $550 million surplus. The *San Francisco Chronicle* said, Governor Reagan has saved the state from bankruptcy [Governor Reagan has saved the state from bankruptcy, source]. The time is now for strong leadership. Reagan for President [Reagan & Bush]. (Reagan, 1980, "Record")

This commercial argues that being the governor of California is very difficult (in 1992, Bush and Perot questioned the relevance and importance of Clinton's experience as governor of Arkansas). Reagan also was proud of the newspaper endorsements his campaign had acquired:

[*Cincinnati Enquirer* plops down] Newspapers all across America [*Plain Dealer* plops down; names of 13 scroll, with 225 more newspapers across America] are endorsing Ronald Reagan for President. One reason is the sad reality of Mr. Carter's record [hostage headline]. A more important reason is the promise of

Ronald Reagan's leadership. As the *Columbus Dispatch* said: Ronald Reagan is by far the best choice to do the job that needs to be done today [Ronald Reagan is by far the best choice to do the job that needs to be done today]. His presidency would return the luster to the American dream [His presidency would return the luster to the American dream, source]. The time is now for Reagan [Reagan & Bush]. (Reagan, 1980, "American Newspapers")

This advertisement manages to include a slap at Carter (for the hostage crisis) while acclaiming the endorsements of the Republican challenger. Reagan's spots also addressed the question of what he would do if elected. He discussed his general goals in this commercial:

Aguirre [Hank Aguirre, Chairman, Medican Industries Inc.]: Governor Reagan's plans for creating jobs are really necessary. But what's he gonna do to get government regulations off our back?

Reagan: It's time we put a stop to government's overregulation of small businesses. Red tape is driving some people out of business. I pledge to help small businesses, and to free them from government interference. Tax incentives will give small business firms more cash to invest, leading to greater productivity, higher profits, and the creation of more jobs.

Announcer: The time is now for Reagan [Reagan for President]. (Reagan, 1980, "Government Regulations")

Thus, Reagan's 1980 campaign attacked his opponent's record, acclaimed his own record as governor—much as Carter had done in 1976.

Carter sounded apologetic about the economy during his term as president in his acclaims during the 1980 campaign, ironically reminiscent of Ford's sandbagging advertisements from four years earlier:

Carter: There's a limit to how much I want the government to stick its nose into people's private affairs, including your family's.

Announcer: The President of the United States, in Mrs. Reed's backyard.

Carter: Back in March, we had absolutely uncontrollable inflation and interest rates—they were both approaching 20%—and we put in some very mild credit restraints. And people like you, all over the nation, in a spirit of cooperation and patriotism, just clamped down on credit and charges, and the results of our very mild restraints were ten times more effective than we had ever dreamed. And it really tightened up credit a little too much. This began to put people out of work. So we had to take those credit restraints off. They served their purpose, and the inflation rate had dropped sharply.

Announcer: President Carter: for the future [Re-elect President Carter]. (Carter, 1980, "Femalation")

This format (appearing in Mrs. Reed's backyard) presumably is intended to give Carter a "common touch," showing him out communing with ordinary citizens. As with Ford's campaign from four years earlier, these excuse-laden acclaims pale in comparison to Nixon's accomplishment spots of 1972.

Carter's campaign adopted another tactic from the Ford campaign in 1976: He used testimony from citizens of Reagan's home state, California.

Man: His problem as Governor was the same as he has now, mainly that he always shot from the hip [Sacramento].

Man: He once stated that if you've, ah, seen one redwood tree you've seen them all [San Francisco].

Man: Statement about if we're gonna have a bloodbath on campus let's get it over with [Sacramento].

Man: Some of the recent goofs that he's pulled with regard to China [Los Angeles].

Man: When you're dealing with governments like Russia [Los Angeles].

Announcer: A lot of Californians feel pretty good about Ronald Reagan, but others feel a sense of continuing concern.

Man: I think it makes a lot of people uneasy, and it certainly makes me uneasy [San Francisco].

Man: I think he's the kind of guy who shoots from the hip [San Francisco].

Woman: He did shoot from the hip [Sacramento].

Man: He shoots from the hip [Fresno].

Man: As a Governor it really didn't make that much difference because the state of California doesn't have a foreign policy, and the state of California isn't gonna be going to war with a foreign nation. And it was just amusing. But as President, ah, you know, it's scary [Sacramento].

Man: Oh, my decision is made, I'm going to stick with President Carter [Los Angeles].

Announcer: On November 4, re-elect President Carter [Re-elect President Carter]. (Carter, 1980, "Shoots from the Hip")

These statements by ordinary citizens from Reagan's home state (and remember he campaigned on his record as governor) questioned his character generally and his leadership ability in particular. Carter's campaign also developed a series of spots built around the question, "What kind of a person should occupy the Oval Office?" These advertisements offered a contrast that favored Carter, of course.

When you come right down to it, what kind of a person should occupy the Oval Office? [next two sentences scroll] Should it be a man who, like Ronald Reagan, has attacked American cities, calling urban aid "one of the biggest phonies in the system"? Calling unemployment insurance "a prepaid vacation"? Or should a man sit here who knows that a decent government should be sensitive to the needs of all Americans, no matter who they are, or where they live? Figure it out for yourself [President Carter]. (Carter, 1980, "Cities")

This commercial contrasts the two candidates in terms that favored Carter. As noted before, voters presumably want a president who will represent the entire country. Another Carter advertisement attempted to counter Reagan's attempt to use Kennedy against Carter with an endorsement from Kennedy:

During the Democratic Convention, I spoke about my deep belief in the ideals of the Democratic Party. And that's why I'm asking you now to make sure your vote will count in 1980. I am convinced that President Carter represents the only real chance to prevent a Reagan victory and preserve our hope for an America of progress and fairness. There is a clear choice in this election, and that is why I am working for the re-election of President Carter [Re-elect President Carter]. (Carter, 1980, "Kennedy")

It is unclear how successful this spot was at controlling damage with this "retraction," but the Carter campaign tried. These examples give an indication of the advertising campaigns in these two election years.

FUNCTIONS OF TELEVISION SPOTS

These campaigns, collectively (64%) and individually, stressed acclaims. For example, in 1976 a Ford commercial acclaimed the president's accomplishments: "In just two years, he has strengthened the ties with our allies in Europe, Japan, and Israel. He has negotiated firmly and fairly with our adversaries, while making sure our military strength is second to none. He has directed the peace efforts in the Middle East, and Africa. And today, there is not a single American soldier fighting anywhere in the world. Let's keep President Ford in charge." In this spot from 1976, Carter praised his record as governor of Georgia: "We had three hundred agencies and departments in the state government. We abolished two hundred-seventy-eight of them and set up a very simple economical structure of government. . . . With a new budgeting technique called zero-based budgeting, we eliminated all the old obsolescent programs, put into effect long-range goals and planning and cut administrative costs more than 50%." Four years later Reagan acclaimed his record as governor of California: "When I became governor of California, we solved many of the same problems America faces today, by bringing in a team of elected officials and private citizens. Working together, we cut the rate of government spending and turned a $194 million deficit into a $554 million surplus. We did it once; we can do it again." In a 1980 spot for Carter, his first-term record is acclaimed:

Table 6.1
Functions of the 1976 and 1980 Campaigns

Year	Candidate	Acclaims	Attacks	Defenses
1976	Ford	**200 (75%)**	59 (22%)	8 (3%)
	Carter	**126 (59%)**	89 (41%)	0
1980	Reagan	**129 (58%)**	93 (42%)	**2 (1%)**
	Carter	**112 (61%)**	68 (37%)	5 (3%)
Total		**567 (64%)**	309 (35%)	**15 (2%)**

In the past four years, working day and night, President Jimmy Carter has hammered out America's first energy program, deregulated airlines and trucking, broken through to an agreement at Camp David. He cut down on federal employees and paperwork, strengthened NATO, brought real help to America's cities, increased our defense capabilities, and kept this nation at peace. And he's not finished yet.

While focusing on his past deeds, this spot also portrays him as a hard and dedicated worker and hints at future accomplishments. Although it mentions more topics than the previous spot from Reagan, it provides considerably less detail about these accomplishments. These excerpts all illustrate how these campaign spots acclaimed (see Table 6.1).

These spots also contained numerous attacks (35%). In one Ford spot, he attacked Carter's future plans: "A middle-income taxpayer earns today around $14,800. Mr. Carter wants to raise taxes on that group in order to pay for these new programs he's proposing. I don't think the $15,000-a-year taxpayer ought to get any more tax increases." Carter attacked Ford's economic record and his leadership ability in this advertisement: "Well, 7.9% unemployment is what you arrive at when incompetent leaders follow outdated, unjust, wasteful, economic policies." This line came back to haunt Carter four years later when Reagan used it to attack Carter:

Jimmy Carter came to Washington promising to do something about unemployment, to give people who were out of work a chance to restore their hopes and dreams. 7.8% unemployment is what you arrive at when incompetent leaders follow outdated, insensitive, unjust, wasteful economic policies. Jimmy Carter did do something about unemployment—two million more people became unemployed this year alone.

That same year, a Carter commercial attacked Reagan's record as governor of California:

When Ronald Reagan speaks of the good old days when he was Governor of California, there are some things he doesn't mention. He increased state spending by 120%. He brought three tax increases to the state. He added 34,000 employees to the state payroll. The Reagan campaign is reluctant to acknowledge the accuracy of these facts today. But can we trust the nation's future to a man who fails to remember his own past?

Notice how this spot begins with policy but then draws a conclusion about his character. These passages illustrate how the spots in these campaigns used attacks.

Defenses occurred in 1976 and 1980, but they were quite rare (2%). Ford tended to rely on defeasibility, suggesting that circumstances beyond his control hampered his efforts at revitalizing the economy. For example, one spot noted that "Two years ago, we were mired in the worst economic crisis since the great depression." Another spot noted that "He came to the office of the president in troubled times," so presumably we shouldn't blame him if things aren't going so well. Four years later, Carter used the same basic approach: "The progress toward a comprehensive peace for the Middle East is very slow and very tedious, but we've got a lot of hatred still in the Mideast." A Carter spot also used transcendence to help justify the grain embargo: "A lot of people think the farmers kinda took it on the chin, but we didn't get into war over it, and so what, what money we might have lost really is a pretty cheap price to pay for freedom, really." Thus, defense did occur occasionally in these advertisements.

POLICY VERSUS CHARACTER

These spots were split almost evenly between policy (51%) and character (49%). One candidate (Reagan) stressed policy (67%), Carter's utterances in 1976 were almost exactly divided between policy and character, and both Ford (57%) and Carter in 1980 (58%) emphasized character (see Table 6.2).

Policy comments were very common in these advertisements. For instance, in 1976 Ford boasted that "We have ended the war in Vietnam and we have peace. We have turned the economy around, and we have reduced the rate of inflation significantly, by better than 50%." That same year Carter found problems in the status quo: "I'll tell you what I've seen. Workers with two jobs to make up for the disappearing income. Homes run down, property taxes skyrocketing. Hospitals closing and welfare lines growing. Enormous waste, unbelievable mismanagement of our tax money. And hard work and our savings thrown away by a far-away, unconcerned bureaucracy." In 1980, Reagan acclaimed his goals: "If we make a deep cut in everyone's tax rates, we'll have lower

Table 6.2
Policy versus Character in the 1976 and 1980 Campaigns

Year	Candidate	Policy	Character
1976	Ford	112 (43%)	**147 (57%)**
	Carter	108 (50%)	107 (50%)
1980	Reagan	**148 (67%)**	74 (33%)
	Carter	75 (42%)	**105 (58%)**
Total		**443 (51%)**	433 (49%)

prices, an increase in production, and a lot more peace of mind." Carter touted his accomplishments in the area of energy policy in 1980: "The energy laws are now on the books. Four years ago the oil companies dominated the Congress, and now we've changed that and the consumers of oil have an equal voice at least." These statements are indicative of the kinds of policy acclaims present in these campaigns.

Character utterances were also frequent topics in these campaigns. Ford argued in 1976 that "We have restored integrity and candor and forthrightness in the White House." A Carter spot in his first presidential campaign acclaimed his character:

In the beginning, Jimmy Carter's campaign was a lonely one. But through the months, more and more people recognized him as a new leader; a man who will change the way this country is run. A competent man, who can make our government open and efficient. But above all, an understanding man, who can make ours a government of the people once again.

Four years later a Carter commercial featured attacks by eleven people from California (who presumably knew best) on Reagan's character. Here are several excerpts from this ad:

Man: His problem as Governor was the same as he has now, mainly that he has always shot from the hip.

Man: Some of the recent goofs that he's pulled with regard to China.

Woman: I'm afraid of him on the foreign policy level.

Woman: He's talking too much and he doesn't know what he's saying.

Man: He talks like nobody else is listening.

Woman: The more he opens his mouth up, I think he's putting himself in a real deep hole.

These candid observations do not enhance Reagan's desirability. A Reagan spot criticized Carter's leadership: "Jimmy Carter's weak indecisive leadership has vacillated before events in Angola, Ethiopia, Afghanistan, and the hostage crisis in Iran. Jimmy Carter still doesn't know that it takes strong leadership to keep the peace, weak leadership to lose it." Thus, character was a recurrent theme in these commercials.

FORMS OF POLICY AND CHARACTER

Consistently the most common form of policy comment was past deeds (63% overall, and the most common form for each candidate and campaign). Ford in 1976 attacked Carter's record as governor of Georgia: "His ads say that he will do the same as President that he did as Governor of Georgia. Then you should know that during his one term as Governor, government spending increased by 58%. Government employees went up 25%. And the state of Georgia went 100% deeper into debt." Carter attacked the Republican status quo in the same campaign: "Gerald Ford voted against Medicare. Against food stamps for the elderly. Against adequate housing. Isn't it bad enough that older people are the worst victims, the easiest victims, of hoodlums and criminals? Must they also be victimized by their own government in Washington?" In 1976, Reagan attacked Carter's record: "In 1976 candidate Carter sold this country a plan he promised would hold prices at a 4% annual increase. Here's what you bought. Here's what he delivered. In only three and a half years consumer prices have skyrocketed 42%. What cost you a dollar three and a half years ago now costs $1.42. And it can get even worse. The Carter record speaks for itself." Carter touted his accomplishments in foreign affairs: "I hope that when I finish my terms in office, that when the history books are written, that one of the most important things there will be that I helped to bring a comprehensive peace to the Middle East." Thus, past deeds were the most common form of policy arguments (see Table 6.3).

Character utterances were divided almost equally between leadership ability (43%) and personal qualities (42%). In 1976, a Ford spot combined both of these appeals: "I believe that President Ford is a strong, honest, and decent man. I believe we can trust his leadership." However, a Carter spot attacked Ford's leadership: "If you agree that it's time we stopped paying for the lack of leadership in our country, do something about it. Vote for Jimmy Carter." Of course, the idea that the United States had been devoid of leadership while Ford was president is a serious accusation. Another ad praised Carter's personal qualities: "If you agree that government should be sensible yet sensitive, vote for Jimmy Carter." A Reagan spot in 1980 reported a newspaper endorsement that discussed: "The promise of Ronald Reagan's leadership. As the *Columbus*

Table 6.3
Forms of Policy and Character in the 1976 and 1980 Campaigns

Year	Candidate	Policy			Character		
		Past Deeds	Future Plans	General Goals	Personal Qualities	Leadership Ability	Ideals
1976	Ford	84 (75%)	21 (19%)	7 (6%)	75 (51%)	54 (37%)	18 (12%)
	Carter	67 (62%)	9 (8%)	32 (30%)	46 (43%)	41 (38%)	20 (19%)
1980	Reagan	79 (53%)	22 (15%)	47 (32%)	20 (27%)	47 (64%)	7 (9%)
	Carter	47 (63%)	13 (17%)	15 (20%)	43 (41%)	43 (41%)	19 (18%)
Total		277 (63%)	65 (15%)	101 (23%)	184 (42%)	185 (43%)	64 (15%)

Dispatch said: Ronald Reagan is by far the best choice to do the job that needs to be done today." A Carter advertisement attacked Reagan's personal qualities, asking what kind of man should "Occupy the Oval Office": "Should it be a man who, like Ronald Reagan, has a fractured view of America, who speaks disdainfully about millions of us as he attacks the minimum wage and calls unemployment insurance 'a prepaid vacation.'?" Thus, these spots emphasized both personal qualities and leadership ability when they discussed character.

SOURCE OF UTTERANCE

In these campaigns, the utterances were decidedly skewed to comments authored by persons other than the candidates. This is true for acclaims (68% others) and attacks (68% others). Defenses were split about evenly. The only exception to this pattern was Carter in his first campaign (1976), when he authored most of his acclaims (58%) and attacks (82%) (see Table 6.4).

CONCLUSION

Carter defeated President Ford in 1976 but then lost to Reagan in 1980. One could argue that the economy was largely responsible for both of these outcomes—and there can be no doubt that it played a major role in both elections. However, voters must be convinced both that the economy is the most important issue and that the economy favored Carter in 1976 and Reagan in 1980. Carter attacked the economy under Ford while acclaiming his record as governor of California. Ironically, Reagan used the same approach in his bid to oust Carter, attacking the economy under Carter and acclaiming his record as governor of Georgia. As we have seen, Carter's commercials in 1976 and Reagan's advertisements in 1980 effectively exploited the opportunities presented by economic conditions in these campaigns.

Table 6.4
Source of Utterances in the 1976 and 1980 Campaigns

Year	Candidate	Acclaims		Attacks		Defenses	
		Candidate	Other	Candidate	Other	Candidate	Other
1976	Ford	32 (16%)	168 (84%)	6 (10%)	53 (90%)	2 (25%)	6 (75%)
	Carter	73 (58%)	53 (42%)	73 (82%)	16 (18%)	0	0
1980	Reagan	48 (37%)	81 (63%)	20 (22%)	70 (78%)	0	2 (100%)
	Carter	26 (23%)	86 (77%)	0	68 (100%)	4 (80%)	1 (20%)
Total		179 (32%)	388 (68%)	99 (32%)	207 (68%)	6 (40%)	9 (60%)

Chapter 7

Republicans in Control: 1984, 1988

Reagan and Bush were nominated by the Republican Party to run again in 1984. Walter Mondale, who had served as vice president with Jimmy Carter (and who lost the bid for re-election in 1980), was nominated as the Democratic candidate for president in 1984. The Democrats selected Congresswoman Geraldine Ferraro as the first woman nominee for vice president.

President Reagan ran on his first-term record in the 1984 campaign. One theme played out in several spots was that it was "Morning in America"—Reagan's accomplishments were revitalizing and renewing the economy and restoring hope to the United States:

It's morning again in America. Today more men and women will go to work than ever before in our country's history. With interest rates and inflation down, more people are buying new homes, and our new families can have confidence in the future. America today is prouder, and stronger, and better. Why would we want to return to where we were less than four short years ago? [President Reagan: Leadership That's Working]. (Reagan, 1984, "Morning in America")

He also repeatedly associated Mondale with his former running mate, Jimmy Carter, and reminded voters of the woes of 1976. Besides comparing the Reagan record to the Carter record of four years earlier, Reagan also contrasted his approach with that of Mondale:

Reagan: The American people have a very clear choice this year about their economic future. And it's a very simple choice between our opponents' old policies and our new policies. When you hear their prescription for the economy—higher taxes, bigger government, sure to follow high inflation—it makes you wonder if they remember how things used to be. There's a better life ahead, but only if we look ahead.

Announcer: President Reagan: Leadership that's working [President Reagan: Leadership that's working]. (Reagan, 1984, "Economic Choice")

Reagan also made use of ordinary people to acclaim his accomplishments and desirability. This spot offered a form of reluctant testimony, presenting the views of Democrats and Independents who acclaimed the Republican candidate:

Announcer: Why Democrats and Independents are voting for President Reagan [Why Democrats and Independents are voting for President Reagan].

[*BF Phillips*]: I am a person that is for the individual that I feel is going to do the most for our nation.

[*Donna Lucien*]: I am a registered Democrat and I've since decided after looking at the candidates that President Reagan is the better choice.

[*Sheila Dennis*]: I'm a registered Democrat, and I am voting for Ronald Reagan because I can see what he's done in the past four years.

[*Anthony Mark*]: I like Ronald Reagan because I believe he's turned the nation around and he's got things back on track again.

[*Karen Gilmore*]: He's helped inflation, brought that down.

[*Hardy Hartzell*]: He's brought the interest rates down so people can afford to borrow money.

[*Cathy Williams*]: I believe Ronald Reagan has brought down the unemployment in this country—he found a lot of jobs for people.

[*Charles Terjesen*]: Well, most of the people when I go on jobs say they're Democrats but they'll vote for Reagan this year.

[*Richard Yanuzzi*]: I'm gonna vote for President Reagan.

[*Marisa Shields*]: I'm gonna vote for Ronald Reagan.

[*Tony Grimes*]: I definitely am gonna vote for Reagan.

[Doris Ott]: He's one of the best presidents we've had in many years.

Announcer: President Reagan: Leadership that's working [President Reagan: Leadership that's working]. (Reagan, 1984, "Man on the Street 2")

This spot focuses on policy matters (inflation, interest rates, jobs) to acclaim Reagan's desirability. The Reagan campaign also used the testimony of ordinary citizens to attack his Democratic opponent:

Announcer: Strong leadership. Does Mondale measure up? [Strong leadership. Does Mondale measure up?].

[*Jerry Thomas*]: Well, I think Fritz Mondale is probably a good man, but I don't think he's a good leader.

[*Abdul Kayoum*]: I don't believe that he has the quality of leadership.

[*John Friedmann*]: He's just a rubber stamp carried over from the Carter administration.

[*Frances Henderson*]: He lacks charisma and he lacks leadership.

[*Arjay West*]: Walter Mondale is wishy-washy.

[*Jenny Scarborough*]: I see no strength in Mondale.

[*Marion Markovich*]: I think we need the strength of President Reagan and his administration and not the weakness of the Carter/Mondale administration.

Announcer: President Reagan: Leadership that's working [President Reagan: Leadership that's working]. (Reagan, 1984, "Man on the Street Mondale")

Unlike the previous advertisement, this attack focused on character topics instead of policy. It also attempts to tie Mondale to the unpopular Carter/Mondale ticket that lost the 1980 campaign to Reagan/Bush. The next spot used "reluctant" testimony from fellow Democrat Gary Hart to attack Mondale:

[Gary Hart talks about Walter Mondale's Record]:

Hart: Walter Mondale may pledge stable prices, but Carter/Mondale could not cure 12% inflation. Walter Mondale has come to Ohio and talked about jobs, but Carter/Mondale watched helplessly as 180,000 Ohio jobs disappeared in the period between 1976 and 1980.

Announcer: Democrats, Maybe Gary Hart is Right [Democrats, Maybe Gary Hart is Right; President Reagan: Leadership That's Working]. (Reagan, 1984, "Hart on Mondale")

Finally, Reagan addressed foreign policy concerns. This spot discussed the importance of being prepared for potential communist aggression using an obvious metaphor.

There's a bear in the woods. For some people, the bear is easy to see. Others don't see it at all. Some people say the bear is tame. Others say it is vicious and dangerous. Since no one can be sure who is right, isn't it smart to be as strong as the bear? If there is a bear [President Reagan: Prepared for Peace]. (Reagan, 1984, "The Bear")

This is a very low-key use of the Communist threat to appeal to voters. These spots give some idea of Reagan's television advertising in the 1984 election.

Democratic candidate Mondale outlined some of his ideals and goals in this 1984 television spot:

Mondale: The government of the United States is not up for sale; it belongs to the people of this country and we want it back.

Announcer: Fritz Mondale, underdog, fighting for what he believes. Tough questions, straight answers. Protecting social security and Medicare. Cleaning up toxic waste. Tax reform, closing loopholes. This is the debate. This is the fight. It must be fought; it will be won [Mondale/Ferraro]. (Mondale, 1984, "Domestic")

Character issues ("straight answers") and policy (social security, Medicare, the environment, taxation) are both used here to acclaim Mondale. The next spot showed voters the Democratic ticket, featuring both Walter Mondale and Geraldine Ferraro:

Ferraro: You want more for your kids than you had, and that's the American dream.

Announcer: Mondale and Ferraro, bringing a new fairness to America. While Mr. Reagan tries to slash Medicare, they fight for seniors. While he forces four million people out of work, they fight for workers. And on tax breaks:

Mondale: I refuse to make your family pay more so that millionaires can pay less [Cheers].

Announcer: They'll be taking a first step in a new direction for America. Mondale/Ferraro [Mondale/Ferraro]: for your future. (Mondale, 1984, "Ticket")

Although this commercial contained an attack on Reagan's tax and unemployment policies, the tone of these spots was generally positive.

Other Mondale spots were much more straightforward attacks on the Republican candidate and on his policies:

Announcer: In this building [Treasury], Mr. Reagan's people are borrowing the money that's putting each of us $18,000 into debt: deficit spending. And who walks away with the money? 90,000 profitable corporations that pay no taxes [business people leaving and getting into limos]. Defense contractors on bloated budgets. Foreign interests who make money on our debt. What the deficit really means is that you're paying for their free ride [limos driving away]. But in November you can stop it: Mondale/Ferraro [Mondale/Ferraro], they're fighting for your future. (Mondale, 1984, "Limo")

This commercial relates the growing federal deficit directly to taxpayers: Reagan's spending is putting every voter $18,000 into debt. To add insult to injury, others (corporations, defense contractors, foreign interests) are benefitting at our expense. Another advertisement from Mondale suggested that Reagan had not put forward a plan for voters to evaluate:

Announcer: Where's the plan, Mr. Reagan? [Where's the plan, Mr. Reagan?] Who's going to pay for your deficits? [Who's going to pay for your deficits?] In your first term you cut aid to seniors, the unemployed, students, and the disabled [photos for each group]. Where are your cuts this time, Mr. Reagan? [Where are your cuts this time, Mr. Reagan?] You gave tax breaks to the rich [man in tuxedo getting cake] and to profitable corporations [limousine], then signed one of the biggest tax increases in history. Who gets the tax breaks this time, Mr. Reagan? [Who gets the tax breaks this time, Mr. Reagan?] Mr. Mondale has told us his plan to reduce your deficit [The Mondale Plan, displayed over a budget proposal document]. Where is your plan? [Where is your plan?] Level with us [Level with us]. Mondale/Ferraro [Mondale/Ferraro]: They're fighting for your future. (Mondale, 1984, "Plan")

This spot also criticizes the president for giving tax breaks to the rich and then for raising taxes. It also suggests that, unlike Mondale, Reagan hasn't proposed an economic plan for his second term of office. Mondale also produced a spot about Reagan's plan to put weapons on satellites.

Ronald Reagan is determined to put killer weapons in space [image of earth on TV screen; pull back to see red phone]. The Soviets will have to match us, and the arms race will rage out of control: orbiting, aiming, waiting [red phone is blinking]. With a response time so short, there'll be no time to wake a President. Computers will take control [numbers, lines on computer screen]. On November 6th, you can take control. No weapons in space for either side [line drawn above and around earth]. Draw the line at the heavens with Mondale [Mondale/Ferraro]. (Mondale, 1984, "Computer")

The red "hot line" telephone makes an appearance in this campaign. Computers (especially when they control weapons) are portrayed as scary. Finally, this spot shows how Mondale used ordinary people—and Reagan's own words—to attack the president on domestic policy:

Reagan: We have preserved the safety net for the people with true needs in this country.

Older Woman: I get $35 in food stamps when I used to get $76, so they've cut me right in half.

Older Woman: That leaves me $12.50 for the month to eat: That's a little hard to take.

Older Woman: I just want enough to get along. That's all I ask.

Reagan: We have no thought of throwing people out into the snow.

Older Woman: No way. No way.

Announcer: Is America back, or can we do better? Mondale for President [Mondale/Ferraro]. (Mondale, 1984, "Safety Net")

This advertisement is designed to evoke sympathy for these older people, while branding Reagan as an uncaring hypocrite. These spots illustrate themes in the Mondale campaign's television advertising.

In 1988, Vice President George Bush was chosen as the Republican
nominee. His running mate was Senator Dan Quayle. Michael Dukakis,
governor of Massachusetts, was the Democratic nominee. Senator Lloyd
Bentsen was the Democratic vice-presidential nominee.

Running on his record succeeded for Reagan in 1984, and Bush took
credit for the Reagan/Bush administration's record when he ran in 1988:

Over the past six years, 18 million jobs were created. Interest rates were cut in
half [scenes of people]. Today, inflation is down, taxes are down, and the economy is stronger. So, while some might try to tell you we're on the wrong road,
or have gone as far as we can go, I believe that today America is better off than
we were eight years ago, and by building on the gains we've made we'll all be
better off in four years, than we are today [George Bush: Experienced Leadership
for America's Future]. (Bush, 1988, "Bush Positive Economy")

He discusses employment, interest rates, and inflation. Bush argues that
we are better off now than in 1980 (when Reagan/Bush ascended to the
presidency) and that we will be better off yet if we elect Bush in 1988.

Several of Bush's spots stressed his experience and qualifications for
the office of the president:

George Bush, effective leadership. Appointed CIA Chief [Appointed CIA Chief],
revitalized the agency [Revitalized the agency] during its toughest time, rebuilt
our intelligence [Rebuilt our intelligence] capability. Headed regulatory reform
[Headed regulatory reform], cut government red tape [Cut government red tape]
saving billions, and sent new life-saving drugs [Sent new life-saving drugs] to
the market place. Represented the President in seventy-four countries [Repre-
sented the President in seventy-four countries]. Knew all the last four Soviet
leaders [Knew all the last four Soviet leaders]. Led the fight for the INF Treaty
[Led the fight for the INF Treaty]. Faced down armed commandantes in El Sal-
vador [Faced down armed commandantes in El Salvador] on human rights.
George Bush: tough, tested Presidential Leadership [George Bush: tough, tested
Presidential Leadership]. (Bush, 1988, "Effective")

Bush has served his country in a variety of positions, working on both
domestic and foreign policy issues. This experience, the ad argues, prepares him very well to be president.

The Bush campaign attacked his Democratic opponent, Michael Dukakis, on several grounds. This spot criticized his record and policy
stands on crime:

A Crime Quiz: [Crime Quiz, Bush on left, Dukakis on right]: Which candidate for President gave weekend passes to first-degree murderers who were not even eligible for parole? [Which candidate for President gave weekend passes to first-degree murderers who were not even eligible for parole?] Michael Dukakis [picture zooms to fill screen]. Who vetoed mandatory jail sentences for drug dealers? [Who vetoed mandatory jail sentences for drug dealers?] Michael Dukakis [picture zooms to fill screen]. Who opposes capital punishment in all cases and even vetoed the death penalty for cop killers? [Who opposes capital punishment in all cases and even vetoed the death penalty for cop killers?] Michael Dukakis [picture zooms to fill screen]. Which candidate for President can you really count on to be tough on crime? [Which candidate for President can you really count on to be tough on crime?] George Bush [Bush's photo zooms to fill screen]: Experienced Leadership for America's Future [Experienced Leadership for America's Future]. (Bush, 1988, "Crime Quiz")

Weekend furloughs, mandatory sentences, capital punishment are all aspects of Dukakis's record on crime. Several spots attacked Dukakis's record on the environment. Boston Harbor was a target for this criticism:

[The Harbor]: As a candidate, Michael Dukakis called Boston Harbor an open sewer [video of polluted harbor]. As Governor, he had the opportunity to do something about it, but choose not to. The Environmental Protection Agency called his lack of action the most expensive public policy mistake in the history of New England. Now Boston Harbor, the dirtiest harbor in America, will cost residents six billion dollars to clean. And Michael Dukakis promises to do for America what he's done for Massachusetts. (Bush, 1988, "The Harbor")

This commercial attacked Dukakis's failure to take action, which will cost taxpayers to correct. It also keys into a theme of the Dukakis advertising campaign: That he (Dukakis) will do for America what he's done for Massachussets (as governor). Bush also used the opinions of ordinary people from Massachussets to indict his record as governor:

Announcer: How good a governor is Michael Dukakis? [How good a governor is Michael Dukakis?]

Man: I don't think that Mike Dukakis has lived up to his promises [Wellesley, MA].

Woman: He raised taxes, and he's raised taxes [Quincy, MA].

Man: He's taken money from the retirement funds that the people have put in there, and, um, you know, to balance his mistakes that he's made [Taunton, MA].

Man: Michael Dukakis should be called Michael Taxkakis [Brighton, MA].

Woman: Dukakis has made one mess out of Massachussets [Hyde Park, MA].

Woman: I'm a Democrat and I've never voted Republican before, but this time I'm voting for George Bush [George Bush: Experienced Leadership for America's Future]. (Bush, 1988, "His Mistakes")

Here, Dukakis's record on taxes and retirement policy is criticized—as is his character, when we are told he has not "lived up to his promises." Thus, these spots give an indication of the nature of the Bush television advertising campaign in 1988.

Dukakis used television spots in the 1988 campaign to articulate his vision for America, orienting viewers toward the future:

[The Debate, 9/25/88]. *Announcer*: He spoke for our concerns.

Dukakis: People all over this country, who, in some cases are living from paycheck to paycheck. The Cases are having a hard time opening up the door to college opportunity for their children.

[Ideas] *Announcer*: With ideas to make life better.

Dukakis: And I think it's time that if you got a job in this country that it came with health insurance.

[Vision] *Announcer*: And vision to build the future.

Dukakis: The best America is not behind us. The best America is yet to come.

Announcer: Michael Dukakis for President [Michael Dukakis for President]: Let's take charge of America's future. (Dukakis, 1988, "Debate")

College opportunity and health care are important to many Americans, and this spot used these issues to acclaim the Democratic nominee. Dukakis also acclaimed his accomplishments as governor of Massachussets in a series of ads acclaiming his "Leadership":

Leadership [Leadership]. It's taking charge, taking responsibility. [The Dukakis Record: Ten Balanced Budgets]. Michael Dukakis balanced ten budgets in a row and still cut taxes five times [The Dukakis Record: Cut Taxes Five Times]. Leadership: It's making life better [The Dukakis Record: Increase Workers; Income]. He increased working people's income at twice the national rate [The Dukakis Record: First Universal Health Care Program]. And pioneered the first universal health care program in the country. And that's why America's governors, both Democrat and Republican, voted Michael Dukakis the most effective governor in the nation [America's governors, both Democrat and Republican, voted Michael Dukakis the most effective governor in the nation]. Michael Dukakis for President [Michael Dukakis for President]. Let's take charge of America's future. (Dukakis, 1988, "Leadership 1")

This spot, and others like it in his campaign, used his record of accomplishments as governor to argue that he was an effective leader and would be a good president.

Dukakis also attacked Bush's policies in several areas. This commercial targets his record on education:

For seven and a half years, George Bush supported cutbacks in American education [BUSH 1981, 1982, 1983, 1984, 1985, 1986, 1987; the word EDUCATION on blackboard is erased bit by bit]. He sat by while college loans for working families were cut. And now suddenly, George Bush says he'll be the education President [Smiling Bush, 1988]. Michael Dukakis won't just give us slogans. He's committed to a new national college loan program to make sure that any American kid can afford to go to college [last two sentences scrolled]. Michael Dukakis for President [Michael Dukakis for President]: A real commitment to education: the best America is yet to come. (Dukakis, 1988, "Education")

This message argued that Bush has not supported education, even though he claims to be the "Education President." This managed to criticize his policy and character. A unique series of ads for Dukakis portrayed Bush's campaign advisors attempting to come up with arguments for Bush's advertising.

[The Packaging of George Bush]:
Man: Well, I think we need another TV commercial on this furlough thing. [Thursday 3: 55 P.M.]
Man: No way. They're beginning to write about Dukakis's real crime record.
Voice: Look, nobody reads anymore.
Man: Let's hope not. Look, first of all, Dukakis changed that furlough program. And look at this, more cops on the street, more drug offenders behind bars, crime down 13% in Massachusetts.
Man: Just what I mean. How long do we expect to get away with this furlough thing?
Man: How many more weeks is the election, Bernie? [laughter].
Announcer: They'd like to sell you a package. Wouldn't you rather choose a president? (Dukakis, 1988, "Packaging of George Bush 1").

This spot managed to acclaim Dukakis's record on crime while portraying the Bush campaign team as unprincipled manipulators. One advertisement attacked the "Packaging of Dan Quayle" as well.

Dukakis also made several spots that responded to Bush's attacks on Dukakis. This illustrates his response to Bush's "The Harbor" spot:

Announcer: George Bush is complaining about Boston Harbor [Bush's False Advertising]. But Bush's administration cut funds to clean up Boston Harbor [The Truth; But Bush's administration cut funds to clean up Boston Harbor; $1.5 billion]. Bush's administration cut funds to clean up California's coast from San Diego Harbor to San Francisco Bay [Bush Record: Bush's administration cut funds to clean up California's coast from San Diego Harbor to San Francisco Bay]. Bush opposed a crackdown on corporations releasing toxic waste [Bush Record: Bush opposed a crackdown on corporations releasing toxic waste]. Bush even favored a veto of the Clean Water Act [Bush Record: Bush even favored a veto of the Clean Water Act]—not once, but twice. The non-partisan League of Conservation Voters has endorsed Mike Dukakis [The non-partisan League of Conservation Voters has endorsed Mike Dukakis]. So when you hear George Bush talk about the environment, remember what he did to the environment [Remember]. (Dukakis, 1988, "Bush's False Advertising 1")

This spot counterattacked Bush's environmental record while rebutting his attacks on Dukakis. These examples convey a flavor for the 1988 advertising campaigns.

FUNCTIONS OF TELEVISION SPOTS

Acclaims were the most common form of utterance, both collectively (64%) and individually. For example, Reagan boasted in 1984 that "During the past year, thousands of families have moved into new homes that once seemed out of reach. People are buying new cars they once thought they couldn't afford. Workers are returning to factories that just four years ago were closed. And America is back, with a sense of pride people thought we'd never feel again." That same year a Mondale commercial declared: "An Army veteran, a solid leader, Mondale's defense plan calls for real growth in military spending, combat readiness, and active pursuit of a mutual verifiable freeze on nuclear arms. It's a plan for peace that deals from strength." In this 1988 spot Bush explained that

I'm a man who sees life in terms of missions: missions defined, and missions completed. I will not allow this country to be made weak again. I will keep America moving forward, always forward, for an endless enduring dream and a thousand points of light. This is my mission and I will complete it.

A Dukakis spot assessed Dukakis's leadership on the basis of his past accomplishments as governor:

Leadership. It's turning around his state's economy, creating 400,000 good jobs, pushing personal income to the highest levels in the country. Leadership. It's balancing ten state budgets in a row, while still cutting taxes five times. Leadership. It's why America's Governors, both Democrat and Republican, voted Michael Dukakis the most effective Governor in the nation.

This spot managed to combine acclaims of Dukakis's past deeds with acclaims of his leadership ability (see Table 7.1).

Attacks comprised 36% of the utterances. For instance, in 1984 a Reagan spot used Gary Hart, a fellow Democrat, to attack Mondale: "Walter Mondale may pledge stable prices, but Carter/Mondale could not cure 12% inflation. Walter Mondale has come to Ohio and talked about jobs,

Table 7.1
Functions of the 1984 and 1988 Campaigns

Year	Candidate	Acclaims	Attacks	Defenses
1984	Reagan	**202 (77%)**	59 (23%)	0
	Mondale	**132 (54%)**	110 (45%)	2 (1%)
1988	Bush	**121 (61%)**	78 (39%)	0
	Dukakis	**206 (61%)**	125 (37%)	4 (1%)
Total		**661 (64%)**	372 (36%)	6 (0.5%)

but Carter/Mondale watched helplessly as 180,000 Ohio jobs disappeared in the period between 1976 and 1980." This excerpt appears to be taken from a spot Hart ran during the Ohio Democratic primary. This Mondale advertisement attacked Reagan's deficit spending: "The four budgets Ronald Reagan sent to Congress, his budgets, his signature, his deficits: Five hundred and six billion dollars. He has never submitted a balanced budget to Congress. He has never submitted a budget that came close." In 1988, a Bush spot showed video of a man (who by the end of the commercial could be identified as Dukakis) riding in a tank:

Michael Dukakis has opposed virtually every new defense system we developed. He opposed new aircraft carriers. He opposed anti-satellite weapons. He opposed four missile systems, including Pershing II missile deployment. Dukakis opposed the Stealth bomber and a ground emergency warning system against nuclear attack. He even criticized our rescue mission to Grenada and our strike on Libya. And now he wants to be our commander-in-chief. America can't afford that risk.

Dukakis did look rather goofy riding around on the tank in this video footage. Dukakis also attacked Bush's record as well as Quayle's promise on fighting illegal drugs in 1988:

George Bush was made responsible for stopping drug traffic from coming into this country. What happened? Cocaine traffic up 300%, more drugs in our classrooms, and Panamanian drug lord Noreiga kept on the government payroll [photo of Noreiga with Bush]. That's the Bush record on fighting drugs. And now George Bush wants to put Dan Quayle in charge for the next four years. If George Bush couldn't handle the job, how do you think Dan Quayle's going to do?

Thus, these campaign spots had numerous attacks on the candidates and their policies.

Defense was quite rare, accounting for a mere 0.5% of the utterances in these advertisements. A Dukakis spot in 1988 began with a television displaying the Bush "Tank Ride" spot. Dukakis turned off the television and declared "I'm fed up with it. Never seen anything like it in twenty-five years of public life. George Bush's negative TV ads. Distorting my record, full of lies, and he knows it. I'm on the record for the very weapons systems his ads say I'm against." While launching a counterattack on Bush for this negative and distorted campaign, this statement clearly denies the accusations in the attack. This is a clear illustration of defense in presidential television spots.

POLICY VERSUS CHARACTER

Policy was the dominant topic in these campaigns, constituting 65% of the remarks in these advertisements. For example, in 1984 Reagan attacked his opponents' policies in this commercial:

The American people have a very clear choice this year about their economic future. And it's a very simple choice between our opponents' old policies and our new policies. When you hear their prescription for the economy—higher taxes, bigger government, sure to follow high inflation—it makes you wonder if they remember how things used to be.

This excerpt ends with a thinly veiled reference to the economy problems under Carter and Mondale. This spot from Mondale mentioned his general policy goals: "Protecting social security and Medicare. Cleaning up toxic waste. Tax reform, closing loopholes. This is the debate. This is the fight. It must be fought; it will be won." In 1988, this Bush advertisement touted his accomplishments: "Appointed CIA Chief, revitalized the agency during its toughest time, rebuilt our intelligence capability. Headed regulatory reform, cut government red tape saving billions, and sent new life-saving drugs to the marked place." In this commercial, Dukakis attacked Bush's policies: "This administration has cut and slashed programs for children, for nutrition, for the kinds of things that can help these youngsters live better lives. Has cut federal aid to education, has cut Pell Grants and loans to close the door to college opportunity to youngsters all over this country." Thus, acclaims and attacks frequently concerned the policies of the candidates (see Table 7.2).

Character was also a common topic for discussion, accounting for 35% of the utterances in these campaigns. In 1984, for example, this Reagan spot used ordinary citizens to attack Mondale:

Table 7.2
Policy versus Character in the 1984 and 1988 Campaigns

Year	Candidate	Policy	Character
1984	Reagan	177 (68%)	84 (32%)
	Mondale	173 (71%)	69 (29%)
1988	Bush	115 (58%)	84 (42%)
	Dukakis	209 (63%)	122 (37%)
Total		674 (65%)	359 (35%)

Man: Well, I think Fritz Mondale is probably a good man, but I don't think he's a good leader.

Man: I don't believe that he has the quality of leadership.

Woman: He lacks charisma and he lacks leadership.

Man: Walter Mondale is wishy-washy.

Woman: I see no strength in Mondale.

This commercial attacked Mondale's leadership ability. This spot for the Democratic candidate contrasted the two contenders on leadership: "Presidential leadership should be exerted to gain control of the federal budget. Mr. Mondale, the challenger, is showing leadership. President Reagan is ducking it." In 1988, this spot for George Bush acclaimed his leadership experience: "He was elected to Congress, selected to serve as UN ambassador, and emissary to mainland China, and later to run the CIA. The more you learn about how George Bush came this far, the more you realize that perhaps no one in this century is better prepared to be president of the United States." This Dukakis ad indicted Bush's character by indicating that Bush did not respect voters' ability to decide on issues: "And what's most amazing [about Bush and the environment]: George Bush doesn't think you'll even bother to look at the facts." The screen then displayed the words, "That's Politics; that's Bush." Thus, character played a part in these campaigns.

FORMS OF POLICY AND CHARACTER

Policy comments were dominated by discussion of past deeds (61%). This 1984 Reagan spot, for example, focused on Reagan's first-term accomplishments:

It's morning again in America. Today more men and women will go to work than ever before in our country's history. With interest rates at about half the record highs of 1980, nearly two thousand families today will buy new homes, more than at any time in the past four years. This afternoon six thousand five hundred young men and women will be married. And with inflation at less than half of what it was just four years ago, they can look forward with confidence to the future. It's morning again in America, and under the leadership of President Reagan, our country is prouder, and stronger, and better.

Although most of this passage concerns Reagan's past deeds, notice that the last sentence included praise of Reagan as a leader. In the same campaign, Mondale asked, "Who's going to pay for your deficits? In your first term you cut aid to seniors, the unemployed, students, and the disabled. Where are your cuts this time, Mr. Reagan? You gave tax breaks to the rich and to profitable corporations, then signed one of the biggest tax increases in history." In 1988, this ad for Bush attacked Dukakis's record on crime:

As Governor, Michael Dukakis vetoed mandatory sentences for drug dealers. He vetoed the death penalty [prison scenes]. His revolving door prison policy gave weekend furloughs to first degree murderers not eligible for parole [revolving door scene]. While out, many committed other crimes like kidnaping and rape [268 escaped] and many are still at large [Many are still at large]. Now Michael Dukakis says he wants to do for America what he's done for Massachusetts. America can't afford that risk.

These actions do not make it appear as if Dukakis was tough on crime as governor. This Dukakis advertisement criticized Bush's record on the environment: "For seven and a half years, George Bush personally weakened regulations on corporate polluters. Failed to push for the clean-up of toxic waste sites. Twice supported the veto of the Clean Water Act. Opposed a ban on ocean dumping." Thus, these campaign commercials frequently focused on policy matters (see Table 7.3).

Character remarks most commonly concerned leadership ability (50%), and personal qualities were the second most frequent form of character utterance (37%). For example, in 1984 this Reagan ad praised his leadership ability when a citizen observed: "There's a lot of things need to be done to this country and I think Ronald Reagan's the man to do it." Perhaps he meant "done for" rather than "done to," but this statement acclaims his ability nevertheless. A spot supporting Mondale also discussed his leadership ability on the nuclear arms freeze issue: "A steady hand. A savvy negotiator, he will direct not delegate the most awesome issue of our time." Four years later, Bush acclaimed his experience and leadership ability in this spot: "For seven and a half years I've worked with a great President. I've seen what crosses the big desk. I've seen the unexpected crisis that arrives in a cable in a young aide's hand. And so I know that what it all comes down to, this election, is the man at the

Table 7.3
Forms of Policy and Character in the 1984 and 1988 Campaigns

Year	Candidate	Policy			Character		
		Past Deeds	Future Plans	General Goals	Personal Qualities	Leadership Ability	Ideals
1984	Reagan	**123 (69%)**	14 (8%)	40 (23%)	12 (14%)	**58 (69%)**	14 (17%)
	Mondale	**72 (42%)**	40 (23%)	61 (35%)	**32 (46%)**	15 (21%)	23 (33%)
1988	Bush	**79 (69%)**	20 (17%)	16 (14%)	25 (30%)	**55 (65%)**	4 (5%)
	Dukakis	**137 (66%)**	13 (6%)	59 (28%)	**64 (52%)**	51 (42%)	7 (6%)
Total		**411 (61%)**	87 (13%)	176 (26%)	133 (37%)	**179 (50%)**	48 (13%)

desk. And who should sit at that desk? My friends, I am that man." To illustrate how personal qualities were used in these campaigns, consider this passage from a Dukakis spot in 1988: "The other side has pursued a campaign of distortion and distraction, of fear and of smear." These are hardly the noble qualities one ought to associate with a president. Thus, these excerpts illustrate how these campaigns addressed character in their spots.

SOURCE OF UTTERANCE

These campaigns showed a decided preference for others rather than candidates as the source of utterances (see Table 7.4). Most of the acclaims (71%) were from other speakers than the candidates and most of the attacks were from others as well (78%). This pattern occurred from every candidate in these campaigns. Again, there were only a few defenses, and a couple more were from others than were from the candidates.

CONCLUSION

Reagan and Bush had beaten the Carter/Mondale ticket in 1980, and they were able to defeat the Mondale/Ferraro team in 1984. The economy was a recurrent theme in these campaigns. Arguably, the economy favored Reagan over Carter. However, in 1984, unlike 1976 and 1980, the economy seemed to be improving. Reagan clearly (and effectively) exploited the economy in his advertisements. Bush defeated Dukakis in his first run for the presidency. He was able to raise questions about Dukakis, especially on the topics of crime, defense, and the environment. Dukakis tried to answer them in his advertising, but it was too little, too late.

Table 7.4
Source of Utterances in the 1984 and 1988 Campaigns

Year	Candidate	Acclaims		Attacks		Defenses	
		Candidate	Other	Candidate	Other	Candidate	Other
1984	Reagan	35 (27%)	97 (73%)	19 (17%)	91 (83%)	0	2 (100%)
	Mondale	85 (42%)	117 (58%)	20 (29%)	39 (71%)	0	0
1988	Bush	28 (23%)	93 (77%)	9 (12%)	69 (88%)	0	0
	Dukakis	42 (20%)	164 (80%)	32 (26%)	93 (74%)	2 (50%)	2 (50%)
Total		190 (29%)	471 (71%)	80 (22%)	292 (78%)	2 (33%)	4 (67%)

Chapter 8

The End of the Millennium: 1992, 1996

George Bush was nominated in 1992 to lead his party to a fourth consecutive term in the White House, with Dan Quayle as his vice president again. Bill Clinton, governor of Arkansas, along with Senator Al Gore, were the challengers in that contest. Millionaire businessman H. Ross Perot created the Reform Party and ran for president as a third-party candidate. His strong showing led the Commission on Presidential Debates to invite him to participate in the 1992 debates.

Just prior to the 1992 campaign, in 1991, Bush had won a great victory in Operation Desert Storm. He worked hard to use this foreign policy and military success into a second term in office. This advertisement exemplifies this approach

Bush [footage from 1991]: Just two hours ago, allied air forces began an attack on military [nighttime missile video; The Persian Gulf Crisis—1991].

News Announcer: President Bush said today that he reassured Mr. Yeltsin the United States would stand by democracy [The Coup Against Gorbachev—1991].

News Announcer: If revolutionaries and terrorists are armed with nuclear and chemical weapons it may pose new challenges to the President [Today's Unknown Threat].

Announcer [Oval Office]: In a world where we're just one unknown dictator away from the next major crisis, who do you most trust to be sitting in this chair? [President Bush: Commander In Chief]. (Bush, 1992, "Persian Gulf Crisis")

This commercial makes explicit the claim that his past record is good evidence about how he will probably respond to future crises. Clinton, as a governor, had no foreign policy experience to speak of. Bush also acclaimed his general goals for a second term in this advertisement:

The world is in transition. We must be a military superpower, an economic superpower, and an export superpower. Here's what I'm fighting for: open markets for American products, lower government spending, tax relief, opportunities for small business, legal and health reform, job training, and new schools built on competition, ready for the 21st century [sporadic high-tech typing of green letters; interspersed with Bush talking and other images] [BUSH, cheering]. (Bush, 1992, "What Am I Fighting For?")

This advertisement listed several desirable policy objectives for his second term in office.

However, Bush also attacked his Democratic opponent repeatedly in this campaign. This spot questioned Clinton's character, arguing that he was inconsistent in a humorous manner:

Announcer [split screen, two candidates with grey dots over faces]: The presidential candidate on the left stood for military action in the Persian Gulf, while the candidate on the right agreed with those who opposed it. He says [candidate who is on the left] he wouldn't rule out term limits. While he says [candidate who is on right] he's personally opposed to term limits. This candidate [on the left] was called up for military service, while this one [on the right] claims he wasn't. One of these [split screen again] candidates is Bill Clinton [left dot removed to reveal Clinton]. Unfortunately, so is the other [other dot removed to reveal Clinton].

Clinton: There is a simple explanation for why this happened. (Bush, 1992, "Grey Dots")

The clip from Clinton at the end adds an additional touch of humor to this condemnation—the simple explanation, of course, is that he has no consistent position on these issues. Bush also used testimony from ordinary citizens to attack Clinton's character and policy:

[October 1992] *Man*: I don't believe him. I don't believe him one bit.

Woman: I don't believe him.

Woman: Trust.

[Where will Bill Clinton get the money for his big promises?]

Man: I don't know much about Clinton except promises.

Man: He tells everybody what they want to hear.

Man: Well, he wants to spend more money and the only place he can get it is from the taxpayers.

Man: Higher taxes.

Woman: Less food on the table.

Man: Broken promises.

Woman: Less clothes on the kids' backs.

Man: I don't know how we can take any more taxes.

Woman: Less money to go to the doctor.

Man: He's raised taxes in Arkansas; he'll raise taxes here.

Woman: Just less of everything [to be continued tomorrow . . .]. (Bush, 1992, "Luke")

This spot declares that Clinton can't be trusted, that he has broken promises, and that he will raise taxes with a variety undesirable consequences. A comment near the end attacks Clinton's record as governor.

The Bush campaign also devoted entire advertisements to criticizing Clinton's record as governor of Arkansas.

In his 12 years as governor, Bill Clinton has doubled his state's debt [Doubled state's debt], doubled government spending [Doubled government spending], and signed the largest tax increase in his state's history. Yet his state remains the 45th worst in which to work [45th worst in which to work; source], the 45th worst for children [45th worst for children; source]. It has the worst environmental policy [Worst environmental policy; source]. And the FBI says Arkansas has America's biggest increase in the rate of serious crime [Biggest increase in serious crime rate; source].

Announcer: And now Bill Clinton says he wants to do for America what he's done for Arkansas. America can't take that risk [America can't take that risk]. (Bush, 1992, "Arkansas Record")

This spot's tag-line (and its general premise) echoes one Bush used successfully in 1988 against Governor Michael Dukakis: "Michael Dukakis says he wants to do for America what he's done for Massachusetts. America can't afford that risk."

Bush also used his advertisements to attack Clinton's policy proposals, often on the grounds that Clinton would increase taxes if elected president:

[To pay for his campaign promises]: Bill Clinton says he'll only tax the rich to pay for his campaign promises. [Here's what Clinton economics could mean to you]. But here's what Clinton economics could mean to you: $1,088 more in taxes [John Cannes, steam fitter], $2,072 more in taxes [Lori Huntoon scientist]. One hundred leading economists say his plan means higher taxes and bigger deficits [100 Economists say higher taxes, bigger deficits]. $2,072 more in taxes [Wyman Winston, Housing Lender, $2,072 more in taxes]. You can't trust Clinton economics [Clinton Economics]. It's wrong for you [Wrong for You]. It's wrong for America [Wrong for America]. To find out how much more in taxes you could pay, Call 1-800-MEGA-TAX [To find our how much more in taxes you could pay, Call 1-800-MEGA-TAX]. (Bush, 1992, "Clinton Economics/Federal Taxes")

Thus, Bush's advertising campaign in 1992 acclaimed his record (especially in the area of foreign policy), outlined domestic goals, and attacked Clinton's character and record in office.

Clinton's advertisements in his first presidential campaign attacked Bush's record, and the Reagan-Bush record as well:

We've been under trickle-down economics for twelve years. Just keep taxes low on the wealthy and see what happens. Well, I'll tell you what's happened. Most Americans are working harder for less money [income is down]. Unemployment is up [higher unemployment]. Health care costs are exploding [Failed health care system]. We are not doing what it takes to compete and win [What it takes:]. I've worked hard on a different plan [booklet, Putting People First]. Let's give incentives to invest in new jobs [new jobs]. Let's spend more on education and training. Let's provide basic health care to all Americans [Cut health care costs]. Putting our people first, rebuilding this economy [For a copy of the plan: 800-272-9763]. Making us competitive. If we do those things, we'll compete and win [Clinton/Gore '92]. And we'll bring this country back. (Clinton, 1992, "Rebuild America")

This spot then moves smoothly into a list of Clinton's proposals for improving America. His proposals for change were also acclaimed in this spot:

Bill Clinton's economic plan. Endorsed by over 600 economists including 10 Nobel Prize Winners [Clinton working at desk; names of endorsers scroll] as the best hope for reviving the nation's economy [best hope for reviving the nation's economy]. More than 400 of America's most respected business leaders say the Clinton Plan will create jobs [More than 400 of America's most respected business leaders say the Clinton Plan will create jobs]. A panel of independent experts convened by *Time* magazine concludes that Clinton's plan has the best solutions to our economic problems [best solutions to our economic problems]. And now even the author of Ross Perot's plan has endorsed Bill Clinton's plan [Clinton is the best choice to lead, John White]. Clinton/Gore: Let's get our economy moving again [Clinton/Gore: Let's get our economy moving again]. (Clinton, 1992, "Economic Plan")

Clinton offers numerous endorsements of his proposals from a variety of sources to bolster his policy positions.

Clinton used some of his advertisements in 1992 to acclaim his record as the governor of Arkansas:

For twelve years he's battled the odds in one of America's poorest states [Clinton working at desk] and made steady progress. Arkansas is now first in the nation in job growth [Arkansas is first in the nation in job growth, source]. Even Bush's Secretary of Labor just called job growth in Arkansas enormous [Job growth in Arkansas enormous, source]. He moved 17,000 people from welfare to work [17,000 people from welfare to work, source]. And he's kept taxes low: Arkansas has the second lowest tax burden in the country [Arkansas has the second lowest tax burden in the country, source]. No wonder his fellow Governors, Democrats and Republicans, have named him the nation's most effective Governor. Bill Clinton: For people for a change. (Clinton, 1992, "Steady")

The implication is that he would be an effective president if given the chance. Thus, Clinton used his advertisements to acclaim his past record and to indicate his plans for a better America.

Clinton attacked Bush's domestic record in his campaign. He used some of Bush's statements against him in this spot.

Announcer 1988 [1988]:

Bush: Thirty million jobs in the next eight years [8/18/88].

Announcer: 1990: America's jobless rate hits three-year high [America's jobless rate hits three year high, Bureau of Labor Statistics].

Bush: I'm not prepared to say we're in recession [11/18/91].

Announcer: March 1992: Jobless rate hits six-year high [Bureau of Labor Statistics].

Bush: The economy is strengthening [10/4/91].

Announcer: George Bush vetoes unemployment compensation [Bureau of Labor Statistics].

Bush: The economy continues to grow [July 3, 1992].

Announcer: July 1992: Unemployment rate is the highest in eight years [Bureau of Labor Statistics]. If George Bush doesn't understand the problem, how can he solve it [If George Bush doesn't understand the problem, how can he solve it]? We can't afford four more years [We can't afford four more years]. (Clinton, 1992, "Curtains")

Not only did this advertisement attack Bush's first-term record, but it also portrayed him as out of touch with reality. The next spot responded to Bush's claim that we can trust him in a crisis.

Announcer: George Bush says you can trust him in a crisis. But we're in a crisis, an economic crisis, and we haven't been able to trust George Bush.

Bush: It is not recession. It does not fit the definition of recession.

Announcer: George Bush has ignored the facts, blamed others, failed to take action.

Bush: Far better than doing something bad to this economy is doing nothing at all.

Announcer: If George Bush can't be trusted to use the powers of the Presidency to get our economy moving, it's time for a President who will. Bill Clinton: For People, For a Change [Clinton/Gore: For the People]. (Clinton, 1992, "Bad")

Notice how this advertisement cleverly shifted from foreign policy (a topic Bush attempted to exploit because it favored him) to domestic policy (a topic that favored Clinton). This spot reminded voters of Bush's famous promise of "No new taxes" during 1988 campaign:

Bush: Read my lips.

Announcer: Remember?

Bush: You will be better off four years from now than you are today.

Announcer: Well, it's four years later. How're ya doin'? (Clinton, 1992, "Remember")

This spot broadens the indictment from his broken promise ("Read my lips: No new taxes") to the state of the economy, reminding viewers that Bush also promised that they would be better off after his first term.

Clinton also criticized Bush for running negative ads, and argued that they made false charges. This ad also managed to acclaim Clinton's record and attack Bush's record simultaneously.

Announcer: George Bush's attack ads [George Bush's attack ads]. He knows they're not true [headlines: "It's lies, damn lies, and George Bush's ads," "Worse than a Lie"]. Under Bill Clinton, Arkansas leads the nation in job growth [Arkansas leads the nation in job growth, source]. The second lowest taxes [Second lowest taxes, source]. The lowest government spending [Lowest government spending, source], and education reforms that are nationally recognized [Education reforms that are nationally recognized]. So what's Bush doing [What's Bush doing, picture of Bush at top of screen]? Trying to hide his own record [Trying to hide his own record]. Nearly ten million people unemployed [Nearly ten million people unemployed]. Health care cost out of control [Health care cost out of control]. The worst economic record in fifty years [Worst economic record in fifty years]. George Bush is trying to scare you about Bill Clinton. But nothing could be more frightening than four more years. [But nothing could be more frightening than four more years]. (Clinton, 1992, "Frightening")

This commercial begins by characterizing Bush as a liar, then it acclaims Clinton's record in Arkansas, and then attacks Bush's economic record. These advertisements give a general idea of the nature of these advertising campaigns.

In 1996, Bill Clinton and Al Gore were selected by the Democratic Party to seek a second term in the White House. Senator Bob Dole, along with Jack Kemp, were the Republican challengers. Ross Perot represented the Reform Party in both campaigns, but was more of a presence in 1992 than in 1996.

Bob Dole ran hard on his proposed 15% tax cut in 1996, and on the character issue as well. This ad acclaimed his proposed tax cut and other policy proposals from the Republican candidate:

The stakes this election? Keeping more of what you earn. That's what Bob Dole's tax cut plan is all about. The Dole plan starts with a 15-percent tax cut for working Americans. That's $1,600 more for the typical family. A $500 per child tax credit. Education and job training incentives. Replacing the IRS with a fairer and simpler tax system. And a Balanced Budget Amendment to stop wasteful spending. The Dole plan. Helping you keep more of what you earn. (Dole, 1996, "The Stakes")

In addition to a specific child tax credit and passing the Balanced Budget Amendment, Dole outlined a general policy proposal (reforming the IRS) here. This campaign also used two spots featuring his wife, Elizabeth Dole. Here is one of them:

My husband is a plain-spoken man from the heart of America, Russell, Kansas. In Russell, you say what you're going to do and you do it. The truth first, last— always the truth. When Bob Dole says he'll cut your taxes 15 percent, he'll cut your taxes 15 percent. This is Bob Dole. He's a workhorse, not a show horse. And he knows whose money it really is: your family's [Bob Dole will cut taxes 15%]. (Dole, 1996, "From the Heart")

This spot extolled his virtues ("plain-spoken," "tells the truth," "a work-horse") and implies that Clinton is merely "a show horse." It also acclaims Dole's 15% tax cut proposal.

Much of Dole's campaign attacked Clinton and his policies. This spot criticized him for tax increases and tried to pin the label of tax and spend liberal onto the Democratic candidate:

Announcer: The truth about Clinton on taxes? [The Truth about Clinton On taxes]. Remember?

Clinton: "I will not raise taxes on the middle class."

Announcer: But he gave the middle class the largest tax increase in history [Clinton gave biggest middle class tax increase in history (CNN "Moneyweek," 8/7/96)].

Announcer: Higher taxes on your salary [Clinton raised taxes on your salary (Clinton's FY'94 budget, OBRA '93)].

Announcer: Gasoline [Clinton raised taxes on gasoline (Clinton's FY'94 budget, OBRA '93)].

Announcer: Social Security [Clinton raised taxes on Soc Sec (Clinton's FY'94 budget)].

Announcer: Clinton even tried higher taxes on heating your home [Clinton tried to raise taxes on heating your home (Clinton's FY'94 budget)].

Announcer: 255 proposed tax and fee increases in all [255 tax and fee increases (Clinton's FY'94-'97 budgets)].

Announcer: Clinton says . . .

Clinton: [September 23, 1996]: "But I don't think that qualifies me as a closet liberal."

Announcer: Sorry Mr. Clinton. Actions do speak louder than words [Actions Do Speak Louder Than Words].

Announcer: The real Bill Clinton. A real spend and tax liberal [The real Bill Clinton. A real spend and tax liberal]. (Dole, 1996, "Sorry—Taxes")

Notice also that this spot began by promising to reveal "The Truth on Clinton on Taxes," strongly suggesting that Clinton was not being honest about his tax record.

Dole repeatedly hammered at the teen drug-abuse problem. This spot was one of several that featured video from Clinton's MTV appearance:

Announcer: We send them off to school [Kids in hallway, school . . .].

And we worry. Teen-age drug use has doubled since 1992.

And Bill Clinton? He cut the White House Drug Office 83 percent [Clinton cut office of National Drug Control Policy 83 percent].

His own surgeon general even considered legalizing drugs [Drugs and kids in school yard].

And in front of our children [In front of our children . . .] on MTV the President himself . . .

Young Man: "If you had it to do over again, would you inhale?"

Clinton: "Sure, if I could . . . I tried before."

Announcer: Bill Clinton doesn't get it [Clinton's liberal drug policy has failed]. But we do. (Dole, 1996, "School")

Once again we see the label "liberal" being hung on Clinton. The attack on his character is quite strong.

The Dole campaign also used defense. This spot responded to Clinton's accusation that Dole and Gingrich had tried to cut Medicare (this controvesy centers around the question of whether a reduction in the proposed rate of increase counts as a "cut" or not—although neither side made this very clear):

Announcer: How many times have you seen this?

Clinton: "Last year Dole/Gingrich tried to cut Medicare $270 billion" [Red DC over ad "Wrong"].

Announcer: It's wrong . . . and the AARP, the largest and most respected senior citizen group, agrees. AARP Letter: Both sides have proposals "which would slow the rate of growth." They said we need "... an end to the political finger-pointing" [AARP agrees with the Dole plan for Bipartisan Agreement]. They agree with Bob Dole we need a bipartisan agreement to fix Medicare, not false political ads that scare seniors [Don't let Clinton fool you]. So next time you see a Clinton ad, don't let him fool you. (Dole, 1996, "Fool")

This controversy centered around the question of whether reducing project growth (of Medicare) is a cut or not. Clearly, in this spot, Clinton was portrayed as trying to misrepresent Dole's proposal. These spots give an indication of the nature of the 1996 Dole general election campaign.

In 1996, Clinton relied on domestic successes (as well as a number of relatively small policy initiatives, like college tax credits) in his second campaign. For example, this spot (while incredibly concise), touts Clinton's first-term accomplishments (and attacks Dole at the end):

Ten million new jobs. Family income up one thousand six hundred dollars. Signed welfare reform—requiring work, time limits. Taxes cut for fifteen million families. Balancing the budget. America's moving forward with an economic plan that works. Bob Dole: $900 billion in higher taxes. Republicans call him tax collector for the welfare state. His risky tax scheme would raise taxes on nine million families. (Clinton, 1996, "Economic Record")

The following spot managed to acclaim Clinton's first-term record and his policy proposals while attacking Dole's character:

The facts Bob Dole ignores in his negative attacks: The deficit cut 60%. 10 million new jobs. Family income up $1,600 [since 1993]. Health insurance you don't lose when changing jobs. President Clinton: moving our economy ahead, helping families. Now a plan to cut taxes for college tuition: $500 per child tax credit. Break up violent gangs. Move one million from welfare to work. Dole resorts to desperate negative attacks. President Clinton is protecting our values. (Clinton, 1996, "Ignores")

Notice that this spot also appropriated a theme from the 1992 Republican campaign: values. Another spot also worked at accomplishing these three goals:

Remember: Recession, jobs lost. The Dole-GOP bill tries to deny nearly a million families unemployment benefits. Higher interest rates, ten million unemployed. With a Dole amendment, Republicans try to block more job training. Today: We make more autos than Japan; record construction jobs; mortgage rates down; ten million new jobs; more women-owned companies than ever. The president's plan: education, job training, economic growth, for a better future. (Clinton, 1996, "The Economy")

Thus, voters had two reasons to prefer Clinton (his past record and his promises for the future) and reasons to reject his opponent.

The Clinton campaign also used several endorsements. One is from James Brady, who was shot during the attempt to assassinate President Reagan:

It was over in a moment, but the pain lasts forever. President Clinton stood up and helped pass the Brady Bill. It wasn't about politics. The president had the integrity to do what was right. When I hear people question the president's character, I say look what he's done. Look at the lives the Brady Bill will save. (Clinton, 1996, "Seconds")

The Brady Bill was named after James Brady, a prominent member (press secretary) of Reagan's White House. This spot acclaimed Clinton for helping to pass the Brady Bill and it responded to criticism of his character.

Several of Clinton's spots used footage from Senator Dole. This one uses Dole's own words and deeds to indict his views on Medicare and on education:

Dole: "I will be the president who preserves and strengthens and protects Medicare. I was there, fighting the fight, voting against Medicare, one of 12, because we knew it wouldn't work."

Announcer: Last year, Dole/Gingrich tried to cut Medicare $270 billion.

Dole: "Give children a chance in life, give them an education. We're going to eliminate the Department of Education. We don't need it in the first place. I didn't vote for it in 1979."

Announcer: Dole tried to slash college scholarships.

Dole: "Voting against Medicare."

Announcer: "Wrong in the past."

Dole: "We're going to eliminate the Department of Education."

Announcer: Wrong for our future. (Clinton, 1996, "Preserve")

Notice also the attempt to use guilt by association. Several of Clinton's spots referred to "Dole/Gingrich" as if they were a single entity (Gingrich's approval ratings had dropped).

FUNCTIONS OF TELEVISION SPOTS

In these campaigns, attacks accounted for 52% of the comments in these spots. For example, in 1992 Bush attacked Clinton's character with these ordinary citizens:

Man: Bill Clinton's not telling anything honestly to the American people.

Woman: I don't think he tells the truth. I think he evades a lot of questions.

Woman: I don't think he's honorable. I don't think he's trustworthy.

Man: One minute he said he didn't, the next he said he did.

Clearly, we want a president who is truthful and trustworthy, or his campaign promises are worthless. In that same campaign Clinton attacked Bush's character in this commercial:

[Irangate, Arms for hostages, The Savings & Loan Bailout, Willie Horton, The Education President, The Environmental President, "I'll do what I have to to be re-elected," "You'll be better off in four years," "It is not a recession," "Read my lips" Four more years?].

Announcer: George Bush is right [George Bush is right]. It is a question of character [It is a question of character].

This spot reminded voters of ten episodes or statements that shed an unfavorable light on the Republican candidate, and tired to turn Bush's assault on Clinton's character back on Bush. In 1996, Dole attacked Clinton on the issue of the increase in teenage drug abuse in this advertisement:

The stakes of this election? Our children. Under Clinton, cocaine and heroin use among teenagers has doubled. Why? Because Bill Clinton isn't protecting our children from drugs. He cut the drug czar's office 83 percent, cut 227 Drug Enforcement agents, and cut $200 million to stop drugs at our borders. Clinton's liberal drug policies have failed. Our children deserve better.

This commercial offers statistics about the teen drug problem and links it to three of Clinton's actions. It also labels him a liberal. During the same campaign Clinton attacked Dole's (and Gingrich's) recent actions in Congress:

Newt Gingrich. Bob Dole. Dole-Gingrich. Against Family Leave.
Against a woman's right to choose. Dole. Gingrich.
Cutting Vaccines for Children. Against Brady Bill and assault weapons ban.
Against higher minimum wage. Cutting college scholarships.

Thus, attacks were common components of these campaigns (see Table 8.1).

Acclaims were also quite common in the 1990s, consisting of 47% of the commercials' remarks. In his first presidential campaign, Clinton acclaimed his policy successes as governor of Arkansas.

Table 8.1
Functions of the 1992 and 1996 Campaigns

Year	Candidate	Acclaims	Attacks	Defenses
1992	Bush	70 (44%)	**90 (56%)**	0
	Clinton	**167 (49%)**	**168 (49%)**	5 (1%)
1996	Dole	111 (37%)	**185 (62%)**	1 (0.5%)
	Clinton	**225 (53%)**	200 (47%)	3 (1%)
Total		573 (47%)	**643 (52%)**	9 (1%)

Twelve years battling the odds in one of our nation's poorest states. Arkansas now leads the nation in job growth [Arkansas leads the nation in job growth]. Incomes are rising at twice the national rate [Incomes rising at twice the national rate]. Seventeen thousand people moved from welfare to work [17,000 people moved from welfare to work]. That's progress, and that's what we need now.

This spot discussed accomplishments on jobs, income, and welfare. Bush acclaimed his foreign policy accomplishments: "Today, for the first time in half a century, America is not at war." In 1996, Dole explained his vision for America:

Before you vote, I want you to know the America I see. I see an America with a government that works for us, not the other way around. Where parents can choose safe schools for their kids. Where the family is strengthened and honored, not battered, by the government. Where we wage a real war on drugs and our leaders set the right example. An America where you keep more of what you earn, because it's your money. If you agree with this America, I'd really appreciate your vote.

These policy goals were given as reasons to vote for Dole. This Clinton spot from his second presidential campaign acclaimed his past accomplishments: "Ten million new jobs. Family income up $1,600 [since 1993]." President Clinton cut the deficit 60%. Signed welfare reform—requiring work, time limits. Taxes cut for 15 million families. This passage succinctly lists five policy accomplishments.

Defenses were uncommon, accounting for 1% of these utterances. Bush used no defense in his advertising. Responding to accusations about his lax drug policies, this Clinton spot rejected Dole's attack:

Dole's attack ad—wrong again. President Clinton expanded the death penalty for drug kingpins. Nearly 40 percent more border agents to stop drugs. Record number of drug felons in federal prisons. President Clinton expanded school antidrug programs. Dole and Gingrich tried to cut them. Voted against 100,000 police. Bob Dole even voted against creating the drug czar. President Clinton appointed a four-star general drug czar—and is leading the fight to protect our children.

In denying Dole's charges, Clinton recounted (acclaimed) his actions in his first term in office on drug abuse.

POLICY VERSUS CHARACTER

These spots focused more on policy (70%) than on character (30%). The only exception was Bush, who devoted 62% of his television spot utterances in 1992 to character. In this spot from 1992, Bush discusses Clinton's tax policy:

Bill Clinton says he'll only tax the rich to pay for his campaign promises [Here's what Clinton economics could mean to you]. But here's what Clinton economics could mean to you: $1,088 more in taxes [John Cannes, steam fitter], $2,072 more in taxes [Lori Huntoon scientist]. One hundred leading economists say his plan means higher taxes and bigger deficits [100 Economists say higher taxes, bigger deficits]. $2,072 more in taxes [Wyman Winston, Housing Lender, $2,072 more in taxes].

This argument used concrete examples as well as experts (economists) to support the criticism of Clinton's proposals. In 1992, Clinton acclaimed his plan for reducing the nation's welfare rolls:

I have a plan to end welfare as we know it, to break the cycle of welfare dependency. We'll provide education, job training, and child care, but then those who are able must go to work—either in the private sector or in public service. I know it can work: In my state we've moved 17,000 people from welfare rolls to payrolls. It's time to make welfare what it should be: a second chance, not a way of life.

Note that Clinton also drew on his accomplishments as governor to reinforce this proposal. In 1996, Dole contrasted his approach to government with Clinton's:

Which plan puts more money in the pockets of seniors? Under Bill Clinton's plan, our huge federal government will grow another 20%, costing us plenty. The Dole plan: our government still grows, but only 14% to protect Medicare and Social Security. See, that's how the Dole plan will cut your taxes 15% and repeal Bill Clinton's big tax on Social Security. The Dole plan: more money in the pockets of seniors.

Table 8.2
Policy versus Character in the 1992 and 1996 Campaigns

Year	Candidate	Policy	Character
1992	Bush	21 (38%)	**35 (62%)**
	Clinton	**125 (77%)**	38 (23%)
1996	Dole	**107 (71%)**	43 (29%)
	Clinton	**225 (71%)**	90 (29%)
Total		**478 (70%)**	206 (30%)

Similarly, this Clinton advertisement contrasted the policies of Dole (and Gingrich) with his own policy proposals:

The Oval Office. If Dole sits here, and Gingrich runs Congress, what could happen? Medicare slashed. Women's right to choose, gone. Education, school drug programs cut. And a risky $550 billion plan balloons the deficit, raises interest rates, hurts the economy. President Clinton says balance the budget, cut taxes for families, college tuition. Stands up to Dole and Gingrich. But if Dole wins, and Gingrich runs Congress, there'll be nobody there to stop them.

This spot associated Dole with Gingrich, using "guilt by association" to attack the Republican candidate. Thus, all of these candidates addressed policy issues in their television spots (see Table 8.2).

The topic of character was also addressed in these campaigns. Bush used these ordinary people to attack Clinton's character in 1992:

Man: Bill Clinton's not telling anything honestly to the American people.

Woman: I don't think he tells the truth. I think he evades a lot of questions.

Woman: I don't think he's honorable. I don't think he's trustworthy.

Man: One minute he said he didn't, the next he said he did.

These are not flattering comments. Clinton explained in 1992 that after he met President Kennedy in 1963, "That's when I decided that I could really do public service 'cause I cared so much about people." In 1996, this Clinton spot managed to attack the Republicans for their criticism of the president while it acclaimed Clinton's character: "I hear people question the president's character and integrity. It's just politics. When it came to protecting children—the president had the courage to make a difference." The Dole campaign argued that he was "The Better Man for a Better America." Thus, candidates in these campaigns discussed character as well as policy.

FORMS OF POLICY AND CHARACTER

These candidates relied heavily on past deeds (56%) when discussing policy (Bush, who discussed past deeds in only 21% of his ad remarks, is the exception). For example, in 1992 this spot for Bush charged that "Arkansas is at the bottom of the list. Why does he keep bragging about Arkansas?" Clinton, of course, had a different view of his record in Arkansas:

For twelve years he's battled the odds in one of America's poorest states [Clinton working at desk] and made steady progress. Arkansas is now first in the nation in job growth [Arkansas is now first in the nation in job growth, source]. Even Bush's Secretary of Labor just called job growth in Arkansas enormous [Bush's Secretary of Labor just called job growth in Arkansas enormous, source]. He moved 17,000 people from welfare to work [moved 17,000 people from welfare to work, source]. And he's kept taxes low: Arkansas has the second lowest tax burden in the country [Arkansas has the second lowest tax burden in the country, source].

Keying into Clinton's pledge to end welfare "as we know it," this Dole spot attacked Clinton's record here: "But he vetoed welfare reform not once, but twice. He vetoed work requirements for the able-bodied. He vetoed putting time limits on welfare. And Clinton still supports giving welfare benefits to illegal immigrants. The Clinton rhetoric hasn't matched the Clinton record." This spot, broadcast in Spanish, acclaimed Clinton's past deeds: "Thanks to President Clinton, over 10 million jobs have been created since 1992. In that same time, a record number of new Hispanic businesses were created. The minimum wage increased." Thus, these spots frequently discussed past deeds when they addressed policy matters (see Table 8.3).

Future plans (24%) and general goals (20%) occurred at roughly the same rate. In 1992, Bush touted his Agenda for American Renewal. One component was his plan for job training: "It provides job training, so workers have the new skills to compete." Clinton attacked Bush's tax cut proposal: "Now George Bush wants to give a $108,000 tax break to millionaires [$108,000 tax break to millionaires, source]. $108,000. Guess who's going to pay? [Guess who's going to pay?]" These utterances illustrate acclaims and attacks on future plans.

The candidates also discussed general goals. In 1996, Dole attacked Clinton for his (failed) health care reform initiative, characterizing his goal as "Government-run health care." Clinton acclaimed his goals in

Table 8.3
Forms of Policy and Character in the 1992 and 1996 Campaigns

Year	Candidate	Policy			Character		
		Past Deeds	Future Plans	General Goals	Personal Qualities	Leadership Ability	Ideals
1992	Bush	21 (21%)	35 (35%)	44 (44%)	47 (78%)	7 (12%)	6 (10%)
	Clinton	125 (56%)	38 (17%)	59 (27%)	93 (82%)	8 (7%)	12 (11%)
1996	Dole	107 (57%)	43 (23%)	39 (21%)	81 (77%)	5 (5%)	19 (18%)
	Clinton	225 (64%)	90 (26%)	34 (10%)	52 (68%)	3 (4%)	21 (28%)
Total		478 (56%)	206 (24%)	176 (20%)	273 (77%)	23 (6%)	58 (16%)

1996: "This country's future [Balance the budget for a growing economy] will be even brighter than its brilliant past." Thus, these spots addressed goals as well as specific plans for the future.

All of these candidates chose to stress personal qualities (77%) when discussing character. This Bush commercial in 1992 attacked Clinton's honesty:

He said he was never drafted. Then he admitted he was drafted. Then he said he forgot being drafted. He said he was never deferred from the draft. Then, he said he was. He said he never received special treatment. But he did receive special treatment. The question then was avoiding the draft. Now for Bill Clinton, it's a question of avoiding the truth.

The question of Clinton and the draft is used to attack his personal qualities. However, integrity was an issue for the Democrats as well. That same year, this advertisement for Clinton impugned Bush's trustworthiness:

George Bush. The *Observer* says new information about Mr. Bush's role in the Iran arms for hostages deal [new information about Mr. Bush's role in the Iran arms for hostages deal, source] and the breaking of his read my lips no tax pledge raise doubts about his trustworthiness [the breaking of his read my lips no tax pledge raise doubts about his trustworthiness, source]. The *Current* says he has been shifty on key issues [he has been shifty on key issues, source]. The *Oregonian*, We refocused on Bush's flip flops on abortion and taxes [Bush's flip flops on abortion and taxes, source], his secret arming of the brutal Iraqi regime [secret arming of the brutal Iraqi regime, source]: Frankly, we no longer trust him [Frankly, we no longer trust him, source]. The *Philadelphia Daily News*: Bush is without a principle or a clue [Bush is without a principle or a clue, source]. It does come down to who you trust. That's why it comes down to Bill Clinton for President. [It does come down to who you trust. That's why it comes down to Bill Clinton for President, source]

In the 1996 campaign, this Dole ad (featuring Elizabeth Dole in part) spoke of his recovery from his war injury to acclaim Dole's personal qualities: "He persevered. He never gave up. He fought his way back from total paralysis." A citizen spoke of Clinton's action on crime legislation, functioning both to defend his character and to acclaim his courage: "President Clinton forced Congress to pass his tough crime bill— life in prison for dangerous repeat offenders, an expanded death penalty. I hear people question the president's character and integrity. It's just politics. When it came to protecting children—the president had the courage to make a difference." These passages illustrate how these campaigns used personal qualities as a topic for character appeals.

Ideals was the second most common topic (16%) and leadership was relatively uncommon (6%). In 1996, this spot (broadcast in Spanish) praised Clinton's ideals: "Clinton wants us to be prepared for the future. ... He wants us to have more opportunities, to improve our quality of life." In this spot from 1992, Clinton questions Bush's leadership ability:

Announcer: George Bush says you can trust him in a crisis. But we're in a crisis, an economic crisis, and we haven't been able to trust George Bush.

Bush: It is not recession. It does not fit the definition of recession.

Announcer: George Bush has ignored the facts, blamed others, failed to take action.

Bush: Far better than doing something bad to this economy is doing nothing at all.

Announcer: If George Bush can't be trusted to use the powers of the Presidency to get our economy moving, it's time for a President who will.

Ignoring the facts, blaming others, and failing to take needed action are not the marks of a skilled leader. Thus, these commercials used several forms of character and policy utterances.

SOURCE OF UTTERANCE

These campaigns showed a clear preference for using others to advance claims in television spots (see Table 8.4). Over three-quarters (77%) of the acclaims were made by people other than the candidates. The only exception was Bush, who made 56% of the acclaims in his advertisements in 1992. Attacks were even more highly skewed toward others: 95% of all attacks were made by other people besides the candidate. In 1996, Clinton did not personally make any of the attacks in his spots. Defenses were made exclusively by other speakers in these campaigns.

CONCLUSION

Clinton won the election of 1992 and was re-elected in 1996. Although Kennedy won in 1960 and Johnson in 1964, the 1990s saw the first time a Democrat had won two terms in the White House in recent memory (Republicans had done so in 1952 and 1956, 1968, and 1972, and 1980 and 1984). The economy surely played a role in Clinton's victories. It was down when he challenged Bush, and was on the upswing when he ran for re-election against Dole. However, Clinton's advertisements effectively exploited the situation by attacking Bush's record in 1992 and by acclaiming Clinton's first-term accomplishments in 1996. Bush was not able to persuasively defend or acclaim his domestic record, and Dole was not able to successfully attack Clinton's first-term record or character in 1996.

Table 8.4
Source of Utterances in the 1992 and 1996 Campaigns

Year	Candidate	Acclaims		Attacks		Defenses	
		Candidate	Other	Candidate	Other	Candidate	Other
1992	Bush	39 (56%)	31 (44%)	5 (6%)	85 (94%)	0	0
	Clinton	45 (27%)	122 (73%)	9 (5%)	159 (95%)	0	5 (100%)
1996	Dole	32 (29%)	79 (71%)	12 (6%)	173 (94%)	0	1 (100%)
	Clinton	13 (6%)	212 (94%)	0	48 (100%)	0	3 (100%)
Total		129 (23%)	444 (77%)	26 (5%)	465 (95%)	0	9 (100%)

Part III

Other Campaigns

Chapter 9

Primary Campaigns: Who Shall Lead Us?

Previous research on presidential primary campaign advertising is relatively sparse. Devlin (1994) provided his interesting insider's perspective on the 1992 New Hampshire primary. Payne, Marlier, and Baukus (1989) examined spots from 1988 using Diamond and Bates' (1992) four categories of identification, argumentative, negative, and resolution spots. Shyles (1983) identified the issues of the 1980 campaign from primary ads and later (1984) discussed the interrelationships of images, issues, and presentation in the same campaign. Pfau, Diedrich, Larson, and van Winkle (1993) conducted an experimental study of relational and competence perceptions of candidates in the 1992 primary. The most extensive study analyzes 1,089 primary spots from 1960 to 1988 (Kaid & Ballotti, 1991); unfortunately, this study has not been published.

It was not always necessary to compete in the primary campaigns to secure a party's nomination. In fact, the first primaries occurred just after the turn of the century in Wisconsin, Pennsylvania, and South Dakota. The number of states with primaries hovered between thirteen and nineteen until 1972. As late as 1968, Hubert Humphrey was nominated without competing in a single primary (Levine, 1995). However, the riots and divisiveness of the Democratic National Convention in Chicago in 1968 (and other factors) prompted reforms in both parties which encouraged more primaries—and earlier primaries. An important goal was to decide who would be the nominee well in advance of the convention so there would be time for the divisions that occur in a contested nomination to heal before the party's showcase event (the nominating convention) on national television. In 1992, there were 37 primary contests which selected about 80% of the delegates to the national conventions (Jackson & Crotty, 1996).

This sample (described in the Appendix) includes a diverse group of primary candidates: 28 are Republicans and 32 are Democrats. The number of spots is also roughly equivalent: 371 (48%) spots are from Republicans and 394 (52%) are from Democrats (Kaid & Ballotti's [1991] study of primary spots included 1,089 spots from 1968 through 1988, but 82% were from Democrats and 18% from Republicans). To provide further balance, the sample for this study includes numerous spots from winners—the eventual nominees—(331; 43%) as well as from losers (434; 57%).

The earliest primary television advertisement I could locate, and quite possibly the first primary spot ever in a presidential race, was by Eisenhower in 1952:

What will Eisenhower do about cleaning up purveyors of influence in Washington? President Truman has made an abortive attempt to clean up the mess in Washington. Eisenhower will clean it up for real. Who will Eisenhower surround himself with if he becomes President? He will come to Washington without commitments. Keep in mind that in every step of his remarkable career he has surrounded himself with outstanding talent. And that throughout his life of significant accomplishments, he has won the determined cooperation of other great men. Thus, at shape, he brought in, in addition to military people, top civilian talent of the United States and Europe. What is Eisenhower's position on censorship in America? Eisenhower says, in my opinion, censorship is a stupid and shallow way to approach the solution to any problem. It is quite clear that if the freedom of the press should disappear, all other freedoms that we enjoy shall disappear. What is Eisenhower's definition of democracy? He says, for my own part, in seeking some definition for the word democracy, I believe this one satisfies me more than any other: Democracy is the political expression of a deeply felt religion. If General Eisenhower wins the nomination, what kind of a political campaign will he wage? Eisenhower has given us these words: If by any chance it should come about that the Republican Party does name me as its standard-bearer, I am determined to lead the entire organization into a fight in which there will be no cessation, no rest, and no lack of intensity until the final decision is made. (Eisenhower, 1952, "Purveyors of Influence")

This commercial attacks the mess in Washington and argues that the incumbent Democratic administration was incapable of solving it. It alludes to his status as a war hero (and leader) and his ideals (freedom of speech, democracy, religion). It ends with a declaration of his intent to campaign hard. Of course, Eisenhower was nominated and won two terms in the White House.

In 1960, Senator Kennedy (from Massachusetts) entered the primaries to demonstrate his viability. Particular concerns had been expressed about his religion (no Catholic had been elected president to this point). He campaigned hard in West Virginia to dispel these fears.

Kennedy [Vote Kennedy May 10]: The question is whether I think that if I were elected president, I would be divided between two loyalties: my church and my state. There is no article of my faith that would in any way inhibit—I think it encourages—the meeting of my oath of office. And whether you vote for me or not because of my competence to be president, I am sure that this state of West Virginia, that no one believes that I'd be a candidate for the presidency if I didn't think I could meet my oath of office. Now you cannot tell me the day I was born it was said I could never run for president because I wouldn't meet my oath of office. I came to the state of West Virginia, which has fewer numbers of my coreligionists than any state in the nation. I would not have come here if I didn't feel I was going to get complete opportunity to run for office as a fellow American in this state. I would not run for it if in any way I felt that I couldn't do the job. So I come here today to say that I think this is an issue.

Announcer: Vote Kennedy May 10 [Vote Kennedy May 10, outline of West Virginia]. (Kennedy, 1960, "Loyalty")

This message draws upon the American Dream that anyone can grow up to be president when he declared that "you cannot tell me the day I was born it was said I could never run for president." Perhaps he could also have referred to freedom of religion (one's religion should not prohibit anyone from becoming president). Kennedy made his point and won the Democratic nomination—and, later that year, the presidency. His primary spots also discussed other issues, like labor, farming, Social Security, and education.

In 1964, Barry Goldwater developed a series of at least seven spots in a consistent format. These advertisements began with an image of Goldwater and a caption displayed upside down. The announcer introduced a topic and reported what "they" are saying about Barry Goldwater. Then he asked, "What did he really say?" and the image turned right-side up and Goldwater stated his actual position. Here is a typical example:

Announcer: They say Barry Goldwater is against social security [image of Goldwater upside down, with label Social Security also upside down]. What did he really say? [image turns right-side up].

Goldwater: I want to strengthen social security, keep the security in it, so you can be paid in real American dollars that are still worth enough to buy the groceries.

Announcer: He said it, you vote it, Goldwater [ballot with X by Goldwater]. (Goldwater, 1964, "Social Security")

This format suggests that Goldwater's critics are wrong (they've turned the truth upside down) and he used this approach to discuss such topics

as Social Security, taxes, war, and civil rights. It clearly functions as defense, denying the accusations as well as acclaiming a general goal.

In 1968, Nixon ran several primary spots that were adapted to individual primary states (perhaps this had occurred earlier, but this campaign
[see also the spot for McCarthy below] is the earliest such audience adap-
tation I found). For example, this commercial uses both ordinary citizens
and a congressman to speak on his behalf in the Wisconsin primary:

[*Susanne Wilmeth, UW Madison*]: Here at school a lot of the kids seem to think
that America is just drifting, that we have no real leadership. I think that Dick
Nixon could provide that leadership.

[*Mrs. Dorothy Krohn, Oshkosh*]: I don't feel safe in my own kitchen, any more,
unless the front doors are locked. My neighbors feel the same way. And I think
that's a tragedy in a country as great as ours. Mr. Nixon shares our concern and
I know he will do something about this rising crime rate.

[*Congressman Glenn Davis, New Berlin*]: My concern is with the careless use of the
taxpayers' money. I know Dick Nixon well. I know of his dedication to efficient
government and a sound dollar. I know of his repugnance to spending money
which we do not have. I shall vote for Dick Nixon on April 2.

Announcer: For times like these, Nixon's the one [Nixon's the one]. (Nixon, 1968,
"Concerns")

Some of Nixon's spots mentioned other states and included other election dates. That same year, Eugene McCarthy challenged Bobby Kennedy
to a primary debate. This is the earliest spot I found to attack another
candidate for refusing to debate:

I'm Eddie Albert. I'd like to ask you a question. Why is Bobby Kennedy afraid
to debate Eugene McCarthy? McCarthy challenged him to a debate but Kennedy
refused. After all it was Bobby's brother John Kennedy who challenged Nixon
to a debate. That certainly helped the country make up its mind. I think a debate
between the two candidates in California would give all of us a chance to decide
which man would make the better President. You know I remember when Gene
McCarthy decided the Vietnam war was wrong, and he had the guts to stand
up in New Hampshire and take on President Johnson. Bobby Kennedy sat on
the fence, and waited to see how Gene McCarthy would make out. It seems to
me that Kennedy wouldn't face Johnson in New Hampshire, and now he won't
face McCarthy in California. Now I admire courage, and that's just one of the
reasons why I'm going to vote for Eugene McCarthy on June 4. (McCarthy, 1968,
"Eddie Albert")

This spot, developed for the California primary, also used a celebrity, actor Eddie Albert, and an unusual form of reluctant testimony: the fact that
Bobby's brother, John, had been willing to debate Nixon eight years earlier.

In 1972, Nixon ran for re-election. He used ordinary people in this
primary spot to acclaim his first-term performance:

Woman: I think President Nixon in his first term has done an absolutely fantastic job.

Woman: And he's getting our boys out of Vietnam, and that's very important, very important to me.

Man: President Nixon did exactly what he said he was going to do.

Woman: He's turned the economy around.

Woman: I certainly do approve of President Nixon's going to Peking.

Man: Without a doubt Mr. Nixon should be re-elected.

Man: I like him.

Woman: You better believe it. I am going to vote for President Nixon.

Announcer: America needs President Nixon, and he needs you. Re-elect the President [Re-elect the President]. (Nixon, 1972, "Approve")

These comments function to acclaim both his policy ("He's turned the economy around") and his character ("I like him").

In 1976, Ronald Reagan challenged Ford for the Republican nomination. In this spot, Reagan alludes generally to his record as governor of California:

I believe that what we did in California can be done in Washington. If government will have faith in the people and let them bring their common sense to bear on the problems bureaucracy hasn't solved. I believe in the people. Now Mr. Ford places his faith in the Washington establishment. This has been evident in his appointment of former congressmen and long-time government workers to positions in his administration. Well, I don't believe that those who've been a part of the problem are necessarily the best qualified to solve those problems [Reagan!]. (Reagan, 1976, "Record")

He also suggests that Ford is part of an entrenched establishment, attacking as well as acclaiming. When Edward Kennedy challenged Carter for the Democratic nomination in 1980, he used Carter's words and campaign promises against him:

Kennedy: Everybody remembers the candidate who said in 1976, "I'll never mislead you, and you can depend on it." But do you remember what else he said? He said he would reduce inflation and unemployment to 4% by the end of his first term, that he would never use high interest rates to fight inflation, that he would never decontrol the price of oil and natural gas, that nuclear power is the resource of last resort, that he would get the ERA passed during his first year in office, that he would balance the budget and reduce the size of government. But now he's secluded in the White House telling us to rally around his failure overseas. He refuses to discuss the issues, but America cannot afford to forget the problems President Carter has left behind. New Hampshire can change that. New Hampshire can make the difference in 1980.

Announcer: Kennedy. (Kennedy, 1980, "Promises")

He refers to Carter's broken promises and failures in both domestic and foreign policy. In 1984, Democrat McGovern contrasted himself with Reagan, who was not challenged for the Republican nomination:

It'd be some fight all right. A classic. [McGovern pictured on left, Reagan on right]: food for peace versus death squads

military cuts versus deficits

home mortgages versus tax breaks

social security versus insecurity

college loans versus B-1s

compassion versus indifference

a nuclear freeze versus space wars

negotiation versus name-calling

coexistence versus no existence

Who says George can't win—are you kidding?

[Massachusetts goes McGovern. McGovern takes Reagan]. (McGovern, 1984, "Some Fight")

Here, he assailed the incumbent, President Reagan. Perhaps McGovern should have concentrated more on his immediate opponent, Walter Mondale, the eventual Democratic nominee, during the primaries.

In 1988, Vice President George Bush sought the Republican nomination. Senator Bob Dole was one of those who contested his nomination. In this spot, unlike the previous one from McGovern, Bush attacked his Republican opponent:

[phone rings, outside Congress] Bob Dole says that President Reagan calls him to get things done. But under Bob Dole's leadership we lost the Bork nomination [under Bob Dole's leadership we lost the Bork nomination]. And in 16 of the 34 votes Reagan lost in the Senate, Dole couldn't deliver even half of the Republicans [Dole couldn't deliver even half of the Republicans]. Senate Republican support for the President hit an all-time low in 1987 [Bob Dole: bar chart], when even Senator Dole failed to support him almost 30% of the time [Senator Dole failed to support him almost 30% of the time]. So when President Reagan wanted a Vice President he could count on, he didn't call Bob Dole: He called George Bush ["He's an executive Vice President," Ronald Reagan, 12/3/87; phone rings]. (Bush, 1988, "16 of 34—Dole Senate Record")

In addition to attacking Dole's record, notice how Bush tried to capitalize on his experience as vice president and on the support of the very popular Republican president, Ronald Reagan.

In the 1992 primary campaign Clinton used a version of the "Which Barry Goldwater" spot Johnson ran in 1964 to attack one of the other Democratic candidates:

[Brown's photo switches from left to right side]: Jerry Brown says he'll fight for we the people. Question is, which people? [which people?] He says he is for working families [He says he is for working families]. But his tax proposal has been called a flat-out fraud [His tax proposal has been called a flat-out fraud, source]. It cuts taxes for the very rich in half and raises taxes on the middle class [It cuts taxes for the very rich in half and raises taxes on the middle class, source]. Jerry Brown says he'll clean up politics and limit campaign contributions [Jerry Brown says he'll clean up politics and limit campaign contributions]. But a year ago he helped lead the fight that killed campaign reform and contribution limits in California [He helped lead the fight that killed campaign reform and contribution limits in California, source]. So the next time Jerry Brown says he's fighting for the people, ask him which people [So the next time Jerry Brown says he's fighting for the people, ask him which people] and which Jerry Brown [which Jerry Brown]. (Clinton, 1992, "Which")

This commercial suggests that Brown's actions don't match his campaign pledges. Voters want a candidate who will follow through with his promises.

That same year, in 1992, Pat Buchanan challenged Bush for the Republican nomination. Bush had won in 1988 in part based on his "Read my Lips—No new taxes" pledge. Several of these spots, like the next one, included a clip from Bush's famous pledge:

Man [Nashua, NH]: The betrayal that I feel in George Bush is now the harder I work, the closer I come to losing my home.

Man [Amherst, NH]: I remember that day he said read my lips, no new taxes and he went against his word.

Woman [Manchester, NH]: That does not go well with the people of New Hampshire because people in New Hampshire keep their word.

Man [Nashua, NH]: And we have to suffer the consequences.

Bush: Read my lips.

Announcer: Send a message [Send a message].

People: Read our lips.

Announcer: Vote Pat Buchanan for President [Vote Pat Buchanan for President]. (Buchanan, 1992, "Betrayed")

This spot works from the same basic premise, that we want to be able to trust candidates to keep their campaign promises.

In 1996, Alexander used a more folksy approach in many of his primary television spots.

Alexander: This race for President is coming down to a zillionaire mudslinger, a grumpy Texan, and a Senator who's been in Washington since before I could vote. I'm Lamar Alexander [Lamar Alexander], and I'm offering new Republican leadership to beat Bill Clinton. Here's my plan. Cut tax rates and unleash free enterprise to create good new jobs [Cut tax rates and unleash free enterprise to create good new jobs]. Make our schools as good as our colleges [Make our schools as good as our colleges]. And replace Washington arrogance with community citizenship [replace Washington arrogance with community citizenship]. So if you're ready for new leadership, I'm your candidate. (Alexander, 1996, "New Leadership")

He begins with unflattering characterizations of his major opponents in the race. Then he describes three general proposals for improving life in America. The spot talks about leadership, but this claim is based on policy proposals. These examples give an indication of how primary spots use acclaims, attacks, and defense, on topics of policy and character.

FUNCTIONS OF PRIMARY SPOTS

Overall, these spots devoted about two-thirds (68%) of their remarks to acclaiming. In the 1996 primary, this commercial praised Alexander's accomplishments:

A conservative Governor who balanced eight budgets [A conservative Governor who balanced eight budgets], kept taxes the fifth lowest of any state [Kept taxes the fifth lowest of any state], reformed education [Reformed education], brought in the auto industry with Saturn [Brought in the auto industry with Saturn], and later helped found a new business that now has 1,200 employees. Lamar Alexander: Governor, businessman, Education Secretary, a Republican running for President from the real world.

Alexander had experience as an elected governor, an appointed cabinet member, and as a businessman. In the 1980 primary, Anderson acclaimed his candidacy in this commercial, addressing several different issues:

I'm John Anderson. I stand alone. If you're concerned about violent crime, I alone stand for the licensing of handguns. If you believe in women's rights, understand that I alone support the ERA extension. I stand alone for the grain embargo. I'm also alone in the conviction that saber rattling is not foreign policy.

He considers four issues (handguns, women's rights, the grain embargo, and foreign policy) and argues that his positions on each are unique. See Tables 9.1 and 9.2 and Figure 9.1 for these data (the functions of primary

Table 9.1
Functions of Primary Spots by Political Party

	Acclaim	Attack	Defense
Republicans	1272 (67%)	604 (32%)	15 (1%)
Democrats	1414 (68%)	644 (31%)	23 (1%)
Total	2686 (68%)	1248 (31%)	38 (1%)

X^2=0.33, ns (acclaims versus attacks)

Table 9.2
Functions of Primary Spots by Outcome

	Acclaim	Attack	Defense
Winners	1340 (68%)	593 (30%)	26 (1%)
Losers	1346 (67%)	655 (33%)	12 (0.5%)
Total	2686 (68%)	1248 (31%)	38 (1%)

X^2=1.82, ns (acclaims versus attacks)

spots are broken out by political party and by outcome, but there are no real differences in these breakdowns).

Attacks accounted for 31% of remarks in these primary advertisements. Dole attacked Forbes in this spot from the 1996 primary campaign:

Have you heard about Steve Forbes' risky ideas [Steve Forbes' risky ideas]? Forbes supports taxpayer-supported welfare benefits for illegal aliens [Forbes supports taxpayer-supported welfare benefits for illegal aliens]. Forbes opposes mandatory life sentences for criminals convinced of three violent felonies [Forbes opposes mandatory life sentences for criminals convinced of three violent felonies]. Forbes' economic plan will add $186 billion a year to the deficit [Forbes' economic plan will add $186 billion a year to the deficit]. No wonder Forbes opposes a constitutional amendment to balance the budget.

This commercial laid out several reasons to oppose Forbes. In 1992, Bush ran this negative advertisement against Buchanan, who was challenging him for the Republican nomination:

Pat Buchanan tells us, America first [Buchanan: Put America First]. But while our auto industry suffers, Pat Buchanan chose to buy a foreign car [Pat Buchanan

Figure 9.1
Acclaims and Attacks in Primary Spots

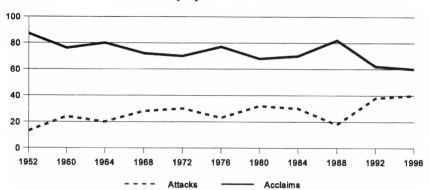

chose to buy a foreign car], a Mercedes-Benz. Pat Buchanan called his American cars "Lemons" [Pat Buchanan called his American cars "Lemons"]. Pat Buchanan: It's America first in his political speeches [Pat Buchanan: It's America first in speeches], but a foreign-made car in his driveway.

The argument here is that he is inconsistent, claiming to put America first in public but privately buying foreign-made products.

Defenses in primary advertisements were relatively rare at 1%. In 1992, Tsongas used denial to respond to charges that he would threaten Social Security if elected:

Now, Bill Clinton is distorting Paul Tsongas's record on Social Security, trying to scare people. But Bill Clinton knows that for ten years in the Congress, Paul Tsongas fought to protect Social Security [Paul Tsongas fought to protect Social Security], to extend Medicare coverage [to extend Medicare coverage], and to end age discrimination [to end age discrimination].

This spot also manages to criticize Clinton for knowingly distorting Tsongas' policy on this issue. In 1996, Gramm used this spot to defend against an accusation from Forbes, although no specific issue is mentioned here:

[Gramm Team New Hampshire] Phil Gramm's team starts to roll [Gramm bus]. Billionaire Steve Forbes starts negative commercials [Forbes in an ad; Malcolm Forbes Jr. Attack Ads]. One problem: They're not true [red FALSE over Forbes' face]. Bob Smith [US Senator Bob Smith] called Forbes' ads deceitful [Forbes' ads deceitful].

This is a clear illustration of a primary commercial's use of simple denial to respond to an attack.

POLICY VERSUS CHARACTER IN PRIMARY SPOTS

Policy was a common topic in these commercials (52%). For instance, Baker acclaimed his agricultural policy in this 1980 spot: "We should start a new trade offensive in our foreign produce. And I want a Vice President who knows how to promote farm exports to run the programs." That same year, Bush attacked President Carter's domestic and foreign policy: "President Carter, what you don't seem to understand is people are really fed up. If we don't get tough with inflation, we're going down the drain. If we don't build up our military capability, we're going to get stung, again. America is in trouble, at home, abroad, with itself. The job has to be done now." The last line lends some urgency to the appeal: We need to correct our domestic and foreign policy shortcomings immediately (see Table 9.3).

Character appeals (48%) were almost as common in primary spots as policy themes. In 1996, this advertisement acclaimed Dole's character: "This courageous man, who understands so much about the privilege and the price of what it is to be an American." Buchanan used a disillusioned voter to charge that Dole was untrustworthy in this spot from 1992:

Woman [Nashua, NH]: Now I don't believe a word that the President says. I don't believe anything that comes out of his mouth anymore. I think it's all double talk, and I just I suspect anything that he says and I don't trust him and I'll never, ever get the trust that I had for Mr. Bush when I elected him, when I voted for him. I'll never get that trust back.

Trust and integrity are important qualities for a president to possess. Thus, many primary commercials addressed questions of character.

FORMS OF POLICY AND CHARACTER IN PRIMARY SPOTS

Primary spots focused primarily on general goals (43%) when they discussed policy topics. For example, in 1996, Alexander explained his goals to viewers: "I thought I'd take a minute to tell you what I'd actually do as President [Lamar Alexander]. I'd cut taxes, and unleash free enterprise to create good, new jobs. I'd help parents make our school as good as our colleges. And I'd help us learn to expect less from Washington and more from ourselves." Alexander acclaims three separate goals in this message. Kerry touted his goals in the 1992 primaries: "As President, I'll force open Japanese markets. That will mean almost 3,000 jobs a day, a million jobs a year, and help put America back to work." While he does not indicate specifically how he will achieve this goal, he does spell out the desirable consequences of his proposal.

Discussions of past deeds occurred almost as often as general goals in

Table 9.3
Policy and Character in Primary Spots

Policy (52%)			Character (48%)		
Past Deeds	Future Plans	General Goals	Personal Qualities	Leadership	Ideals
345/481* (40%)	214/127 (17%)	**764/122** **(43%)**	**600/351** **(51%)**	423/125 (29%)	340/36 (20%)

*acclaims/attacks

these advertisements (40%). Edward Kennedy attacked President Carter's energy policies in 1980: "You pay 98 cents a gallon for home heating oil. Gasoline, now a dollar-sixteen a gallon. Elderly people face a cruel choice between heat for their homes and food on their tables. And oil refiners' profits went up 800% last year. Jimmy Carter decontrolled the price of oil, so you pay while the oil companies profit." Note how Kennedy explicitly links these problems with Carter's action of decontrolling the price of oil. In 1972, Humphrey reminded viewers of several of his past accomplishments:

So many people are seeking the Democratic nomination [list of candidates] it's hard to tell the players without a scorecard. Who created Medicare? Humphrey [check by name]. The job corps? Humphrey [check]. The food stamp program? Humphrey [check]. The first water control bill? Hubert Humphrey [check], and again, and again and again [three checks].

This commercial acclaims Humphrey by listing three specific deeds for which he is responsible and alludes to others as well.

Relatively fewer remarks from these commercials address the topic of future plans (17%). In this spot for Bush in 1992, he acclaimed his proposal for a balanced budget amendment: "To get our economy moving faster, we have to reduce the huge federal deficit by cutting spending [We have to reduce the huge federal deficit by cutting spending]. The only way to do that with certainty, is to pass the balanced budget amendment." That same year, Clinton attacked the future plans of Brown and Tsongas:

Who's going to fight for us? Jerry Brown? Citizens for Tax Justice said "Jerry Brown's national tax proposal would cut taxes for the rich in half, raise taxes for the middle class, and create a new 13% national sales tax." And Paul Tsongas? He proposes another capital gains tax break for the rich, and up to a 50-cent hike in the gas tax over ten years for the rest of us.

Clinton clearly refers to specific taxation proposals advanced by his opponents Brown and Tsongas in this advertisement. Thus, future plans were at times the topics of both acclaims and attacks in primary spots.

When these spots discussed character, they were most likely to address personal qualities (51%). This advertisement for Bush in 1980 acclaimed his personal qualities: "George Bush has the ability and the integrity to earn the complete trust of the American people." In 1976, Wallace praised his own character and background in this commercial:

I came up the hard way. I came up like the average Southerner came up in the years came up in the depression, and therefore I recognize and know for instance what poverty is [Governor George C. Wallace, Democrat Alabama]. I have seen it. I have felt it. I have smelt it. I know it when I see it. I'm not like one of these

Table 9.4
Source of Utterances in Primary Spots by Political Party

Party	Function	Candidate	Other
Republicans	Acclaim	447 (35%)	**825 (65%)**
	Attack	174 (29%)	**430 (71%)**
	Defend	0	**15 (100%)**
Democrats	Acclaim	495 (35%)	**919 (65%)**
	Attack	219 (34%)	**425 (66%)**
	Defend	6 (26%)	**17 (74%)**
Total		1341 (34%)	**2631 (66%)**

Table 9.5
Source of Utterances in Primary Spots by Outcome

Outcome	Function	Candidate	Other
Winners	Acclaim	359 (27%)	**977 (73%)**
	Attack	78 (14%)	**491 (86%)**
	Defend	5 (17%)	**25 (83%)**
Losers	Acclaim	583 (43%)	**767 (57%)**
	Attack	315 (46%)	**364 (54%)**
	Defend	1 (16%)	**7 (84%)**
Total		1341 (34%)	**2631 (66%)**

limousine liberals who has never seen or knows what poverty is unless he reads
it in the dictionary, because he was born with a silver spoon in his mouth, wants
to be the President of the United States and wants to run the country, but he has
no feel of actually what the average citizen feels and understands when he suffers
inflation, unemployment, and no income. Because I have suffered every one of
those—no income, low income, inflation, no employment.

He argues that his background prepares him to better understand the
plight of the ordinary citizen. He also attacks his (unnamed) opponents
for lacking the ability to identify with voters. Muskie acclaimed his likability and trustworthiness in this 1972 spot: "Ed Muskie has always had
a strong sense of community. He's been liked and trusted and involved

here for a long time." Thus, primary spots addressed the candidates' personal qualities.

These advertisements also discussed leadership ability (29%). In this spot from 1992 Bush's exceptional leadership ability was acclaimed: "Perhaps no President in our history has shown the world such strong leadership." In 1984, this commercial for Mondale stressed his experience in government: "A lifetime of leadership. Attorney General of Minnesota, U.S. Senator, Vice President." In the 1976 campaign, a spot promised explicitly that Reagan will "provide the strong new leadership America needs." Gary Hart in 1984 explained that "The South can once more change the course of history, by voting for new leadership, new ideas, and a fresh start for America." So, primary candidates acclaimed their qualifications to be leader of the free world.

Discussions of ideals constituted the smallest topic of character appeals (20%). In 1972, Wallace attacked the ideals of his opponents: "There are six Senators in the race for the Presidential nomination in Florida. In the Senate of the United States a vote was taken on freedom of choice [Governor George C. Wallace (D)]. All six of them voted against freedom of choice." It is clear that Wallace considered freedom of choice to be an important ideal, unlike his opponents. In 1996, an advertisement for Bob Dole acclaimed both his ideals and his personal qualities: "Bob Dole's conservative convictions and character will lead an American renewal." Obviously, conservative ideals should appeal to his Republican audience. These examples illustrate how primary candidates addressed the various forms of character appeals.

SOURCE OF UTTERANCES IN PRIMARY SPOTS

In these primary advertisements, others were more likely than the candidates themselves to be the source of acclaims (65%), attacks (69%), and defenses (84%). Across all three categories, others accounted for 66% of utterances, while the candidates were responsible for 34% of the comments. There was no significant difference in source of acclaims and attacks by Republicans and Democrats. The percentages are identical for acclaims, and there is a non-significant difference in attacks (others were responsible for 71% of Republican and 66% of Democratic attacks). All of the Republican defenses were performed by others, as were 74% of the Democratic defenses (see Table 9.4).

The analysis of source of utterance was more interesting when considered by outcome of the race. Winners (nominees) had a higher percentage of remarks from others (73%) than losers (57%). This difference was even more pronounced for attacks: others provided 86% of the winners' attacks and only 54% of the losers' attacks. Around 85% of the defenses were from others (83% for winners, 88% for losers) (see Table 9.5).

Table 9.6
Kaid and Ballotti (1991) and Benoit Results

Campaign	Positive* (Kaid & Ballotti)	Acclaims (Benoit)	Negative (Kaid & Ballotti)	Attacks (Benoit)
1968	98%	72%	2%	24%
1972	86%	73%	14%	27%
1976	94%	77%	6%	23%
1980	76%	68%	24%	32%
1984	69%	70%	31%	30%
1988	80%	82%	20%	18%
Total	78%	74%	22%	26%

*Positive = Image + Issue

CONCLUSION

These primary advertisements generally prefer acclaims (68%) to attacks (31%) (Table 9.1). Table 9.6 compares Kaid and Ballotti's results with mine. While some years are quite close (e.g., acclaims in 1984: 69%, 70%; in 1988: 80%, 82%), others are quite discrepant (e.g., acclaims in 1968: 98%, 72%; in 1976: 94%, 77%). These differences could be a result of their coding method, which determines the "dominant focus" of an ad (which I think is most likely; this idea is discussed further in Chapter 11), or because their sample includes more spots than my sample. Defenses occurred, but are relatively infrequent in primary spots (1%; Kaid and Ballotti did not code for defenses). There are no apparent differences by political party or by outcome in the functions of these spots.

There is only a slight edge for policy topics (52%) over character (48%) (Table 9.3). This is roughly similar to Kaid and Ballotti's findings: 48% issue and 32% image and 3% combination (exact comparisons are difficult because their approach also classified spots as negative—18%—although we cannot tell if these negative spots discussed policy or character). Discussion of general goals (43%) and past deeds (40%) are more common than future plans (17%) (Table 9.3). When character is addressed, these spots tend to discuss personal qualities most often (51%), with leadership (29%) and ideals (20%) less frequently discussed (Table 9.3). There is a general preference for using others in these commercials more often than the candidates themselves (66% to 34%) (Tables

9.4 and 9.5). There does not seem to be much difference in source for acclaims, attacks, and defense by political party. However, winners are more likely to use others to acclaim than losers, and winners are much more likely to use others to attack than losers. Specific results for each primary candidate are displayed in Table 9.7.

Table 9.7
Forms of Policy and Character in Primary Spots

	Policy			Character			Defense
	Past Deeds	Future Plans	General Goals	Personal Qualities	Leader. Ability	Ideals	
Eisenhower 1952	4/1*	0/1	8/3	9/1	20/1	6/0	0
JF Kennedy 1960	8/9	14/0	8/0	13/9	4/2	16/0	3
Goldwater 1964	0/1	0/0	5/0	1/1	0/0	2/0	4
Nixon 1968	0/14	2/0	6/0	14/0	18/3	6/0	0
McCroskey 1968	0/1	2/1	3/1	6/6	0/3	1/1	0
RF Kennedy 1968	0/2	0/0	7/0	3/0	4/0	8/0	0
Rockefeller 1968	0/1	0/0	3/0	0/0	0/0	1/0	0
Nixon 1972	16/0	0/0	1/0	10/0	3/0	0/0	0
Humphrey 1972	4/0	1/1	6/1	2/0	0/0	12/0	0
McCarthy 1972	0/1	0/0	0/0	0/0	0/0	1/0	1
McGovern 1972	1/9	0/0	6/0	2/5	2/1	6/0	0
Muskie 1972	0/3	1/0	4/2	5/0	1/1	10/0	0
HM Jackson 1972	3/6	3/0	10/1	13/1	4/0	2/0	0
Wallace 1972	0/22	2/0	22/5	0/4	0/1	4/0	0
Udall 1976	0/4	1/3	7/0	4/9	3/0	1/0	0

Wallace 1976	0/7	0/0	9/0	6/4	4/0	8/1	2
Carter 1976	1/3	0/1	1/0	3/0	3/3	5/1	1
Ford 1976	44/0	0/0	8/0	34/0	51/0	5/0	8
Reagan 1976	1/19	0/0	6/0	½	2/4	2/1	0
Anderson 1980	0/2	11/3	14/3	49/16	5/0	4/0	0
Baker 1980	5/1	2/0	5/0	3/6	12/0	8/0	0
Bush 1980	0/13	1/0	19/0	14/7	25/13	3/0	0
Connally 1980	0/4	0/0	7/1	22/0	32/1	10/0	0
Crane 1980	0/8	0/0	9/0	9/0	0/2	0/0	0
Reagan 1980	3/5	0/0	12/6	2/1	7/1	6/4	0
Brown 1980	7/5	0/0	19/2	1/0	½	6/0	0
Carter 1980	17/3	0/5	4/0	18/12	6/4	14/1	1
E Kennedy 1980	10/43	0/0	7/0	29/8	15/31	13/1	0
Cranston 1984	0/0	2/0	10/0	0/2	0/0	1/0	0
McGovern 1984	6/0	0/0	0/6	1/3	0/0	2/0	0
Glenn 1984	0/0	0/0	1/0	6/4	2/1	2/0	0
Hart 1984	0/8	0/0	7/3	3/9	6/0	9/0	0

Table 9.7 (continued)

	Policy			Character			Defense
	Past Deeds	Future Plans	General Goals	Personal Qualities	Leader. Ability	Ideals	
Mondale 1984	9/37	9/2	62/0	32/10	54/17	22/2	0
Haig 1988	1/1	1/0	4/0	8/0	10/0	0/0	0
DuPont 1988	0/5	4/0	7/16	0/0	0/0	4/0	0
Dole 1988	5/3	0/0	12/1	10/5	6/0	0/0	0
Bush 1988	0/0	1/0	4/0	2/5	9/1	1/0	0
Kemp 1988	4/7	1/1	19/7	7/2	2/0	4/0	0
J Jackson 1988	4/0	0/0	10/0	6/0	0/0	0/0	0
Gore 1988	4/0	0/0	5/0	2/0	3/0	2/0	0
Dukakis 1988	33/5	2/2	16/0	21/9	16/0	10/0	0
Gephardt 1988	7/2	1/0	31/6	18/1	5/0	3/0	0
Babbitt 1988	0/0	0/0	8/0	4/2	3/1	1/0	0
Simon 1988	2/2	1/0	10/0	10/0	4/1	2/0	0
Brown 1992	6/5	1/3	2/0	6/5	0/0	1/0	0
Clinton 1992	33/23	34/32	64/8	48/25	10/5	8/2	8
Harken 1992	0/1	2/3	13/2	5/0	2/0	1/0	0

Kerry 1992	2/4	6/1	14/0	4/3	2/0	2/0	0
Tsongas 1992	5/5	0/3	14/0	9/7	3/1	0/0	3
Buchanan 1992	0/19	5/8	11/1	5/35	7/0	4/0	0
Bush 1992	7/7	9/0	31/11	2/8	8/3	3/0	0
Alexander 1996	15/2	9/0	15/0	17/14	6/2	21/5	1
Buchanan 1996	1/32	14/1	10/0	17/6	3/1	6/5	0
Forbes 1996	8/34	27/18	18/1	21/40	9/1	8/0	7
Gramm 1996	9/12	1/4	4/1	7/5	2/1	8/0	1
Lugar 1996	0/1	0/0	1/0	10/5	3/0	6/0	0
Taylor 1996	0/4	3/2	7/0	13/8	6/1	3/0	0
Wilson 1996	10/0	0/0	0/0	3/1	0/0	4/0	0
Dole 1996	4/33	10/11	61/20	27/35	19/15	20/12	4
Clinton 1996	46/42	31/42	77/14	3/10	1/0	22/0	4
Total	345/481	214/127	764/122	600/351	423/124	340/36	48

*acclaims/attacks

Chapter 10

Third-Party Candidates: Another Choice

In the modern era, presidential campaigns have been dominated by the two major political parties. However, third-party candidates regularly seek the presidency. Humphrey decided to attack Wallace in several of his 1968 spots, while a Nixon advertisement cautioned citizens against "wasting" their vote on a third-party candidate (in an interesting twist, in 1996 Perot urged "Don't waste your vote on politics as usual"). Perot clearly exerted an influence on the 1992 campaign, and was selected to participate in the presidential debates. Third-party candidates—and their spots—are relatively uncommon. I located 60 spots from four campaigns (1968, 1980, 1992, 1996) and four candidates (Wallace, Anderson, Perot [twice], and Browne). While much more limited than the sample for either general or primary spots, I was unable to locate any study in the literature that focused on third-party spots (of course, third-party candidates are sometimes mentioned in articles devoted to a single campaign).

The earliest third-party candidate for which I located television spots was Wallace, in his 1968 campaign. His spots hammered away at issues like forced public school busing, crime and violence, and foreign aid. Another theme was that he has the courage to lead America in the proper direction. Here is one of his advertisements:

Announcer [1968; scenes of riots, poverty, violence]: 1968, a time of international crisis and domestic chaos. In times like these we need a President who can meet the challenges of America. A man of sufficient courage to return the nation to its proper course.

Wallace: And the most recent mistake they made was when Castro was in the hills of Cuba, the *New York Times* wrote that he was the Robin Hood of the Caribbean. He was introduced on nationwide television as being the George Washington of Cuba.

Announcer [photo of Nixon with Castro]: At informal discussions designed to seek an upward revision of Cuba's sugar quota, it was Mr. Nixon who said, quote: "The United States is nationally interested in working with Cuba." Is this the kind of man we want to trust with the future of America? (Wallace, 1968, "1968")

This spot used a quotation from (and a picture of) Nixon. Especially given Nixon's history as an opponent of Communism, this is a potentially damaging attack. In 1980, Anderson ran against Carter and Reagan. This spot illustrates his approach:

Fact: Former President Gerald Ford once said of John Anderson, "He's the smartest guy in Congress, but he insists on voting his conscience instead of his party" [He's the smartest guy in Congress, but he insists on voting his conscience instead of his party].

Fact: 69% of Americans believe John Anderson has the courage to talk straight [ABC News-Harris Survey, October 8, 1980: 69% agree: "John Anderson has the courage not to make the easy promises to the voters . . ."].

Fact: The *LA Times* poll shows John Anderson ahead of Carter when he is given a chance to win [*LA Times*-National Poll, October 15, 1980: When Anderson is given a real chance: Reagan 34%, Anderson 26%, Carter, 25%]. So we can have a President we respect. Don't we need more than a Jimmy Carter or a Ronald Reagan now? Don't we really need John Anderson? (Anderson, 1980, "Fact 1")

Repetition of the word "fact" is surely intended to provide more force to these claims. Because the major parties have dominated presidential politics for so long, it is important for third-party candidates to establish their viability in the election (that a vote for them would not be wasted). This spot argues strongly that Anderson is a credible candidate. Perot ran in the 1992 election. Many of his advertisements focused on the huge federal debt. However, he also discussed our country's potential for improvement under his leadership:

Announcer: Ross Perot on what this country can be [Ross Perot on what this country can be].

Perot: We can be a country whose people are working hard at their jobs instead of working hard just to find a job. We can be a country where once again the diversity of our people is our greatest strength, instead of division being our greatest weakness. We can be a country leading the way instead of a country falling behind. We can be all of these things tomorrow if we would just make the tough choices today.

Announcer: Ross Perot for President [Ross Perot for President]. (Perot, 1992, "What This Country Can Be")

Perot juxtaposes the problems of today (unemployment, division, falling behind) with the goals that he would help achieve if elected. In his 1996 campaign, Perot focused on two other themes: complaints about being omitted from the presidential debates, and the problem of special interests in Washington. This spot illustrates the latter argument:

[The image metamorphoses through a series of ordinary people]: Don't throw your vote away on politics as usual. Just vote for Ross. We can make the twenty-first century the greatest in our history. We can take our country back from the special interests. Just vote for Ross.

Perot: Because it is your country [Perot 96]. (Perot, 1996, "Your Country")

The most radical of the third-party candidates for whom I found spots was Browne, the Libertarian candidate in 1996. This advertisement illustrates his campaign:

Browne [Harry Browne, Libertarian for President]: Social Security is headed for collapse, yet neither Bill Clinton nor Bob Dole will admit it [his telephone number and www address]. We must get the government completely out of Social Security by selling off federal assets and using the proceeds to buy a private annuity for everyone who needs it. And then you will be free forever from that 15% tax that you know is just money down the drain. I'm Harry Browne, the Libertarian candidate for President. This year, vote for freedom. Vote to get your life back. Vote for Harry Browne. (Browne, 1996, "Social Security")

He offers proposals for change that are quite different from those advocated by the major party candidates. These commercials illustrate the third-party campaigns in this study.

FUNCTIONS OF THIRD PARTY SPOTS

Third-party candidates acclaimed in 68% of their spot utterances. For example, in 1968, Wallace announced that "As President, I shall within the law turn back the absolute control of the public school systems to the people of the respective states." Forced busing was a heated topic of discussion during that campaign, and Wallace acclaimed his goal. A spot for Anderson in 1980 reported that "My purpose in running for President is not to weaken the two-party system in America. Rather, it is to strengthen that system in the future by making it aware that it must respond to the people." Surely we want our political system to be responsive to our will. Perot acclaimed his ideals in 1992 in this commercial: "If you want a government that comes from the people instead of at the people, let your vote say so." In 1996, Browne proposed this so-lution: "Let's repeal the income tax and replace it with nothing. Let's make the government live by the Constitution and pass the savings on to you." Although this proposal might seem radical, some voters would surely embrace it. Thus, these candidates employed extensive acclaiming in their campaigns (see Table 10.1).

These candidates attacked in 32% of their remarks. Wallace attacked foreign aid in this advertisement: "Watch your hard-earned dollars sail away to anti-American countries [video of ship sailing off]." Anderson argued that in 1980, "Our nation faces deep problems, and this year's presidential campaign is one of them. Issues are being ignored, problems papered over, personal attacks, easy promises, easy answers, and none of it feels true. What does it mean for a great democracy when the two major candidates for our highest elected office refuse to face up to the crucial issues?" Here, he managed to allude to policy problems while attacking the character of both Carter and Reagan. In 1996, Perot com-plained bitterly that he had been left out of the presidential debates: "Why are they [Dole and Clinton video] desperate to keep Ross Perot out of the debate [What are they so afraid of?] when 76% of the voters want him [76% of the voters want Ross to debate]?" Browne attacked his Republican opponent in this spot: "Bob Dole wants to give you a tiny tax cut, but he has no plans to reduce the size of government." Thus, attacks were common in these spots. None of these third-party candi-dates used defenses in their advertisements (party because attacks from the major party candidates on third-party candidates [like the one from Humphrey in Chapter 5] are quite rare).

POLICY VERSUS CHARACTER IN THIRD-PARTY SPOTS

Third-party candidates addressed policy topics in slightly more than half of their comments (52%). For example, Wallace promised that he would be tough on crime and lawlessness: "As President, I will stand up for your local police and firemen in protecting your safety and prop-erty." In 1980, Anderson acclaimed his record on several important is-sues: "He has fought for equal rights, campaign reform [Leader in Fight for Campaign Reform], a strong economy, and John Anderson's pro-posed a bold new energy program for America [Leader for Energy In-dependence]." Perot directed our attention to the federal budget deficit in this advertisement from 1992: "Our children dream of the world that we promise them as parents, a world of unlimited opportunity. What would they say to us if they knew that by the year 2000, we will have left them with a national debt of eight trillion dollars?" Browne focused on governmental spending in this 1996 advertisement: "The major issue in this election is whether we're going to stop the Democratic and Re-

Table 10.1
Acclaims and Attacks by Third-Party Candidates

Candidate	Acclaims	Attacks
Wallace 1968	18 (56%)	14 (44%)
Anderson 1980	80 (95%)	4 (5%)
Perot 1992	59 (54%)	50 (46%)
Perot 1996	46 (70%)	20 (30%)
Browne 1996	21 (55%)	17 (45%)
Total	224 (68%)	105 (32%)

publican organizations from taking your money and throwing it away. From stealing your freedoms while promising you benefits they can't deliver. From destroying our cities, our schools, our health care system, and our country." He accuses both major parties of complicity in these problems. Thus, third-party spots are replete with policy appeals (see Table 10.2).

Character was almost as common in these advertisements (48%). In 1968, one spot noted that "Wallace has the courage to stand up for America," acclaiming his personal qualities. An advertisement for Anderson asked voters, "Don't we really need that independence, that intelligence, that conscience in a President? Don't we really need John Anderson now?" These are desirable qualities in a president. In 1996, this commercial for Perot declared: "I'm voting for the only candidate who is not for sale at any price. I'm voting for Ross. He has never taken a penny of special interest money. Never will." Clearly integrity is an important trait for a candidate for president to possess. Browne acclaimed his ideals in this advertisement: "This year, vote for freedom. Vote to get your life back. Vote for Harry Browne." Thus, these spots devoted a good deal of their time to addressing character issues.

FORMS OF POLICY AND CHARACTER IN THIRD-PARTY SPOTS

When third-party commercials discussed policy topics, they focused most on general goals (51%), then on past deeds (39%), and least often on future plans (10%). For example, Wallace acclaimed this goal, should the Paris peace talks fail to resolve the Vietnam War: "As your President, I shall call upon the Joint Chiefs of Staff to bring a military conclusion to the war with conventional weapons and bring American servicemen

Table 10.2
Policy versus Character by Third-Party Candidates

Candidate	Policy	Character
Wallace 1968	24 (75%)	8 (25%)
Anderson 1980	27 (32%)	57 (68%)
Perot 1992	65 (60%)	44 (40%)
Perot 1996	25 (38%)	41 (62%)
Browne 1996	33 (75%)	11 (25%)
Total	174 (52%)	161 (48%)

home and turn the security of South Vietnam over strictly to the South Vietnamese forces." In 1996, this spot mentioned Perot's "pledge to reform campaign spending [reform campaign spending] and influence peddling by lobbyists [reform influence peddling by lobbyists]." Browne appealed to past deeds in this spot: "Your paycheck is being ravaged by the income tax. Your retirement is being subverted by a fraudulent scheme called Social Security, and your city is being destroyed by an insane war on drugs." Clearly he sees these problems as reasons to turn away from the traditional parties. Anderson attacked plans for tax reduction from the other candidates: "Multi-billion dollar tax cuts, proposed by my opponents, sound good. I can't support them. They will increase inflation, the cruelest tax of all." In 1992, Perot rejected his opponents' plans to reduce the federal debt: "We have a national debt of four trillion dollars. . . . This is a bomb that is set to go off and devastate the economy, destroy thousands and thousands of jobs. The other two candidates have told you to ignore the ticking. They've given you plans that will only delay dealing with the issue. But I've spelled out a solution that will fix this problem starting now." He attacks Bush's and Clinton's future plans while acclaiming his own proposal in this commercial. Thus, these spots illustrate use of the three forms of policy topics (see Table 10.3).

When third-party spots addressed character topics, they emphasized ideals most (57%), followed by personal qualities (33%), and occasionally leadership ability (11%). Anderson spoke out against certain religious figures, basing his objection on an important ideal: "I'm repelled by those television preachers who call themselves a moral majority. They want to tell us how to vote, influence legislation, and reveal whose prayers God listens to. That's not for me. It violates a basic constitutional principle that I believe in: separation of church and state." In 1992, Perot explained

Table 10.3
Forms of Policy and Character Utterances by Third-Party Candidates

Candidate	Policy (52%)			Character (48%)		
	Deeds	Plans	Goals	Qualities	Leadership	Ideals
Wallace 1968	0/13*	0/0	11/0	5/1	1/0	1/0
Anderson 1980	10/0	8/0	9/0	34/4	11/0	8/0
Perot 1992	0/28	0/3	34/0	2/14	15/3	8/2
Perot 1996	5/1	0/0	19/0	13/19	0/0	9/0
Browne 1996	0/11	2/4	11/5	0/1	0/0	8/2
Total	15/53 (39%)	10/7 (10%)	84/5 (51%)	54/39 (33%)	27/3 (11%)	34/4 (57%)

*acclaims/attacks

Table 10.4
Source of Utterances in Third-Party Candidates' Spots

Candidate	Acclaims		Attacks	
	Candidate	Other	Candidate	Other
Wallace 1968	**12 (67%)**	6 (33%)	1 (7%)	**13 (93%)**
Anderson 1980	8 (10%)	**72 (90%)**	1 (25%)	**3 (75%)**
Perot 1992	24 (41%)	**35 (59%)**	21 (42%)	**29 (58%)**
Perot 1996	7 (15%)	**39 (85%)**	0	**20 (100%)**
Browne 1996	**21 (100%)**	0	**17 (100%)**	0
Total	74 (33%)	**152 (67%)**	40 (38%)	**65 (62%)**

simply that "I want you to have the American dream." In 1980, Anderson acclaimed his experience in government: "He served on the powerful House Rules Committee." Wallace acclaimed his leadership ability and his personal qualities in this advertisement: "In times like these we need a President who can meet the challenges of America. A man of sufficient courage to return the nation to its proper course." These excerpts reveal how these third-party candidates used the three forms of character utterances in their spots.

SOURCE OF UTTERANCES IN THIRD-PARTY SPOTS

Third-party candidates' advertisements were more likely to rely on others for two-thirds of the acclaims in their commercials and these candidates presented one-third of the self-praise themselves. Others were also more likely to present attacks (62%) than did the candidates (38%) (see Table 10.4).

CONCLUSION

No third-party candidate has won the presidency during the modern era (in which television spots played a role in the campaign). I take this as evidence of the continued importance of the two major political parties. As I argued earlier, neither party can win the election without "help" from the economy, foreign affairs, and campaigning. However, the parties still wield enough power that the candidate must represent one of them to win the presidency.

However, this does not necessarily mean that third-party candidates are irrelevant. For example, Perot in 1992 focused attention on the federal debt. Benoit and Wells (1996) argue that his presence influenced the course of the presidential debates because he tended to attack Bush more than Clinton—and neither candidate devoted many attacks to Perot (hoping not to alienate Perot's followers, who might have voted for Bush or Clinton at the last minute).

These spots from third-party candidates were more likely to acclaim (68%) than attack (32%) and did not contain defenses (Table 10.1). Humphrey did attack Wallace in 1968, but that was unusual. There are probably no defenses from third party candidates because they are subject to few attacks. They were only slightly more likely to discuss policy (52%) than character (48%) (Table 10.2). When they addressed policy, they focused on general goals (51%) most often, followed by past deeds (39%), and, least often, on future plans (10%). On character, they discussed ideals (57%) personal qualities (33%), and leadership least often (11%) (Table 10.4). These advertisements relied more heavily on others (66%) than on the candidates themselves (34%).

Part IV

Comparisons

Chapter 11

Contrasts

This chapter will explore eight topics based on the results of the analyses presented in earlier chapters. The first five points will address the sample of general campaign spots from the two major party candidates each year. Initially, I will consider trends in general television spots, indicating contrasts that emerge over time. Then I will contrast the commercials of incumbent party candidates with those of challenger party candidates. Third, I will compare the advertising generated by Republican and Democratic candidates. Next, I will contrast the spots from winning and losing campaigns. Fifth, I will examine the source of utterances in spots: candidates versus other speakers. Then I will broaden the discussion to include the other groups of spots in my sample, discussing the functions of (all) presidential television advertisements. This will be followed by a contrast of primary and general election campaign advertising. Finally, I will compare general spots by the major party candidates with those from third-party candidates.

TRENDS IN GENERAL TELEVISION SPOTS

In this section I address four topics. First, I will discuss the number of themes addressed in general presidential television spots. Second, I will address the average length of these advertisements. Then, I take up the topic of the functions of presidential television commercials. Fourth, I will contrast these spots' reliance on policy and character topics. I will also discuss their use of the three forms of policy and the three forms of character.

Figure 11.1
Number of Themes by Party

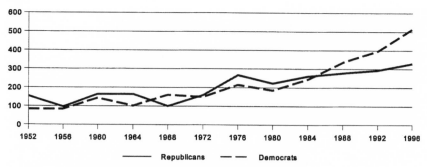

Increasing Density: Number of Themes per Spot

First, there has been a trend over time for candidates to use more themes in their spots. However, given that I was not able to achieve my goal of obtaining 30 minutes of spots for each candidate in every campaign, it was difficult to be sure that this apparent trend was not caused by the fact that the fewest spots were obtained from the earliest campaigns (of course, I could not locate 30 minutes of different spots for five of the six most recent candidates, either). In order to better investigate this trend I conducted a separate analysis in which I adjusted the totals for number of themes in those campaigns for which I had obtained less than 30 minutes of spots, to reflect the number of themes that probably would have occurred if I had located 30 minutes of spots. I divided the number of seconds of the advertisements I had into 1,800 (30 minutes) and multiplied the result by the number of acclaims, attacks, and defenses observed (I didn't bother to adjust the totals within 20 seconds of 1,800). This produces an estimate for the number of each kind of utterance the candidate would have produced in 30 minutes of spots. Controlling this way for sample size, Figure 11.1 reveals that the number of themes per 30 minutes of spots has increased steadily over time for both parties. In the last three election years, however, the increase is especially dramatic for Democrats. To illustrate this phenomenon, contrast a 30-second spot from McGovern in 1972 with a 30-second spot from Clinton in 1996:

President Nixon has received ten million dollars in secret campaign contributions from men and interests whose names Mr. Nixon refuses to reveal to the American people. Who are these men, and what do they want? (McGovern, 1972, "Secret Nixon Contributions")

The facts Bob Dole ignores in his negative attacks. The deficit cut 60%. Ten million new jobs. Family income up $1,600. Health insurance you don't lose when

Figure 11.2
Percent of 20/30-and 60-Second Spots

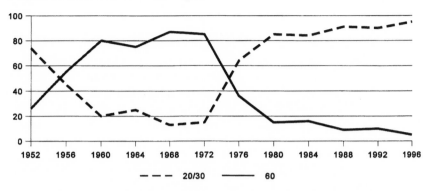

changing jobs. President Clinton: moving our economy ahead, helping families. Now a plan to cut taxes for college tuition: $500 per child tax credit. Break up violent gangs. Move one million from welfare to work. Dole resorts to desperate negative attacks. President Clinton is protecting our values. (Clinton, 1996, "Ig-nores")

The McGovern ad articulates only one theme: that Nixon accepts huge secret campaign contributions. In contrast, in the same amount of time the Clinton spot hurriedly mentions nine themes: Dole's negative attacks, the deficit, jobs, family income, health insurance, college tuition tax credit, gangs, welfare, our values. Experimental research would be necessary to determine whether there is more benefit from focusing entirely on one theme (depth) or mentioning several themes (breadth)—but there is no doubt that political spots are moving in the direction of saying less and less about more and more topics.

Sound Bites: Average Length of Spots

I will also mention a related finding, although surely a less surprising one. After candidates experimented with this new kind of campaign message in the 1950s, most television spots in the 1960s (and in 1972) were 60 seconds long. In the mid-1970s and 1980s the length of spots gradually shifted to 30 seconds, until by the 1990s virtually all television spots were 30 seconds in length (see Figure 11.2).

Thus, there is a trend toward producing shorter spots and toward airing a smaller body of spots. Surely the cost of producing and broadcasting television spots has fueled this trend to shorter spots. Similarly, the fact that the news media have been quoting shorter and shorter bits of candidate statements (see Chapter 1) has also encouraged the move toward shorter messages. I doubt that the electorate is well served by this trend.

The Function of General Presidential TV Spots

Presidential candidates used their television commercials most frequently to acclaim: 60% of the utterances in these messages engaged in self-praise. For example, in 1984, Reagan boasted of his first-term accomplishments: "Today, inflation is down, interest rates are down. We've created six and a half million new jobs. Americans are working again, and so is America." He discussed policy in this acclaim, identifying three particular successes: reducing inflation, reducing interest rates, and creating jobs. In 1960, Nixon stressed his experience: "Above everything else, the American people want leaders who will keep the peace without surrender for America and the world. Henry Cabot Lodge and I have had the opportunity of serving with President Eisenhower in this cause for the last seven and a half years. We both know Mr. Krushchev. We have sat opposite the conference table with him." This acclaim stresses the character of the Republican ticket, in the form of boasting of their leadership ability. Every candidate repeatedly used acclaiming in their television commercials, with the least amount of self-praise at 31% (Eisenhower, 1952). The more desirable a candidate appears to voters, the more likely that candidate will seem preferable to opponents (see Table 11.1 and Figure 11.3).

Attacks also occurred with frequency: 39% of the remarks in these spots were attacks. For example, in one of his "Eisenhower Answers America" spots, Eisenhower responded to this prompt: "General, the Democrats are telling me I never had it so good" by attacking the past deeds of the current, Democratic, administration: "Can that be true when America is billions in debt, when prices have doubled, when taxes break our backs, and we are still fighting in Korea?" He attacks on policy grounds here, leveling four separate criticisms, bemoaning the federal debt, inflation, taxation, and the Korean War. In 1988, Dukakis attacked his opponent's character: "The other side has pursued a campaign of distortion and distraction, of fear and of smear." These are not the actions of an honorable person. Every candidate used at least some attacks in their television spots, although in 1956 Eisenhower attacked in but 2% of his remarks (Nixon in 1960 used just 9% attacks). The less desirable an attacked opponent appears to voters, the more likely the sponsoring candidate will seem preferable.

In general, acclaims occur more often than attacks (about one and a half times as often). Both strategies can improve a candidate's apparent preferability. However, voters profess not to like mudslinging (Stewart, 1975; Merritt, 1984). There is some concern that attacks could create back-

Table 11.1
Functions of General Presidential TV Spots

Year	Candidate	Acclaims	Attacks	Defenses
1952	Eisenhower	22 (31%)	48 (69%)	0
	Stevenson	30 (64%)	17 (46%)	0
1956	Eisenhower	78 (98%)	2 (2%)	0
	Stevenson	41 (62%)	25 (38%)	0
1960	Nixon	140 (85%)	14 (9%)	10 (6%)
	Kennedy	105 (73%)	38 (27%)	0
1964	Goldwater	98 (60%)	55 (34%)	11 (7%)
	Johnson	59 (58%)	42 (42%)	0
1968	Nixon	71 (71%)	29 (29%)	0
	Humphrey	119 (73%)	36 (23%)	5 (3%)
1972	Nixon	124 (78%)	35 (22%)	0
	McGovern	58 (39%)	90 (60%)	1 (1%)
1976	Ford	200 (75%)	59 (22%)	8 (3%)
	Carter	126 (59%)	89 (41%)	0
1980	Reagan	129 (58%)	93 (42%)	**2 (1%)**
	Carter	112 (61%)	68 (37%)	5 (3%)
1984	Reagan	202 (77%)	59 (23%)	0
	Mondale	132 (54%)	110 (45%)	2 (1%)
1988	Bush	121 (61%)	78 (39%)	0
	Dukakis	206 (61%)	125 (37%)	4 (1%)
1992	Bush	70 (44%)	90 (56%)	0
	Clinton	167 (49%)	168 (49%)	5 (1%)
1996	Dole	111 (37%)	185 (62%)	1 (.5%)
	Clinton	225 (53%)	200 (47%)	3 (1%)
	Total	2746 (60%)	1755 (39%)	**57 (1%)**

Figure 11.3
Functions of General TV Spots

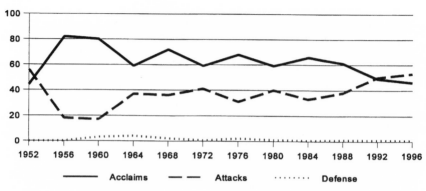

lash with some voters. Thus, it is perfectly reasonable to expect acclaims to be more frequent than attacks, as this data reveals. However, Figure 11.3 suggests that (after a highly negative campaign in 1952, especially from Eisenhower) the percentage of acclaims is slowly dropping while the proportion of attacks is growing over time. In 1992, the overall percentage of attacks was higher than the percentage of acclaims for the first time since 1952 (and that distribution held true in 1996 as well). Notice that primary spots are also becoming more negative over time (see Figure 9.1).

Every candidate employed both acclaims and attacks. However, four candidates bucked the general trend, using more attacks than acclaims in their television spots. Eisenhower (1952), McGovern (1972), Bush (1992), and Dole (1996) all employed more attacks than acclaims in their spots. In 1992, Clinton's utterances were divided evenly between acclaims and attacks (49% each). The remaining nineteen candidates/ campaigns used more acclaims than attacks in their television advertisements.

Defenses were also used in presidential television spots, but far less frequently than acclaims or attacks: Defenses accounted for only 1% of the total utterances in these advertisements. For example, in 1984, Reagan spots accused Mondale of wanting to increase taxes, declaring that "Walter Mondale thinks you can squeeze more money out of your budget." A Mondale advertisement used a woman to respond to this attack: "I think you've got it all wrong. Mondale thinks I'm paying too much." This clearly denies the attack. Over half (thirteen) of these candidates did not defend in any of the spots examined here, while the other candidates used defense sparingly. If candidates can effectively dissipate attacks, threats to their desirability can be reduced or eliminated with defense. This increases the likelihood that they will seem preferable.

There are several possible reasons for the proportion of defenses to be consistently lower than that of acclaims and attacks. First, candidates may not wish to remind voters of attacks from their opponents. Indeed, if a voter hasn't been exposed to an attack, a defense will inform them about attacks against the ad's sponsor. Second, candidates may wish to "stay on message." Typically, each campaign has a theme and a set of issues to emphasize which are different from the opponent's theme and issues. For example, in 1996 Clinton discussed education more than Dole, and Dole talked about his proposed tax cut more than Clinton talked about taxes. Presumably, opponents will attack on the issues that favor them, so to defend against an attack means the candidate must spend time on the opponents' issue. Finally, candidates may not wish to appear to be on the defense. They may wish to look active rather than reactive. Note that these factors are not equally important for all types of campaign messages. For example, in a presidential debate, there is no question that the audience has been exposed to an attack (it may also be more difficult to resist the impulse to respond to attacks in a live confrontation than when writing the script for a spot). As might be expected, defenses are more common in debates than in spots (Benoit, Blaney, & Pier, 1998).

How do these data compare with previous research? Kaid and Johnston (1991) provide figures for the number of positive and negative spots from 1960 to 1988. Table 11.2 displays their data and the results of this study for those years. For some years, the figures are quite comparable: 1968: 75% acclaims and 78% positive ads; 1984: 66% acclaims and 65% positive ads; 1988: 62% acclaims and 63% positive ads. However, the data are less consistent for some campaigns: 1960: 82% acclaims and 93% positive ads; 197,: 59% acclaims and 72% positive ads. The totals are also somewhat discrepant: 66% acclaims and 71% positive ads.

There are three possible explanations for these discrepancies. One is that we have operationalized "acclaim" and "positive" differently (and, of course, "attack" and "negative"). Chapter 2 presents these definitions of "acclaim" and "attack":

- Themes that portrayed the sponsoring candidate or the candidate's political party in a favorable light were *acclaims*.
- Themes that portrayed the opposing candidate or opposing candidate's political party in an unfavorable light were *attacks*.

Kaid and Johnston explained their coding system this way: "Each spot was classified as positive or negative according to its focus; a negative spot focused on the opposition, and a positive spot focused on the candidate sponsoring the ad" (p. 56). The only difference is that my definitions focus on both the target (candidate or opponent) and content

Table 11.2
Functions of General Presidential TV Spots: Kaid and Johnston (1991) and Benoit (this volume)

Year	Acclaims (Benoit)	Positive (Kaid & Johnston)	Attacks (Benoit)	Negative (Kaid & Johnston)
1960	82%	93%	18%	7%
1964	64%	60%	36%	40%
1968	75%	78%	25%	22%
1972	59%	72%	41%	28%
1976	69%	76%	31%	24%
1980	60%	64%	40%	36%
1984	66%	65%	34%	35%
1988	62%	63%	38%	37%
Total	66%	71%	34%	29%

(favorable or unfavorable light). However, given that candidates say positive things about themselves and negative things about their opponents, this does not seem to be a serious difference. Our respective operationalizations are unlikely to be the cause of the differences that occurred.

A second possibility is that our samples are different. While the number of spots are essentially the same for some campaigns (e.g., 1964, 1972)—and given that we both relied heavily on the Oklahoma Archive, these may well be the same spots. However, they have 38 more spots from 1976 and 153 more from 1980 (see Table A.5 in the Appendix). However, given that there was no bias in the spots I selected to obtain 30 minutes of advertising, this seems unlikely as an explanation of differences in our results.

A third possible explanation concerns our coding units. I code each theme in a spot rather than characterize an entire spot as positive or negative. Kaid and Johnston (1991), like most research in this area, code entire spots as positive or negative: "Our unit of analysis was the commercial spot" (p. 56). They address the possibility that this procedure could skew the results: "Our method of dichotomizing the sample into positive and negative ads by determining a dominant focus on the candidate or his opponent is useful for analysis but may understate the amount of negative information about an opponent present even in a positive ad" (p. 62). Based on the comparison of results, it appears that their speculation was correct. In six of the eight discrepancies, they found more positive (and fewer) negative ads, and their mean percent of positive ads (71%) is higher than the mean number of acclaims (66%) in my study.[1]

To illustrate this potential problem, consider the following spot from Dole's campaign in 1996:

Dole: *Americans are working harder and longer but taking home less. In fact, the typical American family spends more on taxes than on food, clothing and housing combined. The American people deserve better.*

Announcer: Bob Dole's economic plan will cut taxes 15 percent for every single taxpayer. The typical family of four will save over $1,600 a year. The Dole plan: Americans keep more of what they earn. Bob Dole: The better man for a better America.

The italicized portion of this spot is negative, attacking Bill Clinton's first-term record. The underlined portion is positive, acclaiming Bob Dole's future plans for taxation. To describe this entire spot as *either* positive *or* negative clearly ignores or misclassifies about half of what is being said to voters. Thus, while I certainly agree that their research is useful, I am convinced that my method of classifying each theme in a spot offers a more accurate indication of the amount of attacking and acclaiming (or positive and negative ideas) in a spot.

West (1997) analyzes 379 "prominent" (primary and general) presidential television spots from 1952 to 1996. His results are also different from mine (see Table 11.3). Like Kaid and Johnston, West classifies entire spots rather than themes. However, there is an additional limitation on his results. His sample is by no means drawn randomly, nor should it be assumed to represent typical television spots. He selected spots mentioned in Jamieson's (1992) book (for 1952–1988) and broadcast on the *CBS Evening News* (for 1992 and 1996). As a communication scholar, I am delighted to see that a political scientist is aware of work in our discipline, and chooses to rely on our scholarship so highly. However, it seems highly unlikely to me that Jamieson was trying to select spots that would be typical for West's purposes (nor is it clear what basis Jamieson could have used for selecting representative spots, even if that had been her purpose). Furthermore, West's decision to include spots from 1992 and 1996 because they were broadcast on the *CBS Evening News* may have been convenient, but it too is questionable. West, Kern, Alger, and Goggin (1995) argued that Bush and Perot used national ad buys in 1992, but "Clinton targeted more expenditures on local markets in selected states. There were also important differences in ads aired in different cities" (p. 288). Local ad buys were also used in the 1996 pres-

Table 11.3
Acclaiming and Attacking in Primary and General Spots: West (1997) and
Benoit (this volume)

Campaign	Positive West (1997)	Acclaims Benoit	Negative West (1997)	Attacks Benoit
1952	75%	58%	25%	42%
1956	62%	79%	38%	21%
1960	88%	71%	12%	29%
1964	50%	63%	50%	37%
1968	31%	73%	69%	27%
1972	67%	65%	33%	35%
1976	67%	60%	33%	40%
1980	40%	73%	60%	27%
1984	26%	68%	74%	32%
1988	17%	71%	83%	29%
1992	34%	57%	66%	43%
1996	40%	55%	60%	45%
Total	54%	65%	46%	35%

idential campaign. As West (1997) explained, "presidential candidates
have begun to bypass national networks in their ad buys and purchase
time directly from selected local stations" (p. 19). This means, of course,
that presidential spots that were broadcast nationally (i.e., on the CBS
Evening News) did not accurately reflect the campaign's advertising in
1992 and 1996. Thus, West's results, while interesting, must not be assumed to reflect typical presidential advertising.

Policy versus Character in General Presidential TV Spots

Overall, candidates discussed policy matters in more utterances than
character concerns: 60% of the utterances in these spots addressed policy,
while 40% concerned character. For example, in 1960 Kennedy discussed
federal aid to education:

But I believe in the passage by this Congress and I hope the next administration,
of a federal aid to education bill, which would provide assistance to the various

states for school construction and for teachers' salaries. And we want good class-rooms. And we want each child to have an advantage of getting the best education he can get. So I strongly support federal aid to education.

This is clearly an acclaim based on policy. Similarly, this spot for Nixon in 1972 acclaimed his policy accomplishments:

He has brought home over 500,000 men from the war, and less than 40,000 remain. None engaged in ground combat. He has overhauled the draft laws and made them fair for everyone, black and white, rich and poor. He certified an amendment giving 18-year-olds the right to vote. He has created an economy that is growing faster than at any time in years. The rate of inflation has been cut in half. He has taken a strong stand for equal education but against massive busing as a means to accomplish it. He has named common sense judges to the Supreme Court. He's gone to China to talk peace with Mao Tse Tung. He's gone to the Soviet Union to talk peace with Leonid Breshnev.

The Vietnamese war, the right to vote, the economy, education and bus-ing, judicial appointments, and foreign policy topics are all touched on in this spot. In sharp contrast, this spot for Bush in 1992 attacked Clin-ton's character:

Man: I don't believe him. I don't believe him one bit.

Woman: I don't believe him.

Woman: Trust.

In 1976, this Ford commercial acclaimed his personal qualities: "Sensi-tivity and concern. A willingness to listen and to act." Thus, these tele-vision spots addressed both policy and character (see Table 11.4 and Figure 11.4).

Figure 11.4 reveals that from 1956 through 1976, campaigns sometimes focused more on policy and sometimes more on character. Starting with 1980, however, there has been a persistent trend toward heavier reliance on policy than character. Joslyn (1980), in a study of spots from 1960 to 1976, found that there was less issue content from 1970 to 1976 (75.5%) than from 1960 to 1968 (79.6%). His figures are higher than my data for the same years, but he dichotomized spots into those with issue content and those with issue content, rather than focusing on themes.

Policy utterances were divided into three sub-forms: past deeds, future plans, and general goals. The most common form of policy utterance is past deeds, which accounted for 58% of policy utterances. For example, in 1972, a citizen attacked Nixon's record in this spot for McGovern: "I voted for Nixon in 1968. I never voted for a Republican before until he came along and says he's gonna stop this war. But he didn't." General

Table 11.4
Policy versus Character in General TV Spots

Year	Candidate	Policy	Character
1952	Eisenhower	60 (86%)	10 (14%)
	Stevenson	23 (49%)	24 (51%)
1956	Eisenhower	35 (44%)	45 (56%)
	Stevenson	37 (56%)	29 (44%)
1960	Nixon	56 (36%)	98 (64%)
	Kennedy	71 (50%)	72 (50%)
1964	Goldwater	73 (48%)	80 (52%)
	Johnson	66 (65%)	35 (35%)
1968	Nixon	54 (54%)	46 (46%)
	Humphrey	67 (43%)	88 (57%)
1972	Nixon	98 (62%)	61 (38%)
	McGovern	94 (64%)	54 (36%)
1976	Ford	112 (43%)	147 (57%)
	Carter	108 (50%)	107 (50%)
1980	Reagan	148 (67%)	74 (33%)
	Carter	75 (42%)	105 (58%)
1984	Reagan	177 (68%)	84 (32%)
	Mondale	173 (71%)	70 (29%)
1988	Bush	115 (58%)	84 (42%)
	Dukakis	209 (63%)	122 (37%)
1992	Bush	100 (63%)	60 (37%)
	Clinton	222 (66%)	113 (34%)
1996	Dole	189 (64%)	107 (36%)
	Clinton	349 (82%)	76 (18%)
	Total	2711 (60%)	1791 (40%)

Figure 11.4
Policy versus Character

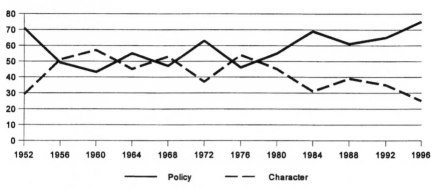

goals were the second most common kind of policy remark at 27%. In 1960, Kennedy adopted these goals: "We will build and expand our forest programs. We will cleanse our rivers of pollution. We will carry out reclamation and conservation programs on our land. And we will try to move ahead in those areas which have been cut back." Figure 11.5 reveals that general goals have been used less often in recent years. Finally, specific future plans comprised 16% of the utterances in these television spots. In 1964, a Johnson spot declared that "Even his running mate William Miller admits that Senator Goldwater's voluntary plan would destroy Social Security," attacking Goldwater's future plan. Figure 11.5 shows that future plans are somewhat more common in recent years (see Table 11.5).

Joslyn (1986) analyzed 506 spots from 1960 to 1984. He found that 37% concerned future policy. This is fairly close to the combined total of utterances devoted to future plans and general goals: 43%. He also discovered that past governmental policy accounted for 60% of the spots in his sample. This is quite close to the figure for past deeds: 58%.

Character remarks were also subdivided, into themes addressing personal qualities, leadership ability, and ideals. The most common kind of character utterance addressed personal qualities, at 49%. Joslyn (1986) reported that 57% of the spots from 1960 to 1984 mentioned personal qualities. West (1997) reported that personal qualities were used in 39% of spots. For example, President Ford acclaimed his character in 1976: "So tonight it is not the power and the glamour of the Presidency that leads me to ask for another four years. It is something every hard-working American will understand: the challenge of a job well begun but far from finished."

The candidates talked about leadership ability in 38% of the remarks. In 1968, this Nixon spot acclaimed his leadership ability, particularly in

Figure 11.5
Forms of Policy

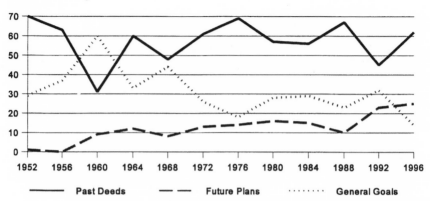

foreign affairs: "Well, I think Richard M. Nixon probably is more qualified in world affairs than anyone else that I know." The smallest group of character utterances, concerning the candidates' ideals, accounted for 17% of their character comments. An example of this topic occurs in this 1980 spot for Carter: "And I would like to serve eight years in the White House and have our nation stay at peace, but at the same time enhance the quality of life of people in other nations and promote freedom and human rights and democratic principles as well." See Figure 11.6, which reveals that the distribution of forms of character utterances are more chaotic than the allocation of policy remarks.

It is interesting to note that acclaims and attacks were not distributed equally across the two topics of policy and character. Attacks were more common on policy (45%) than on character (32%), while acclaims were more plentiful on character (68%) than policy (55%). Nor were acclaims and attacks distributed equally on the six sub-forms of policy and character. These results, incidentally, do not support the view that attacks primarily focus on personalities.

Past deeds were more often used to attack (58%) than to acclaim (42%). Future plans were also more likely to be used for attacks (58%) than acclaims (42%). Perhaps these figures reflect the prevalence of imperfections in the world, so that more of the candidate's past and future actions lend themselves to attacks than acclaims. Personal qualities were split more equally, occurring in 53% of acclaims and 47% of attacks. This could indicate that these candidates have about as many good qualities as bad.

The remaining three topics are all far more frequently used to acclaim than attack. Leadership ability was used in 82% of acclaims and 18% attacks, ideals were employed in 84% of acclaims and 16% of attacks, and general goals were utilized in 91% of acclaims and only 9% of attacks. By their very nature, both general goals and ideals are general and usually desirable. For example, it is far easy to acclaim than attack a general goal like balancing the budget or an ideal like freedom of speech. (Conversely, it is relatively easy to attack a future plan for accomplishing that goal, like increasing taxes 10% or closing sixteen military bases.) Given that candidates for the presidency have managed to ascend to the leadership role in their political party (they just aren't like ordinary citizens in their governmental experience), it may be easier to acclaim than attack leadership ability as well.

INCUMBENTS VERSUS CHALLENGERS

In the general spots examined here, incumbents acclaimed more than challengers (66% to 54%). Challengers, on the other hand, attacked more than incumbents (45% to 33%). Although every candidate made use of both acclaims and attacks, it is clear that incumbents are more likely to acclaim than attack in television spots, and challengers are prone to attack more than they acclaim in their commercials. A X^2 calculated on function (acclaims and attacks) versus incumbency was significant (df = 1, X^2 = 73.11, p < .001; defenses were excluded from he calculations because there were so few of them). These findings are consistent with our earlier (and smaller) study of television spots in from 1980 to 1996 (Benoit, Pier, & Blaney, 1997), which found that incumbents acclaimed more than challengers (53% to 44%), while challengers attacked more than incumbents (59% to 46%) (see Table 11.6, and Figures 11.7 and 11.8).

Figure 11.7 reveals that incumbents have a fairly consistent advantage over challengers in use of acclaims. Conversely, challengers tend to use attacks more often than incumbents, as Figure 11.8 demonstrates. Kaid and Johnston (1991) found only slight differences on this dimension: there were more positive incumbent than challenger spots (72% to 70%), and there were more negative challenger than incumbent spots (30% to 28%). This discrepancy may well be related to the difference in our coding procedures, discussed earlier.

I also broke out the five candidates who won a first term as a challenger and campaigned for a second term as an incumbent (Eisenhower, Nixon, Carter, Reagan, and Clinton; while Bush participated in two campaigns, he was clearly not a challenger in 1988). Surely this would provide the strongest test for a contrast between incumbents and challengers: When a specific candidate is a challenger, does he (all of these candidates were men) attack more than when that same individual is an incumbent? First, in general, this subset of candidates acclaimed more as incumbents (67%) than they did as challengers (55%). This was true on policy (477 to 289) and character (264 to 226). These candidates

Table 11.5
Forms of Policy and Character Utterances in General TV Spots

Year	Candidate	Policy			Character		
		Past Deeds	Future Plans	General Goals	Personal Qualities	Leadership Ability	Ideals
1952	Eisenhower	45	0	15	5	3	2
	Stevenson	13	1	9	13	6	5
1956	Eisenhower	21	0	14	26	16	3
	Stevenson	24	0	13	6	9	14
1960	Nixon	13	9	34	17	67	14
	Kennedy	27	2	42	28	31	13
1964	Goldwater	40	2	31	46	7	27
	Johnson	39	14	13	15	12	8
1968	Nixon	24	2	28	8	26	12
	Humphrey	34	8	25	44	28	16
1972	Nixon	54	22	22	23	23	15
	McGovern	63	3	28	47	2	5

1976	Ford	84	21	7	75	54	18
	Carter	67	9	32	46	41	20
1980	Reagan	79	22	47	20	47	7
	Carter	47	13	15	43	43	19
1984	Reagan	123	14	40	12	58	14
	Mondale	72	40	61	32	15	23
1988	Bush	79	20	16	25	55	4
	Dukakis	137	13	59	64	51	7
1992	Bush	21	35	44	47	7	6
	Clinton	125	38	59	93	8	12
1996	Dole	107	43	39	81	5	19
	Clinton	225	90	34	52	3	21
	Total	1563 (58%)	421 (16%)	727 (27%)	868 (49%)	617 (38%)	304 (17%)

Figure 11.6
Forms of Character

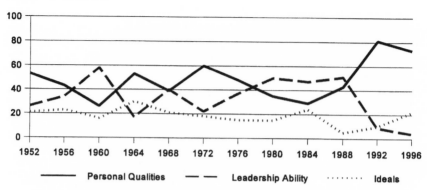

attacked more as challengers (45%) than as incumbents (33%). This re-lationship occurred on policy (303 to 257) and character (124 to 107). Furthermore, in all five cases the percent of remarks devoted to acclaims was higher for each candidate as an incumbent than as a challenger, while the percent of attacks was lower for each candidate as incumbent than as challenger (see Table 11.7). Thus, in presidential television spots, there is an indisputable tendency for challengers to attack—both on pol-icy and character—while incumbents tend to acclaim—on policy and character (see also Trent & Trent, 1974; Trent & Trent, 1995).

Previous research on debates, keynotes, acceptance addresses, and tel-evision spots has addressed the question of incumbent versus challenger party. Benoit and Wells' (1996) analysis of the 1992 presidential debates found that "Clinton, the challenger, engaged in more persuasive attack than Bush, the incumbent, or Perot, the third party candidate" (p. 71). Although they did not break acclaims out as separate from defenses, an important part of defense is bolstering, or recounting favorable infor-mation—a part of acclaiming. They found that "Bush engaged in more bolstering than Clinton or Perot" (p. 84). Thus, the incumbent acclaimed more than the challenger (or challengers), while the challenger (or at least one of the two challengers) attacked more than the incumbent in the 1992 debates.

Our study of presidential nomination Acceptance Addresses from 1960 to 1996 found similar results (Benoit, Wells, Pier, & Blaney, in press). Incumbents were more likely to acclaim (77%) than challengers (67%), while challengers were prone to attack (32%) more than incumbents (22%). Our study of nominating convention keynote speeches is also con-sistent with these findings (Benoit, Blaney, & Pier, 1996). We found that incumbent party keynoters acclaimed (59%) more than challengers (42%), while challenger party speakers attacked (58%) more than incum-

Table 11.6
Functions of TV Spots by Incumbents and Challengers

Year	Candidate	Acclaims	Attacks	Defenses
1952	Eisenhower C	22 (31%)	48 (69%)	0
	Stevenson I	30 (64%)	17 (46%)	0
1956	Eisenhower I	78 (98%)	2 (2%)	0
	Stevenson C	41 (62%)	25 (38%)	0
1960	Nixon I	140 (85%)	14 (9%)	10 (6%)
	Kennedy C	105 (73%)	38 (27%)	0
1964	Goldwater C	98 (60%)	55 (34%)	11 (7%)
	Johnson I	59 (58%)	42 (42%)	0
1968	Nixon C	71 (71%)	29 (29%)	0
	Humphrey I	119 (73%)	36 (23%)	5 (3%)
1972	Nixon I	124 (78%)	35 (22%)	0
	McGovern C	58 (39%)	90 (60%)	1 (1%)
1976	Ford I	200 (75%)	59 (22%)	8 (3%)
	Carter C	126 (59%)	89 (41%)	0
1980	Reagan C	129 (58%)	93 (42%)	**2 (1%)**
	Carter I	112 (61%)	68 (37%)	5 (3%)
1984	Reagan I	202 (77%)	59 (23%)	0
	Mondale C	132 (54%)	110 (45%)	2 (1%)
1988	Bush I	121 (61%)	78 (39%)	0
	Dukakis C	206 (61%)	125 (37%)	4 (1%)
1992	Bush C	70 (44%)	90 (56%)	0
	Clinton I	167 (49%)	168 (49%)	5 (1%)
1996	Dole C	111 (37%)	185 (62%)	1 (.5%)
	Clinton I	225 (53%)	200 (47%)	3 (1%)
	Incumbents	1577 (66%)	778 (33%)	36 (2%)
	Challengers	1169 (54%)	977 (45%)	19 (1%)
	Total	2746 (60%)	1755 (39%)	**57 (1%)**

Figure 11.7
Acclaims by Incumbents and Challengers

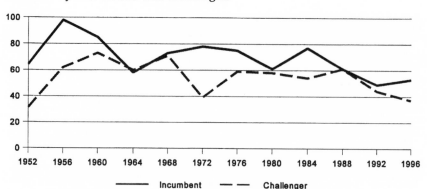

bents (38%). Our smaller study of television spots from 1980 to 1996 found similar results (Benoit, Pier, & Blaney, 1997): Incumbents acclaimed more (53%) than challengers (44%), while challengers attacked more (59%) than incumbents (46%).

The most obvious difference between incumbents and challengers is that incumbents have a record in the very office sought. This is important both for themselves and for their opponents. An incumbent's record provides a source of ideas for acclaiming. Even our less distinguished presidents have some bright spots that provide potential resources for self-praise. Of course, it is unrealistic for a president to take credit for everything that happens (or increases, or decreases) while serving in office. However, because challengers want to promise desirable outcomes to voters if elected, they may well be hesitant about pointing this out (Benoit & Wells, 1996). Thus, an incumbent's record in office is an important source of material for acclaiming.

On the other hand, even our outstanding presidents cannot hope to solve every problem or provide every possible benefit. Thus, apparent shortcomings are available to challengers for attack. Again, it is unreasonable to expect a president to create perfection on earth, but incumbents may be reluctant to point out their actual limitations to voters. Thus, incumbents' records from the first terms in office are an important resource for them to acclaim and for their opponents to attack.

Other sources of acclaims and attacks exist besides the incumbent's record in office. Thus, Ford attacked Carter's record as governor, just as Carter attacked Reagan in 1980, and as Bush attacked Dukakis in 1988 and Clinton in 1992. Kennedy, Goldwater, and Dole ran on (and were attacked for) their records in the Senate. Reagan, Carter, Dukakis, and Clinton all acclaimed on the basis of their records as governor. Perot acclaimed his business experience (as did Steve Forbes, George Bush,

Figure 11.8
Attacks by Incumbents and Challengers

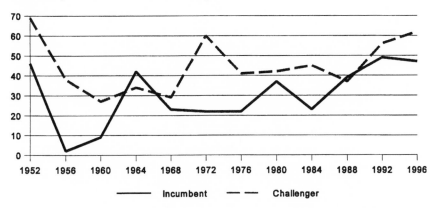

and Lamar Alexander, for example). However, I believe that the incumbent's record in the office sought is viewed as an especially relevant (and fertile) ground for both acclaims (by the incumbent) and attacks (by the challenger).

A second possible explanation concerns the advantages enjoyed by incumbents. Incumbents have a variety of potential advantages, like greater recognition, easier access to media, and perks of the office (see, e.g., Trent & Friedenberg, 1995). The challenger may feel it necessary to attack in order to overcome the benefits of incumbency.

REPUBLICANS VERSUS DEMOCRATS

Recall that 60% of the total utterances in these television advertisements are acclaims and 39% are attacks (Table 11.1). Overall, Republicans acclaimed more frequently than the mean, 64% of the time, while Democrats acclaimed less frequently than the mean, 57% of the time. On the other hand, Democrats attacked 42% of the time, somewhat more than the average of 39%, while Republicans attacked less often, 35% of the time. A X^2 calculated on function (acclaims and attacks) versus party was significant (df = 1, X^2 = 21.88, p < .001; defenses were excluded from the calculations because there were so few of them). Finally, candidates from both parties defended in about 1% of their remarks (see Table 11.8). Figure 11.9 contrasts acclaims in spots by Republicans and Democrats. Figure 11.10 compares attacks made by Republicans and Democrats.

These results are inconsistent with our previous study of television spots from 1980 to 1996 (Benoit, Pier, & Blaney, 1997), which found Republicans attacked 55% of the time and Democrats acclaimed 52% of the time. However, as Table 11.8 (and Figures 11.9 and 11.10) reveals, these

Table 11.7
Acclaims and Attacks by Candidates Who Were Both Challengers and
Incumbents

Year	Candidate	Acclaims	Attack
1952	Eisenhower C	22 (31%)	**48 (69%)**
1956	Eisenhower I	**78 (98%)**	2 (2%)
1968	Nixon C	71 (71%)	**29 (29%)**
1972	Nixon I	**124 (78%)**	35 (22%)
1976	Carter C	126 (59%)	**89 (41%)**
1980	Carter I	**112 (61%)**	68 (37%)
1980	Reagan C	129 (58%)	**93 (42%)**
1984	Reagan I	**202 (77%)**	59 (23%)
1992	Clinton C	167 (49%)	**168 (49%)**
1996	Clinton I	**225 (53%)**	200 (47%)
	Challengers	515 (55%)	**427 (45%)**
	Incumbents	**741 (67%)**	364 (33%)

years buck the overall trend from 1952 to 1996. Keynote speeches from
1960 to 1996 (Benoit, Blaney, & Pier, 1996) found that Republicans tend
to acclaim more (55%) while Democrats were prone to attack (53%).
However, acceptance addresses (Benoit, Wells, Pier, & Blaney, in press)
found that Democrats (77%) acclaimed more than Republicans (68%),
while Republicans (30%) attacked more than Democrats (23%). Kaid and
Johnson (1991) also found that slightly more Republican than Democratic
spots were positive (72% to 69%), and there were more Democratic than
Republican negative spots (31% to 28%). In my opinion, these mixed
results indicate that situation (incumbent or challenger party) exerts
more influence on the functions of political campaign messages than political party. If one believes in counting, two of the three message forms
(television spots, keynote speeches) suggests Democrats are more negative, while only one (acceptance addresses) suggests that Republicans are
more negative.

WINNERS VERSUS LOSERS

Overall, winners acclaimed (62%) more than losers (59%) in these presidential television spots. Losers attacked slightly more often than win-

Table 11.8
Functions of TV Spots by Political Party

Year	Candidate	Acclaims	Attacks	Defenses
1952	Eisenhower R	22 (31%)	48 (69%)	0
	Stevenson D	30 (64%)	17 (36%)	0
1956	Eisenhower R	78 (98%)	2 (2%)	0
	Stevenson D	41 (62%)	25 (38%)	0
1960	Nixon R	140 (85%)	14 (9%)	10 (6%)
	Kennedy D	105 (73%)	38 (27%)	0
1964	Goldwater R	98 (60%)	55 (34%)	11 (7%)
	Johnson D	59 (58%)	42 (42%)	0
1968	Nixon R	71 (71%)	29 (29%)	0
	Humphrey D	119 (73%)	36 (23%)	5 (3%)
1972	Nixon R	124 (78%)	35 (22%)	0
	McGovern D	58 (39%)	90 (60%)	1 (1%)
1976	Ford R	200 (75%)	59 (22%)	8 (3%)
	Carter D	126 (59%)	89 (41%)	0
1980	Reagan R	129 (58%)	93 (42%)	**2 (1%)**
	Carter D	112 (61%)	68 (37%)	5 (3%)
1984	Reagan R	202 (77%)	59 (23%)	0
	Mondale D	132 (54%)	110 (45%)	2 (1%)
1988	Bush R	121 (61%)	78 (39%)	0
	Dukakis D	206 (61%)	125 (37%)	4 (1%)
1992	Bush R	70 (44%)	90 (56%)	0
	Clinton D	167 (49%)	168 (49%)	5 (1%)
1996	Dole R	111 (37%)	185 (62%)	1 (.5%)
	Clinton D	225 (53%)	200 (47%)	3 (1%)
	Republican	1366 (64%)	747 (35%)	30 (1%)
	Democrat	1380 (57%)	1008 (42%)	25 (1%)
	Total	2746 (60%)	1755 (39%)	**57 (1%)**

Figure 11.9
Acclaims by Political Party

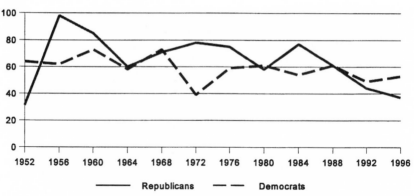

ners (39% to 38%). Although defense is generally uncommon, as noted before, defense is a characteristic of losers, who defended about six times as frequently as winners (2% to 0.4%). However, a X^2 calculated on function versus outcome revealed that these differences were not significant (df = 1, X^2 = 1.38, n.s.; defenses were excluded because of their infrequency). Thus, winners are not distinguished from losers based on the functions employed in their television advertisements (see Table 11.9 and Figures 11.11 and 11.12).

In order to further explore the relationship between outcomes and functions, I decided to conduct a different analysis that considered whether the presidential race was close throughout the campaign. I used *Gallup Opinion Index* to locate tracking polls and divided the candidates into three groups.

- Candidates who led throughout the campaign: Eisenhower: 1952, 1956; Johnson: 1964; Nixon: 1972; Reagan: 1984; Clinton: 1992, 1996.
- Candidates who trailed throughout the campaign (opponents of the candidates in the first group): Stevenson: 1952, 1956; Goldwater: 1964; McGovern: 1972; Mondale: 1984; Bush: 1992; Dole: 1996.
- Candidates who participated in closely contested races: Nixon and Kennedy: 1960; Nixon and Humphrey: 1968; Ford and Carter: 1976; Reagan and Carter: 1980; Bush and Dukakis: 1988.

When these data are broken out in this fashion, some interesting differences emerge. Acclaiming was most common among candidates who ran in tight races (67%) and those who led throughout the campaign (61%). These candidates had correspondingly fewer attacks (32%, 38% respectively). On the other hand, candidates who trailed in the polls were prone to attack (51%) more than acclaim (48%). Although the numbers

Figure 11.10
Attacks by Political Party

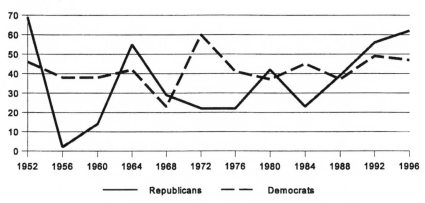

are small, defense was most common in closely contested campaigns (2%) and least common from candidates who led (0.5%). A two by three X^2 calculated on function (acclaims and attacks) by type of race (leaders, trailers, and close) was significant at the .001 level, 110.50 (df = 2, X^2 = 110.50, p< .001) (see Table 11.10 and Figures 11.13 and 11.14).

It is possible that the functions addressed in television spots do not cause election outcomes as much as they respond to situational differences. Those candidates who trail throughout the campaign may feel forced to attack more (51%) than the norm (39% of the comments in all spots are attacks). Attacks do attract attention, and they can reduce the apparent favorability of their target. Of course, there is the risk of a backlash from voters, many of whom profess to dislike mudslinging (e.g., Stewart, 1975; Merritt, 1984). However, those candidates who are clearly losing the election may be willing to run this risk if there is a chance that negative ads can "move the [poll] numbers" in their favor. Those in close races may be even more sensitive to the dangers of voter backlash to attacking ads, which could lead them to acclaim more (67%) than is usual (60% of the utterances in all spots are positive).

SOURCES OF UTTERANCES: CANDIDATES VERSUS OTHERS

There appears to be a trend over time for less reliance on candidates and more on others in television spots. In general campaigns, others were responsible for more of the utterances (71%) in campaign spots than the candidates themselves (29%). However, this was not split evenly among the functions. Others made 68% of the acclaims, 76% of the attacks, and 51% of the defenses (see Table 11.11 and Figure 11.15).

Table 11.9
Functions of TV Spots by Winners and Losers

Year	Candidate	Acclaims	Attacks	Defenses
1952	Eisenhower W	22 (31%)	48 (69%)	0
	Stevenson L	30 (64%)	17 (46%)	0
1956	Eisenhower W	78 (98%)	2 (2%)	0
	Stevenson L	41 (62%)	25 (38%)	0
1960	Nixon L	140 (85%)	14 (9%)	10 (6%)
	Kennedy W	105 (73%)	38 (27%)	0
1964	Goldwater L	98 (60%)	55 (34%)	11 (7%)
	Johnson W	59 (58%)	42 (42%)	0
1968	Nixon W	71 (71%)	29 (29%)	0
	Humphrey L	119 (73%)	36 (23%)	5 (3%)
1972	Nixon W	124 (78%)	35 (22%)	0
	McGovern L	58 (39%)	90 (60%)	1 (1%)
1976	Ford L	200 (75%)	59 (22%)	8 (3%)
	Carter W	126 (59%)	89 (41%)	0
1980	Reagan W	129 (58%)	93 (42%)	**2 (1%)**
	Carter L	112 (61%)	68 (37%)	5 (3%)
1984	Reagan W	202 (77%)	59 (23%)	0
	Mondale L	132 (54%)	110 (45%)	2 (1%)
1988	Bush W	121 (61%)	78 (39%)	0
	Dukakis L	206 (61%)	125 (37%)	4 (1%)
1992	Bush L	70 (44%)	90 (56%)	0
	Clinton W	167 (49%)	168 (49%)	5 (1%)
1996	Dole L	111 (37%)	185 (62%)	1 (.5%)
	Clinton W	225 (53%)	200 (47%)	3 (1%)
	Winners	1429 (62%)	881 (38%)	8 (0.4%)
	Losers	1317 (59%)	874 (39%)	47 (2%)
	Total	2746 (60%)	1755 (39%)	**57 (1%)**

Figure 11.11
Acclaims by Winners and Losers

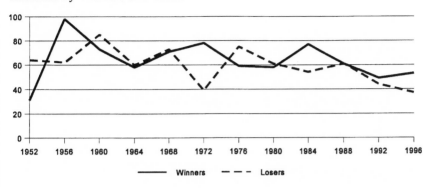

When we break this data out by acclaims and attacks, some differences emerge. First, Figure 11.16 reveals that only in two campaigns did the candidates make more of the acclaims than others. Generally, these campaigns are fairly consistent in using others to do most of the acclaiming. The data are more chaotic for attacks: Figure 11.17 reveals that in several early campaigns the candidates uttered more attacks than others in their advertisements. However, in 1980 and thereafter, others made most of the attacks in these spots. Furthermore, this trend seems more pronounced for attacks in recent years than for acclaims: even more of the attacks are made by others since 1980 than is true for acclaims. Kaid and Johnson found that 53% of positive ads and 14% of negative ads featured the candidates speaking, while 47% of positive and 86% of negative ads featured anonymous announcers or surrogate speakers. While the figures are not identical, both samples found that others make a higher percentage of attacks than acclaims.

Using another person to make an acclaim may appear somewhat more modest (and somewhat less self-serving) than using the candidate himself (again, all of these presidential candidates were men). Of course, the candidate should be visible in the campaign—voters want to see what the candidates have to say for themselves—so candidates may not wish to allow all acclaims to be made by others. Given the concerns over alienating some voters with mudslinging, it is not surprising to see an even higher percentage of attacks from others (76%) than from the candidate (24%). There is experimental research which suggests that attacks from spots sponsored by the candidate create more backlash than those sponsored by other organizations (e.g., PACs; see Garramone, 1985; Garramone & Smith, 1984; Kaid & Boydston, 1987). It is not clear that effects ad sponsor transfer to source of utterance, but these studies suggest that it might be wise for candidates to allow others to make some of the attacks. Defenses were split almost evenly between candidates and oth-

Figure 11.12
Attacks by Winners and Losers

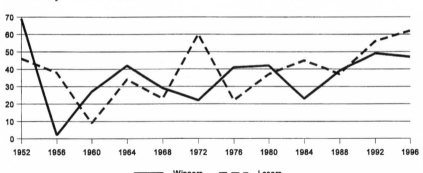

ers, but there are so few defenses that it is not clear whether this finding is meaningful.

FUNCTIONS OF TELEVISION SPOTS

The tenor of candidates' television advertising is largely positive. Across all campaigns (primary and general, major and third-party candidates), 65% of utterances are acclaims. The second most common form of utterances is attacks, which constitute 34% of the remarks in these spots. Finally, defenses are relatively infrequent at 1% of the comments in these commercials (see Table 11.12).

PRIMARY VERSUS GENERAL ADVERTISING CAMPAIGNS

These data show that commercials in primary campaigns devote a larger percentage of their remarks to acclaims (68%) than the general campaign (60%). Conversely, general campaigns tend to be more negative (39%) than primaries (31%). A Chi-square calculated on acclaims versus attacks for primary and general spots is significant ($X^2 = 44.6$, p $<$ .001). Defense remained constant at 1% of the utterances (see Table 11.13).

Our study of television spots in the 1996 campaign (Benoit, Blaney, & Pier, 1998) found roughly similar results (although the Democratic primary was uncontested). In 1996, more utterances were acclaims in the primary (58%) than in the general campaign (54%). Attacks were more common in the general campaign (46%) than in the primaries (40%).

To further explore the relationship between campaign stage and function of spots, I conducted a separate analysis using candidates for whom

Table 11.10
Functions of TV Spots by Closeness of the Race

Candidate	Acclaim	Attack	Defense
Led Throughout Race			
1952 Eisenhower	22 (31%)	48 (69%)	0
1956 Eisenhower	78 (98%)	2 (2%)	0
1964 Johnson	59 (58%)	42 (42%)	0
1972 Nixon	124 (78%)	35 (22%)	0
1984 Reagan	202 (77%)	59 (23%)	0
1992 Clinton	167 (49%)	168 (49%)	5 (1%)
1996 Clinton	225 (53%)	200 (47%)	3 (1%)
Led Race	**877 (61%)**	554 (38%)	8 (0.5%)
Close Races			
1960 Nixon	140 (85%)	14 (9%)	10 (6%)
1960 Kennedy	105 (73%)	38 (27%)	0
1968 Nixon	71 (71%)	29 (29%)	0
1968 Humphrey	119 (73%)	36 (23%)	5 (3%)
1976 Ford	200 (75%)	59 (22%)	8 (3%)
1976 Carter	126 (59%)	89 (41%)	0
1980 Reagan	129 (58%)	93 (42%)	**2 (1%)**
1980 Carter	112 (61%)	68 (37%)	5 (3%)
1988 Bush	121 (61%)	78 (39%)	0
1988 Dukakis	206 (61%)	125 (37%)	4 (1%)
Close Race	**1329 (67%)**	629 (32%)	34 (2%)
Trailed Throughout Race			
1952 Stevenson	30 (64%)	17 (46%)	0
1956 Stevenson	41 (62%)	25 (38%)	0

Table 11.10 (continued)

Candidate	Acclaim	Attack	Defense
1964 Goldwater	98 (60%)	55 (34%)	11 (7%)
1972 McGovern	58 (39%)	90 (60%)	1 (1%)
1984 Mondale	132 (54%)	110 (45%)	2 (1%)
1992 Bush	70 (44%)	90 (56%)	0
1996 Dole	111 (37%)	185 (62%)	1 (0.5%)
Trailed Race	540 (48%)	**572 (51%)**	15 (1%)

Figure 11.13
Acclaims by Race Position

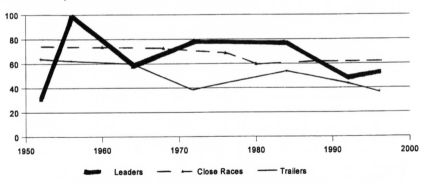

I had obtained both primary and general campaign spots. This would provide the strongest test of whether there is a difference in function by campaign stage, because it compares the same candidates (it is conceivable that the results for primary spots are skewed by unusual ads from primary losers, who are excluded from this analysis—although that is very unlikely, because there was no significant differences between primary winners [nominees] and losers). I compared the percentage of attacks by each candidate in primary spots with the percentage of attacks in general spots (the opposite pattern would, of course, hold for acclaims, given the relative infrequency of defenses). I found that in *every single case* these candidates devoted a greater percentage of the remarks to attacks in general than in primary ads. Frankly, I was surprised that out

Figure 11.14
Attacks by Race Position

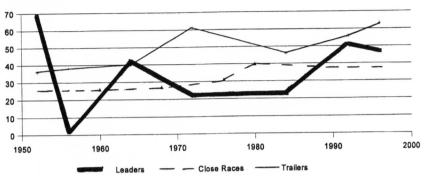

Leaders ▬▬▬   Close Races ▬ ▬   Trailers ▬▬▬

of sixteen comparisons, there was not a single exception to this rule (see Table 11.13).

Kaid and Ballotti (1991) studied 1,089 primary television spots from 1968 through 1988. They found that 48% were issue ads (focusing on the sponsor's policy stances), 32% were image ads (focusing on the sponsor's characteristics or qualifications), 18% were negative ads (focusing on the opponent or comparing the sponsor and the opponent), and 3% were combinations (no dominant focus). While our categories are not identical, their study suggests that primary spots are less negative than the data obtained here (18% to 32%). These discrepancies are akin to the ones between my study of general spots and that of Kaid and Johnston (1991), discussed above.

There are four possible explanations for these somewhat discrepant results. The first and second potential explanations concern the sample and coding definitions of "acclaim," "positive," "attack," and "negative." The arguments made above (about Kaid & Johnston, 1991) apply here as well. Third, primary spots have gotten more negative over time and I included 280 primary spots from 1992 and 1996, after their study was completed. Thus, I broke out just the primary spots in my sample from 1968 to 1988 (omitting defenses) to make my data directly comparable to Kaid and Ballotti's results. For those years 73% of the utterances were acclaims and 27% were attacks. Thus, the fact that more recent primaries are more negative (than the ones in the campaigns studied by Kaid & Ballotti) does not entirely account for the discrepancy.

The final possible explanation is that some of the discrepancy occurs from our different methods of analysis: Their method classifies entire spots according to their "primary focus" while I analyze each theme separately. Consider these two primary spots from 1980. The italicized portions are attacks; the underscored parts are acclaims. The first spot is from Edward Kennedy's primary campaign:

Table 11.11
Candidates and Others as Sources of Utterances

Year	Candidate	Acclaims		Attacks		Defenses	
		Candidate	Other	Candidate	Other	Candidate	Other
1952	Eisenhower	15 (68%)	7 (32%)	36 (75%)	12 (25%)	0	0
	Stevenson	0 (0%)	30 (100%)	0 (0%)	17 (100%)	0	0
1956	Eisenhower	8 (10%)	70 (90%)	0 (0%)	2 (100%)	0	0
	Stevenson	27 (66%)	14 (44%)	20 (80%)	5 (20%)	0	0
1960	Nixon	66 (47%)	74 (53%)	9 (64%)	5 (36%)	7 (70%)	3 (30%)
	Kennedy	59 (56%)	46 (44%)	25 (66%)	13 (34%)	0	0
1964	Goldwater	56 (57%)	42 (43%)	17 (31%)	38 (69%)	6 (55%)	5 (45%)
	Johnson	33 (56%)	26 (44%)	12 (29%)	30 (71%)	0	0
1968	Nixon	25 (35%)	46 (65%)	19 (66%)	10 (34%)	0	0
	Humphrey	43 (36%)	76 (64%)	15 (42%)	21 (58%)	5 (100%)	0
1972	Nixon	17 (14%)	107 (86%)	0 (0%)	35 (100%)	0	0
	McGovern	32 (55%)	26 (45%)	28 (31%)	62 (69%)	1 (100%)	0

1976	Ford	32 (16%)	168 (84%)	6 (10%)	53 (90%)	2 (25%)	6 (75%)
	Carter	73 (58%)	53 (42%)	73 (82%)	16 (18%)	0	0
1980	Reagan	48 (37%)	81 (63%)	20 (22%)	70 (78%)	0	2 (100%)
	Carter	26 (23%)	86 (77%)	0 (0%)	68 (100%)	4 (80%)	1 (20%)
1984	Reagan	35 (27%)	97 (73%)	19 (17%)	91 (83%)	0	2 (100%)
	Mondale	85 (42%)	117 (58%)	20 (29%)	39 (71%)	0	0
1988	Bush	28 (23%)	93 (77%)	9 (12%)	69 (88%)	0	0
	Dukakis	42 (20%)	164 (80%)	32 (26%)	93 (74%)	2 (50%)	2 (50%)
1992	Bush	39 (56%)	31 (44%)	5 (6%)	85 (94%)	0	0
	Clinton	45 (27%)	122 (73%)	9 (5%)	159 (95%)	0	5 (100%)
1996	Dole	32 (29%)	79 (71%)	12 (6%)	173 (94%)	0	1 (100%)
	Clinton	13 (6%)	212 (94%)	0 (0%)	48 (100%)	0	3 (100%)
Total		879 (32%)	1867 (68%)	386 (24%)	1214 (76%)	27 (47%)	30 (53%)

Figure 11.15
Candidates and Others as Sources of Utterances

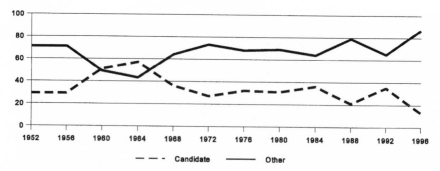

Figure 11.16
Source of Acclaims

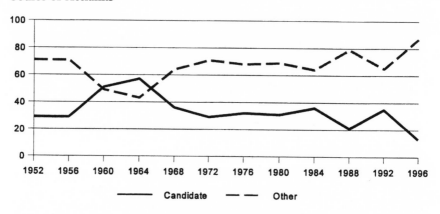

[Carroll O'Connor]: *Friends, I've seen some oddities off stage as well as on, but never anything odder than Jimmy Carter in a Democratic primary, because he may be the most Republican president since Herbert Hoover. And he may give us a depression that'll make Hoover's look like prosperity. Our money is worth less and less every day because of runaway prices. Soon it won't be worth the paper used to print it. We're looking at industrial lay-offs and unemployment in all parts of the country. We have a foreign policy nobody understands. And Jimmy stays in Washington making warm-hearted speeches. Maybe that's a smart political strategy, but I hope it doesn't fool too many people.* I hope you'll support a man who's out there facing problems. I mean my friend Senator Ted Kennedy. I've always liked him politically and personally, and I believe in his friends, in every way. So let's give him our vote, and give ourselves the best chance for a future with confidence and security.Thank you.

The following advertisement is from George Bush's Republican primary campaign that same year:

Figure 11.17
Source of Attacks

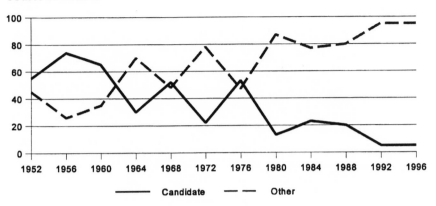

Table 11.12
Primary versus General Campaigns

Campaign	Acclaims	Attacks	Defenses
Primary	2868 (68%)	1248 (31%)	38 (1%)
General	2746 (60%)	1755 (39%)	**57 (1%)**
Total	5614 (65%)	3003 (34%)	**95 (1%)**

I'm George Bush. *In 1976, candidate Jimmy Carter said we didn't have an energy policy. We still don't.* Sure we have to conserve, but let's be more specific about what we have to do: get the government out of the energy business, tax dollars would go into research, not more bureaucracy. We've got to produce more energy; that means coal, safe nuclear, solar. We've pulled together before; we can do it now.

It is misleading to classify either advertisement as entirely positive or as negative. Each ad contains both positive (acclaiming) and negative (attacking) elements. The first example is clearly more negative than positive, while the second is more positive than negative. Even classifying them as "comparative" advertisements is misleading, because neither one is divided equally into positive (acclaiming) and negative (attacking) components. Again, their research is an extremely important contribution to the literature, but I believe that the most accurate way to analyze political television spots is by theme.

Why would general spots rely more heavily on attacks than primary spots? It seems likely that this is a function of the differences in a can-

Table 11.13
Attacks in Primary and General Presidential TV Spots

Candidate/Year	Primary	General
Eisenhower 1952	13%	69%
Kennedy 1960	23%	27%
Goldwater 1964	14%	34%
Nixon 1968	27%	29%
Nixon 1972	0%	22%
Ford 1976	0%	22%
Carter 1976	36%	41%
Reagan 1980	36%	42%
Carter 1980	29%	37%
Mondale 1984	27%	45%
Bush 1988	26%	39%
Dukakis 1988	14%	37%
Bush 1992	33%	56%
Clinton 1992	32%	49%
Dole 1996	47%	62%
Clinton 1996	39%	47%

didate's opponents in each stage of the campaign. In the primaries, a candidate runs against other members of his (again, all of these candidates were male) own party. Although there are differences among Republicans (and among Democrats), for the most part two candidates of the *same party* should have more in common—and therefore possess fewer differences to attack—than two candidates from *different parties*. Of course, there are differences between candidates from the same party, and these can develop into areas for attack. The point is that there are comparatively fewer differences between members of the same party than between members of different parties (and, of course, there are some similarities between candidates of different parties, but there are probably fewer points of commonality than between two candidates of the same party).

Table 11.14
Major Party versus Third-Party Candidates

Campaign	Acclaims	Attacks	Defenses
Major Party	2746 (60%)	1755 (39%)	57 (1%)
Third Party	224 (68%)	105 (32%)	0
Total	2970 (61%)	1860 (38%)	57 (1%)

There are also pressures which encourage candidates not to attack too much in the primaries. Candidates know that if they win their party's nomination, they will want their primary opponents to endorse them (if not actively campaign on their behalf) in the general campaign. Thus, savvy primary candidates may wish to avoid alienating their primary opponents by attacking them too much. Also, we have seen that attacks from the primaries can be used by the other party in the general campaign. For example, in 1964 Johnson used statements from Goldwater's primary opponents to attack Goldwater, and in 1980 Reagan spots used clips from Edward Kennedy's primary ads attacking Jimmy Carter. This could be another factor which moderates to a certain extent the amount of attack in primary campaigns. Of course, attacks are still quite common in the primaries; they are just less frequent at that stage than in the general campaign.

West (1997) reported that personal qualities were a more common topic in primary (39%) than in general campaigns (31%). My sample indicates that the percentage of personal qualities appeals (out of total character utterances) was 51% in the primaries and 49% in the general campaign. Thus, I do not agree that there is a significant difference in use of personal qualities by stage of the campaign (recall my reservations about West's sample, expressed earlier).

MAJOR VERSUS THIRD-PARTY CANDIDATES

Television spots from third-party candidates tend to be more positive (68%) than general campaign commercials from the major parties (60%). General campaign advertisements from Republicans and Democrats use more attacks (39%) than political spots from third-party candidates (32%). None of the third-party advertisements examined here included defenses (see Table 11.14).

Third-party candidates often try to portray themselves as an alternative to "politics as usual" in the major parties. This may account for the fact that they use somewhat fewer attacks than Republicans and Democrats: Their advertising strategies as well as their policy stands may be

Table 11.15
Functions of Presidential Television Spots

Campaign	Acclaims	Attacks	Defenses
Primary Republican	1260 (67%)	611 (32%)	14 (1%)
Primary Democrat	1415 (68%)	647 (31%)	23 (1%)
General Republican	1366 (64%)	747 (35%)	32 (1%)
General Democrat	1380 (57%)	1008 (42%)	25 (1%)
General Independent	224 (68%)	105 (32%)	0 (0%)
General	3020 (61%)	1860 (38%)	57 (1%)
Primary	2868 (68%)	1281 (31%)	38 (1%)
Total	5888 (65%)	3141 (34%)	95 (1%)

used to distinguish themselves from major party candidates. The major party candidates tend to battle one another, rarely attacking the third-party candidate. To my knowledge, no one has studied third-party candidates (Kaid, 1994, did study Perot in 1992). However, Benoit and Wells (1996) found that in the 1992 presidential debates, Clinton and Bush tended to attack each other much more than they attacked Perot. They speculated that Clinton and Bush may have hoped to attract some of Perot's supporters, which led them to eschew attacks against Perot.

Third-party candidates also produced no defenses in these spots. Fewer attacks on Perot meant that he needed, and produced, fewer defenses than the other candidates. Given that these third-party candidates were the target of fewer attacks than the major party candidates, they had less to defend, and in fact produced no defenses in these spots.

PRESIDENTIAL TELEVISION ADVERTISING: OVERALL FINDINGS

The tenor of presidential candidates' television advertising in general is largely positive. Across all campaigns (primary and general, major and third-party candidates), 65% of utterances functioned as acclaims. The second most common form of utterance is attacks, which constitute 34% of the remarks in these spots. Finally, defenses are relatively infrequent at 1% of the comments in these commercials (see Table 11.15).

The overall sample indicates that candidates' television spots focused more on policy (58%) than on character (42%). Policy utterances addressed past deeds (46%) most often, followed by general goals (32%), and finally future plans (22%). Character remarks discussed personal qualities (50%), leadership ability (31%), and ideals (19%). When these spots addressed past deeds, they were more likely to attack (59%) than acclaim (41%). This was also true of future plans (65% attacks, 35% acclaims). General goals were a different story: Goals were the basis of far more acclaims (89%) than attacks (11%). Turning to character, we see that acclaims were more common than attacks for each type of character utterance (personal qualities: 58%/42%; leadership ability: 80%/20%; ideals: 88%/12%) (see Table 11.16).

In these spots, acclaims were more likely to be uttered by others (67%) than by the candidates themselves (33%). Attacks were even more likely to originate with other sources (72%) than with the candidates (28%). Defenses were attributed to others (65%) more than to the candidates (35%). Thus, these spots rely more heavily on other speakers besides the candidates. The candidates have a strong presence (33%, 38%, 35%) in these advertisements, but not a dominating one (see Table 11.17).

Finally, I would like to address the question of these candidates' use of specific strategies for defense. As Table 11.18 reveals, the most common strategy was simple denial, accounting for more than seven out of ten defenses. As the name implies, this is a straightforward defense. It directly rejects the accusation as false. As such, it is relatively easy to develop and relatively simple for voters to evaluate. The second most common form of defense, defeasibility (18%), was used by Ford (1976) and Carter (1980) to excuse the relatively poor performance of the economy. The argument is that forces beyond the president's control, not the president himself, are responsible for the problem. The idea that there are multiple causes is more complex, and less satisfying for voters: Although it may be realistic, the idea that the president cannot control events is not one that encourages them to return Ford or Carter to the White House. Of course, they couldn't persuasively deny that the economy was troubled, so they used this strategy instead. However, it doesn't surprise me that simple denial was the most common defense in these television spots (and it was most common in both primary and general spots).

I also examined Table 11.1 to see if there is a relationship between attack and defense. In eight instances out of twelve, the candidate who defended (or, if both defended, the candidate who defended the most) was the target of a greater percentage of attack. Thus, it appears that attacks tend to provoke defenses. Benoit and Wells (1996) report that in the 1992 presidential debates, "the most attacks (from Clinton and Perot) were aimed at Bush, who has the largest number of defenses utterances, and the fewest attacks were leveled (by either Bush or Clinton) at Perot, who presented the least number of defenses" (p. 112). The idea that attacks provoke defenses seems quite reasonable.

Table 11.16
Forms of Policy and Character Utterances

Campaign	Policy (58%)			Character (42%)		
	Deeds	Plans	Goals	Qualities	Leadership	Ideals
Primary	345/481*	214/127	764/122	600/351	423/124	340/36
General	649/913	186/236	642/62	465/414	507/110	257/48
Third Party	15/53	10/7	84/5	54/39	27/3	34/4
Total	1009/1447 (46%)	410/770 (22%)	1490/189 (32%)	1119/804 (50%)	957/237 (31%)	631/88 (19%)

*acclaims/attacks

Table 11.17
Candidates and Others as Sources of Utterances

Campaign	Acclaim		Attack		Defense	
	Candidate	Other	Candidate	Other	Candidate	Other
Primary	942	1744	393	855	6	32
General	879	1867	386	1214	27	30
Third Party	74	152	40	65	0	0
Total	1895 (33%)	3763 (67%)	819 (28%)	2134 (72%)	33 (35%)	62 (65%)

Table 11.18
Use of Defensive Strategies

Campaign	Strategy				
	Simple Denial	Defeasibility	Differentiation	Shift Blame	Transcendence
Primary	28	9	-	-	-
General	41	8	3	3	2
Total	69 (73%)	17 (18%)	3 (3%)	3 (3%)	2 (2%)

CONCLUSION

Thus, I have identified and documented several trends in presidential television advertising (including greater density and increasing reliance on shorter spots). Incumbents are more likely to acclaim more than challengers, who, in contrast, attack more than incumbent party candidates. Republicans tend to acclaim somewhat more than Democrats, who attack more than Republicans. There is no clear difference in the spots of winners and losers, but there are systematic differences by position in the race. Candidates in closely contested elections acclaim the most, followed by those who lead their campaigns. The most attacks originate with candidates who trail throughout the campaign. There has been a gradual trend for presidential spots (both general and primary spots) to be more negative—although the single most negative advertising campaign in history was conducted by Eisenhower in 1952 (attacks accounted for 69% of his utterances). Only three other presidential candidates devoted more than half of their utterances to attacks (McGovern, 1972: 60%; Bush, 1992: 56%; Dole, 1996: 62%). Both primary and third-party spots are less negative (and more positive) than general spots. There has been a clear trend toward others speaking more than candidates in spots, and this is even more pronounced for attacks than acclaims.

NOTE

1. Kaid and Tedesco (1999) analyzed television spots from 1996, concluding that 61% of Dole's spots were negative, while 68% of Clinton's spots were negative. My analysis, in contrast, found more of Dole's themes to be negative (62%) than Clinton's (47%). They offer this example of a negative spot from Clinton:

> America's values. The President bans deadly assault weapons; *Dole/Gingrich vote no.* The President passes family leave; *Dole/Gingrich vote no.* The President stands firm: a balanced budget, protects Medicare, disabled children; *No again. Now Dole resigns, leaves gridlock he and Gingrich created.* The president's plan: balance the budget, protect Medicare, reform welfare. Do our duty to our parents, our children. America's values. (p. 213; emphasis added)

I underlined the positive parts (acclaims) and italicized the negative portions (attacks). The beginning of this spot is positive (primacy). The final three utterances are positive (recency). A word count reveals 44 words develop acclaims while fewer than half as many, 19, enact attacks. The first part of the spot balances acclaims of Clinton with corresponding attacks of Dole, but the end of the spot features acclaims of Clinton without corresponding attacks of Dole. Clearly, part of this spot is negative, but for these reasons, the "dominant content" of this spot should be considered positive rather than negative (this spot was coded 75% acclaims and 25% attacks in my analysis). This difference in coding procedures may explain the disparity in our results.

Chapter 12

Conclusions

This chapter is designed to highlight some of the most important implications of this study. First, this project has demonstrated the utility of the functional approach to televised political campaign discourse. This perspective has allowed us to develop an understanding of television spots from the inception of this message form through the most recent presidential contest. Candidates produce advertising that is replete with acclaims and attacks, and that also contains occasional defenses. Acclaims can help a candidate persuade voters that he (as mentioned earlier, all presidential candidates to this point have been men) is a desirable choice. Attacks can help reduce the apparent desirability of a candidate's opponent (or opponents, in the primary or in a campaign with a prominent third-party candidate). Defenses can be used in an attempt to restore lost desirability. Furthermore, these functions can occur on policy and character topics, and the functional theory of campaign discourse analyzes each of these broad topics into useful categories (policy: past deeds, future plans, general goals; character: personal qualities, leadership ability, ideals). While further breakdowns are possible (into topics of policy [e.g., foreign trade, national defense, taxation, the federal deficit, crime, education, transportation] or into kinds of personal qualities [e.g., honesty, courage, compassion]), this theory provides us with useful concepts for describing and understanding political campaign messages.

Past research on political spots has served us well. However, in my opinion, it is time to abandon the practice of classifying entire spots with a method that categorizes by themes. The traditional approach worked better when spots tended to focus on a single theme. However, candidates are likely to string together six or eight diverse topics in a single ad, combining acclaims and attacks as well as policy and character appeals. Consider this sample spot from Bush in 1992, which uses statements from ordinary citizens:

I saw the debate last night, and I've just got one conclusion, it's all George Bush.

I have, I still have a lot of confidence in my President.

I think we need Bush to keep us from a big spending Congress.

I don't trust Clinton.

The man says one thing and does another.

First he denies it and then he says well maybe it happened: you can't trust him.

If Clinton gets in what we're gonna see are more taxes.

One thing that's got me definitely for Bush is I remember what happened the last time we did things the way Bill Clinton wants to do 'em. (Bush, 1992, "Debate")

This commercial freely mixes acclaims of Bush (e.g., "I still have a lot of confidence in my President," "we need Bush to keep us from a big spending Congress") with attacks on Clinton (e.g., "I don't trust Clinton," "The man says one thing and does another," "If Clinton gets in we're gonna see more taxes"). This advertisement also discusses character (trust) as well as policy (taxes). Trying to categorize this spot as *either* acclaiming (positive) *or* attacking (negative), or as *either* policy (issue) *or* character (image), clearly ignores part of what voters see and hear. Even the expedient of classifying spots as "comparative" is only accurate if all spots devote an equal number of utterances to each function. The fact that spots are becoming increasingly dense (more themes per unit of time) renders the traditional approach increasingly problematic. My approach, classifying each theme in a spot (and classifying each theme according to both function and topic) is clearly superior.

There are several trends that emerge in this study. First, television spots are increasingly dense: The typical presidential advertisement crams more ideas into the same amount of time. Figure 11.1 vividly documents this trend. For example, Clinton ran this spot in 1996 ("Ignores"):

The facts Bob Dole ignores in his negative attacks: The deficit cut 60%. 10 million new jobs. Family income up $1,600 [since 1993]. Health insurance you don't lose when changing jobs. President Clinton: moving our economy ahead, helping families. Now a plan to cut taxes for college tuition: $500 per child tax credit. Break up violent gangs. Move 1 million from welfare to work. Dole resorts to desperate negative attacks. President Clinton is protecting our values.

This 30-second spot mentions eleven topics: Dole is engaging in negative campaigning, Clinton cut the deficit, created new jobs, increased family income, made health insurance portable; Clinton is helping economy, helping families, proposing a tuition tax credit, fighting gangs, moving people from welfare to work, protecting values. This trend means that candidates address a wider range of topics in a spot; however, it also means that they spend less time on each idea.

I believe this trend is a manifestation of several related trends in contemporary American society. As I pointed out in Chapter 1, Hallin's (1992) study found that the network news quotes candidates in far shorter segments (down from an average of 43 seconds in 1968 to only 9 seconds in 1988). The news media, in my opinion, are encouraging development and use of sound bites. Furthermore, it is quite possible that the "MTV" style of videography (which is not limited to MTV), with a series of shots of small duration either encourages, or reflects, a decreased attention span. The increasing diversity of the electorate combined with the skyrocketing costs of television time may also encourage candidates to take this shotgun approach of mentioning several topics without really discussing them. However, whatever the cause, it doesn't seem reasonable to believe that this trend is good for the electorate or for our democracy. The issues addressed in our presidential campaigns can be very complex, and five to ten seconds (or less) is just not enough to do them justice.

The presidential debates help to offset this tendency to some extent, but two factors mitigate against that. First, presidential debates frequently limit candidates to one to two minutes for their statements. The hour or hour and a half devoted to a debate is chopped up by format into much smaller units of time. Second, candidates may choose to spend their minute or two discussing many topics, so that their debate answers may sound much like their television spots. Most of the same potential pressures (all but cost) that encourage candidates to cover many topics in a television spot exist in a presidential debate as well.

Second, and consistent with this idea, is the fact that television spots have become shorter over time. Again, Figure 11.2 clearly reveals this trend. The turning point was 1976, the first time (since the experimentation of the 1950s) that 30-second spots outnumbered 60-second spots. Again, smaller spots mean less time for voters to learn about the candidates and their policies (remember that people obtain four times as much information from spots as from the news: Patterson & McClure, 1976; Kern, 1989).

A third pattern that emerges from this study is the fact that presidential television spots have become more negative over time (again, after the highly negative campaign in 1952). Figure 11.3 clearly reveals that campaign spots in 1956 and 1960 were over 80% acclaims (and fewer than 20% attacks), but this gap gradually narrowed until, in the 1990s, attacks were more prevalent than acclaims. Interestingly, people often think of 1988 (and Bush's campaign in particular) as a highly negative campaign. These advertisements may have had a more vicious tone (no one that I know codes this factor), and perhaps they were more misleading (e.g., Jamieson, 1996) than earlier commercials. However, Eisenhower in 1952 used the largest percentage of attacks of any presidential candidate in the history of televised political advertising.

Recently, there was more emphasis on policy than character in these spots. As Figure 11.4 demonstrates, since 1980 presidential television spots have consistently spent more time on issues than on character (although, as suggested above, they do not go into depth on these issues). They are not simply campaigning on image. Of course, these two topics are tightly intertwined. Surely candidates can attempt to influence voters' perceptions of the candidates by the policy stances attributed to candidates in their spots. As demonstrated earlier, policy attacks (e.g., inconsistent stands on policy issues) can be used to indict the candidates' character. Still, there is more of an emphasis on policy than character— despite George Bush's and Bob Dole's attacks on Bill Clinton's character in 1992 and 1996.

Furthermore, Figure 11.5 reveals that there is a fairly consistent distribution of policy remarks among past deeds (most common), general goals, and future plans (least common). However, the use of future plans has increased in the 1990s, which I take as a generally good sign. This means that the candidates are being more specific in their discussions of future policy. However, Figure 11.6 suggests that the candidates' use of the forms of character utterances are not as consistent as their use of the forms of policy. Personal qualities is often most common—especially so in the 1990s, when Bush and Dole were attacking Clinton's character.

This study reveals that defenses occur in presidential television spots, but not very frequently. Some candidates never defend at all in their spots. Other research (Benoit & Wells, 1996; Benoit, Blaney, & Pier, 1998) reveals that defenses are more common in presidential debates than in television spots. Several reasons account for the infrequency of defenses in advertisements. First, candidates may not want to remind (or inform) voters of attacks against them. They surely would be reluctant to spend their own campaign funds to disseminate attacks from their opponents! Furthermore, candidates may wish to stay "on message," devoting spots to the topics that favor themselves, not the topics that favor opponents. Furthermore, presidential candidates may wish to appear active rather than reactive. They may wish to avoid creating the impression that they are on the defensive. However, some attacks are so damaging that candidates feel forced to reply. The fact remains that defenses are relatively uncommon in these spots.

We can also make comparisons among different kinds of campaigns, or of different kinds of candidates, with the data from this study. Primary spots tend to be more positive than general campaign spots. Third-party spots are often more positive than spots from the major party candidates. This may reflect a conscious desire on the part of third-party candidates to appear distinct from "politics as usual" from the major party candidates, which as we've seen, are increasingly negative.

Incumbents are more positive than challengers, while challengers are more negative. Studies of the 1996 campaign (Benoit, Blaney, & Pier, 1998), the 1992 presidential debates (Benoit & Wells, 1996), Keynote Speeches from 1960 to 1996 (Benoit, Blaney, & Pier, 1996), and Acceptance Addresses from 1960 to 1996 (Benoit, Wells, Pier, & Blaney, in press) all found the same pattern. Incumbents have a record in office which serves as an important resource for acclaims by the incumbent and for attacks from the challenger. Furthermore, the incumbents often have a lead (five of the seven candidates who led throughout the race were incumbents), which may encourage them to acclaim and their (challenger) opponents to attack.

In television advertising, Republicans tended to be more positive than Democrats. However, this trend may not be as important as the previous one. Research on Acceptance Addresses (from 1960 to 1996) finds Republicans tend to attack more than Democrats (Benoit, Wells, Pier, & Blaney, 1998), but our study of Keynote Speeches (also from 1960 to 1996) revealed that Democrats attacked more than Republicans (Benoit, Blaney, & Pier, 1996). It may well be that situation (incumbency) is a more important influence on the functions of television spots than agent (political party).

There are no consistent differences in the television spots of winners and losers. However, their position in the race may influence the nature of their spots. Candidates in close races tend to use the most acclaims and fewest attacks (67%). Perhaps they are most concerned about alienating voters who profess to dislike mudslinging (Stewart, 1975; Merritt, 1984). Candidates who trail their opponents in the polls throughout the campaign use the most attacks (51%). They have the least to lose, and may feel it is worth the risk created by attacking so much. Finally, candidates who lead throughout the race acclaim at fairly high levels (61%), but still attack opponents with some frequency (38%), presumably to keep them from catching up.

Finally, as Figure 11.5 demonstrates, there is a trend for candidates to speak less in their spots, which are increasingly featuring other persons as sources. Figure 11.16 shows that this trend has nearly always been the case for acclaims. Figure 11.17 reveals that attacks in early campaigns were sometimes more from candidates and sometimes more from others.

Table 12.1
Clinton's and Dole's Use of Past Deeds and Future Plans in 1996

	Acclaims		Attacks	
	Past Deeds	Future Plans	Past Deeds	Future Plans
Dole	**No**	Yes	Yes	**No**
Clinton	Yes	Yes	Yes	Yes

SUGGESTIONS FOR CANDIDATES

This study helps us to understand what options are available to candidates. First, the functional theory of political campaigns makes it clear that candidates have three potential functions (acclaim, attack, defend) and two general topics (policy, character). It suggests that candidates can be specific (past deeds, future plans) or more general (general goals, ideals). Candidates can also discuss the past (past deeds), encouraging retrospective voting, or the future (future plans, general goals), encouraging prospective voting. Our study of the 1996 campaign (Benoit, Blaney, & Pier, 1998) found that Dole did not make use of these opportunities as well as Clinton. Clinton acclaimed both his past deeds and his future plans. Dole, in contrast, hardly ever developed acclaims concerning his past deeds. Clinton attacked both Dole's past deeds and his future plans. Dole, in contrast, rarely attacked Clinton's future plans. Thus, Clinton gave voters more information about the two candidates. Dole left out two very important parts of the story (the good things about his past; the bad things about Clinton's future). Finally, candidates can discuss their leadership ability or their personal qualities in their television spots (see Table 12.1).

This study has also revealed that candidates have many options for their acclaims and attacks, depending upon their own (and their opponents') circumstances. Incumbents (Eisenhower in 1956, Johnson in 1964, Nixon in 1972, Ford in 1976, Carter in 1980, Reagan in 1984, Bush in 1992, Clinton in 1996) have a record in the office sought. Surely this is one of the best, if not the best, possible source(s) of evidence about their likely performance if re-elected. These candidates acclaimed their record, and their opponents attacked it. Candidates who are "almost" incumbents (Vice Presidents Nixon in 1960, Humphrey in 1968, Bush in 1988) can attempt to take credit for current successes—and their opponents can blame them for current failures. Their opponents can also argue, as Kennedy did in 1960, that the vice president wasn't really responsible for successes of their administration. Some candidates have other governmental experience besides being president. Jimmy Carter (1976), Ronald Reagan (1980), Michael Dukakis (1988), Bill Clinton (1992) had been governors. They acclaimed their successes while their opponents attacked their failures. Bob Dole was a U.S. Senator, although as we saw above he rarely acclaimed his past deeds. Clinton certainly attacked his past deeds in the 1996 race. Candidates who have no governmental experience (e.g., Ross Perot, Steve Forbes, Pat Buchanan) acclaim their business experience (as did George Bush in 1988 and Lamar Alexander in 1996, who both had governmental experience as well). Those who are "outsiders" (like Ross Perot, Steve Forbes, and Pat Buchanan) can attempt to parlay this into an advantage by attacking the Washington establishment, and distancing themselves from it. If you've worked in government, stress your experience; if you haven't worked in government, stress your independence and new ideas.

Candidates also have a variety of options available for source of message. The obvious first decision is whether the candidate or others should speak in spots. When others do speak there are other choices. Should an anonymous narrator or announcer be used? Should the spot use an ordinary citizen or voter to speak? Some spots use celebrity endorsers or other political figures. Bob Dole used General Colin Powell in 1996. Occasionally, the candidates' wives (e.g., Nancy Reagan in 1980) appear in a commercial. At times one candidate uses an opponent's words (or video) as "reluctant testimony" to argue for inconsistency or broken promises. Pat Buchanan attacked George Bush in 1992 for having broken his "Read my lips: No new taxes" pledge. Kennedy's "Ike's Press Conference" spot in 1960 must have embarrassed (and angered) Nixon. Sometimes one campaign (e.g., Reagan in 1980) will use clips or statements from a contested primary to get another form of reluctant testimony (e.g., Edward Kennedy attacking fellow Democrat Jimmy Carter).

Although it does not emerge in the data I generated for this study, my analysis of political spots revealed that sources like charts, graphs, and video footage of criminals or polluted harbors are being used increasingly in political spots. Although I did not attempt to quantify its occurrence, spots from recent campaigns have begun to provide the source of evidence in a sort of footnote at the bottom of the screen. Perot used video "morphing" technology to have one voter transform into another in several of his commercials. Thus, as technology is increasing, candidates have more options for producing their television spots.

FUTURE RESEARCH ON POLITICAL ADVERTISING

Clearly, more work remains to be done on understanding political spots. As mentioned earlier, there has been sporadic study of primary spots (e.g., Devlin, 1994; Payne, Marlier, & Baukus, 1989; Shyles, 1984) or unpublished work on spots (Kaid & Ballotti, 1991) and sporadic study of non-presidential campaigns (Benze & Declercq, 1985; Johnston & White, 1994; Latimer, 1984, 1989; Nowlan & Moutray, 1984; Payne & Baukus, 1988; Prisuta, 1972; Rose & Fuchs, 1968; Tinkham & Weaver-Lariscy, 1995; or Tucker, 1959; Weaver-Lariscy & Tinkham, 1987). Only one study that I found focuses on radio spots (Shapiro & Rieger, 1992). Relatively little work has been conducted on political newspaper advertisements (Bowers, 1972; Humke, Schmitt, & Grupp, 1975). However, more work could clearly be done in each of these areas. Barbatis (1996) examines images, or "pictorial enactment," in negative spots. Boynton and Nelson (1997; Nelson & Boynton, 1997) have begun to study the audio portion of political spots (voices, music, and sound effects). Hughes (1994) focused on formal logic and fallacies to examine television spots. Kaid (1996; cf. Jamieson, 1996) has analyzed spots for technological distortion that raise ethical issues. My study also revealed a trend away from candidates speaking in their ads—especially in attacks. While quantitative studies have shown that sponsors can affect viewer perceptions (Garramone, 1985; Garramone & Smith, 1984; Kaid & Boydston, 1987), I am not aware of any experimental research that contrasts candidates and others as sources of utterances within spots.

Furthermore, there are areas in which this study could be developed further. For example, research could break down the nature of appeals to personal qualities, as suggested above (e.g., trustworthiness, tenacity, empathy). Policy utterances could be coded for topic (e.g., foreign trade, taxation, crime, education), and this could be compared with public opinion data on the topics most important to voters. Of course, new election years will inevitably bring forth an onslaught of new political spots for our study.

Appendix: The Sample

I began by buying as many videotapes of presidential television spots as I could afford (the Central States Communication Association Federation Prize provided much of these funds, along with the Loren Reid Fund, the Department of Communication, and the College of Arts and Sciences at the University of Missouri). I transcribed each advertisement into separate computer files for each campaign. I focused on verbal aspects of the ads (and described important visual and aural elements as well; however, many ads are simply "talking heads" where the candidate, a citizen, or another endorser stands or sits in front of the camera and talks). I was awarded a Big Twelve Fellowship to spend two weeks at the University of Oklahoma Political Communication Archive. When I worked in the Archive, I focused on locating and transcribing ads that were not on any of the videotapes I had purchased. As I watched an ad at the Archive, I used a word processor to search the file for that campaign to see if I had already transcribed that commercial from one of the tapes I had purchased. If so, I skipped to the next ad. On the other hand, if the spot was new to me, I transcribed it. Thus, I tried to make my stay at Oklahoma as efficient as possible, concentrating on adding spots that I could only find and view there.

I began with general election spots, which were my first priority. Then I tried to find a variety of primary spots, looking for ads from diverse campaigns and candidates. Finally, I wanted to locate some general election spots by third-party candidates. This would give me a variety of kinds of televisions spots, from a variety of candidates and campaigns, to compare and contrast.

GENERAL CAMPAIGN SPOTS

The length of television spots varied quite a bit. For example, in 1952, Eisenhower made at least twenty-nine 20-second "Eisenhower Answers America" spots. For 1956, I was able to locate only one 20-second spot for Eisenhower, along with a 2-minute spot, and five spots of about 4 minutes and 20 seconds. Historically, the most common formats for presidential television spots are 30 seconds and 60 seconds, but even there the 60-second spots are twice as long as the 30-second advertisements. Thus, because television spots vary in length, comparing the number of spots could be misleading. That is, thirty 60-second spots have twice as much opportunity to influence viewers as thirty 30-second spots. Therefore, I decided not to try to find an *equal number of commercials* for each candidate. Instead (in the general campaigns), I tried to locate an *equal amount of time* for each candidate. For general campaigns from the two major parties, my goal was to acquire one-half hour of television commercials from each candidate.

I did not expect to be able to obtain that much commercial time from the earliest campaigns (and I could not find that much for either 1952 or 1956): It is not certain that these early campaigns produced a half-hour of television spots (or, if they did, that they have all been preserved). Oddly enough, I also had trouble meeting this goal in the most recent campaigns. I suspect there are at least two reasons for my inability to locate 30 minutes of spots from recent campaigns. First, in recent years several spots were aired, for example, both as Bush/Quayle ads and as Republican National Committee ads. When this happened, what appeared to be two different commercials were actually just one spot (and so I treated them as a single commercial, rather than as two different ones). Second, during the 1960s most of the presidential advertisements I found were 60 seconds, and in the 1990s most were 30 seconds. However, the more recent campaigns did not appear to produce twice as many 30-second spots (as earlier campaigns made 60-second spots). Cost may well play a role here, assuming the costs of producing a television spot have increased dramatically in recent years as production values have increased. Also, campaigns may prefer to spend their money broadcasting a smaller group of more powerful spots than a large number (60 or more) of commercials. The sample of presidential television spots I obtained from the two major parties' general campaigns are described in Table A.1.

I was pleased that of the 24 candidates in these campaigns, I was able to obtain approximately 30 minutes of television advertisements for 15, 25 minutes for 6, and 14 or 15 minutes for the remaining 3 candidates. I worked hard to find 30 minutes from each of these candidates, but I could not locate any other general election spots for the 9 candidates for

Table A.1
General Election Democrat and Republican Presidential Spots

Campaign	Democrat		Republican	
1952	Stevenson	1010 (secs.)	Eisenhower	820 (secs.)
1956	Stevenson	1490	Eisenhower	1525
1960	Kennedy	1800	Nixon	1800
1964	Johnson	1810	Goldwater	1800
1968	Humphrey	1800	Nixon	1800
1972	McGovern	1800	Nixon	1780
1976	Carter	1820	Ford	1800
1980	Carter	1800	Reagan	1800
1984	Mondale	1800	Reagan	1800
1988	Dukakis	1800	Bush	1550
1992	Clinton	1575	Bush	980
1996	Clinton	1620	Dole	1530
Total	Democrats	20125	Republicans	18985

whom I have less than 30 minutes at the University of Oklahoma Archive. I would not be surprised if a some other spots for these candidates exist, but I believe my search was fairly exhaustive given the limitations on my time at the Archive (and the Curator was very helpful in locating my requests). Of course, as remarkable as the Archive's collection is—and I was very impressed by it—the Archive does not have every spot that was produced for these candidates (and some candidates may not have produced a half-hour of spots for the general campaign).

PRIMARY SPOTS

Once again I began collecting primary advertisements by purchasing videotapes and transcribing them into computer files so I could focus on ads not otherwise available to me while at the Oklahoma Archive. The picture for the sample of primary spots is somewhat chaotic. There are, of course, far more candidates, and the number of spots available for each varies widely. I suspect there are several reasons for this. First, primaries were less important in the nomination process in early years.

It was not necessary for the candidates to compete in all primaries, and there were fewer primaries in early years. As recently as 1968, for example, Humphrey was nominated without campaigning in a single primary (Levine, 1995). Thus, I believe there were far fewer primary ads produced in early years than recently. Second, I speculate that general campaign spots are more likely to be preserved than primary spots. Although in point of fact the primary campaign may in a very real sense determine who is elected (if one party is stronger, or conditions favor one party than the other), more attention is lavished on the general campaigns. Third, unsuccessful contenders may only produce a few spots and drops out of the race, while the leading contenders (and those with more money, usually the same candidates) make more spots throughout the primary campaign. This means the pool of primary ads varies considerably from candidate to candidate. Whatever the reason or reasons, I was unable to adopt the strategy used for collecting general spots from the two major parties (attempt to get a large block of time, like 30 minutes of spots, for each candidate)—there were simply too many candidates for whom there were few primary spots available. Nor did I have enough time to transcribe every primary spot in the Archive's collection.

So, I adopted two strategies for collecting primary advertisements. First, I wanted to obtain primary spots from many different campaigns and many different candidates. I preferred to have at least some spots from as many campaigns and candidates as possible rather than to have many spots from a few candidates in a few campaigns. Second, I tried to obtain primary spots from both successful (the eventual nominees) and unsuccessful candidates. Trying to include a wide variety of primary candidates sometimes meant limiting myself to five or ten spots from a given candidate (in Rockefeller's case, I have but a single primary spot). More primary spots were available for study at the Archive than I transcribed, but my time was limited. Third, when direct contrasts between candidates were obvious and there were numerous spots available, I tried to obtain an equal amount of advertising (e.g., in 1992 only Buchanan challenged Bush in the primaries, and I have nineteen Bush and nineteen Buchanan spots, about ten minutes each; for 1996, I found 40 Dole and 40 Clinton primary spots, about 20 minutes each, to contrast the eventual major party nominees). This is a compromise, but I had a limited amount of time to spend at the Archive (among my particular regrets is my inability to obtain any primary spots, if they were made, from Stevenson, Nixon in 1960, Johnson in 1964, Humphrey in 1968, or Reagan in 1984). Still, I obtained primary spots from both parties and from a variety of both successful and unsuccessful candidates. This procedure resulted in the sample of primary spots listed in Table A.2.

Table A.2
Presidential Primary Television Spots

Campaign	Republican	Time (secs.)	Democrat	Time (secs.)
1952	Eisenhower	645		
1960			Kennedy	1040
1964	Goldwater	210	McCarthy	360
1968	Nixon	720	Kennedy	310
	Rockefeller	60		
1972	Nixon	120	Humphrey	420
			Muskie	540
			Wallace	690
			McGovern	770
			McCarthy	90
			Jackson	300
1976	Reagan	450	Carter	240
	Ford	1080	Udall	300
			Wallace	300
1980	Anderson	840	Brown	330
	Baker	480	Carter	780
	Bush	840	Kennedy	1080
	Connally	600		
	Crane	270		
	Reagan	450		
1984			Cranston	90
			Glenn	120
			Hart	300
			McGovern	90
			Mondale	1450

Table A.2 (continued)

1988	Bush	180	Babbitt	180
	Dole	180	Dukakis	750
	DuPont	150	Gephardt	450
	Haig	150	Gore	120
	Kemp	300	Jackson	300
			Simon	210
1992	Buchanan	660	Brown	180
	Bush	630	Clinton	1290
			Harkin	180
			Kerry	240
			Tsongas	330
1996	Alexander	750	Clinton	1200
	Buchanan	390		
	Dole	1260		
	Forbes	1080		
	Gramm	360		
	Lugar	210		
	Taylor	240		
	Wilson	90		
Total	Republicans	13395	Democrats	15030

THIRD-PARTY CANDIDATE SPOTS

For third-party candidates, I adopted yet a third strategy. This was my lowest priority, so I selected only a few third-party candidates. When I saw what was available, I obtained every general election spot I could find (on my videotapes and at the Archive) for these third-party candidates. I believe my search was fairly exhaustive for these candidates (I decided not to include any of Perot's half-hour "infomercials" because I

Table A.3
Third-Party General Election Presidential Spots

Candidate/Campaign	Time (secs.)
Wallace 1968	340
Anderson 1980	840
Perot 1992	1230
Perot 1996	360
Browne 1996	300
Total	3070

believe spots that long are inherently different from spots of more traditional lengths in terms of audience attracted and how the audience processed them). I could have included other third-party candidates, but, again, my time was limited. My sample for third-party candidates is described in Table A.3.

Thus, my sample includes 371 Republican primary spots (over 220 minutes) and 394 Democratic primary spots (about 250 minutes). It has 423 Republican general ads (over 300 minutes) and 406 Democratic general ads (335 minutes). The sample also includes over 60 general television commercials from third-party candidates (over 50 minutes) (see Table A.4).

IDENTIFICATION OF SPOTS

There are a few other issues I would like to discuss concerning my sample. First, I acknowledge the possibility that a few advertisements could be misclassified. Many spots have slates that describe the candidate and the date (and other information, like the advertising agency). When an advertisement has a date of January or February, it is a safe bet that it is a primary spot; when a commercial has a date of September or October, it must be a general election spot. However, slates are not always present on reels of political spots, and so other clues must be used. In 1988, for example, a spot that lists "Bush for President" as the sponsoring organization would be a primary ad, while "Bush/Quayle" is a general ad. In 1992, that trick would not work, because both primary spots and general spots that year were sponsored by "Bush/Quayle." At times the advertisements mention a particular state's primary (several of George Wallace's ads talk about the Florida primary, for example). Other commercials may explicitly refer to the nomination (I found some

Table A.4
Total Sample of Presidential Television Spots

Campaign	Spots	Seconds	Minutes
Republican Primary	371	13395	223
Democratic Primary	394	15030	251
Republican General	423	18985	316
Democratic General	406	20125	335
Third Party	62	3070	51
Total	1656	70605	1177

1952 Eisenhower primary spots this way). Some spots implore voters to go to the polls, and a November date indicates a general campaign ad while a February or March date reveals a primary spot. However, not every spot has such information. Thus, while I was very careful to try to distinguish primary from general spots, I cannot guarantee that every advertisement is correctly classified.

Another factor is that some ads are produced but never broadcast. While such ads may allow inferences about the candidate and the ad agency, they tell us nothing about the messages to which voters were exposed during the election. Accordingly, I decided not to include in my sample any spots that I was certain had not been televised. Some spots were marked this way (as having never been aired) in the videotapes I purchased, so I skipped past them. However, videotapes I examined at the Archive did not indicate whether the ads had aired. Thus, I tried to include only spots that had been televised, but not all spots are clearly identified as broadcast or not. So it is possible that my sample includes some spots that were never viewed by voters.

Other information about these advertisements would be valuable, but either does not exist or is not available to me. I would find it very interesting to know when (and how often and where) a given spot was broadcast, which could be correlated with public opinion poll data, but that information simply is not readily available.

Finally, I would like to compare the sample in this study with the samples in Kaid and Johnston (1991), Kaid and Ballotti (1991), and West (1997). As Table A.5 shows, this sample has more primary and more general spots than West. It has virtually the same number of spots as Kaid and Johnston, but they are distributed differently, more evenly, and across more campaigns. It has fewer spots than Kaid and Ballotti, distributed over more campaigns.

Table A.5
Kaid & Johnston (1991), Kaid & Ballotti (1991), West (1997), and Benoit (this volume) Samples

Year	Kaid & Johnston (general)	Kaid & Ballotti (primary)	West		Benoit		
			Primary	General	Primary	General	Third Party
1952	-	-	0	16	3 (645*)	47 (1830*)	-
1956	-	-	8	8	0	21 (2935)	-
1960	97	-	2	14	16 (1040)	69 (3600)	-
1964	58	-	0	26	7 (210)	59 (3610)	-
1968	74	52	12	14	34 (1450)	58 (3600)	9 (340*)
1972	58	203	5	34	59 (2930)	58 (3580)	-
1976	122	180	8	28	60 (2490)	84 (3600)	-
1980	247	139	18	44	163 (5670)	94 (3600)	-
1984	93	272	1	22	61 (2050)	84 (3600)	6 (840)
1988	81	243	0	29	82 (2970)	87 (3090)	-
1992	-	-	37	16	108 (3510)	68 (2525)	22 (1230)
1996	-	-	44	11	172 (5580)	100 (3150)	25 (660)
Total	830	1089	262	135	765 (2845)	829 (38720)	62 (3070)

*seconds

References

Aden, R. C. (1989). Televised political advertising: A review of literature on spots. *Political Communication Review, 14*, 1–18.

Ansolabehere, S., & Iyengar, S. (1995). *Going negative: How political advertisements shrink and polarize the electorate.* New York: Free Press.

Atkin, C., & Heald, G. (1976). Effects of political advertising. *Public Opinion Quarterly, 40*, 216–28.

Atkin, C. K. (1977). Effects of campaign advertising and newscasts on children. *Journalism Quarterly, 54*, 503–8.

Barbatsis, G. S. (1996). "Look, and I will show you something you will want to see": Pictorial engagement in negative political campaign commercials. *Argumentation and Advocacy, 33*, 69–80.

Basil, M., Schooler, C., & Reeves, B. (1991). Positive and negative political advertising: Effectiveness of ads and perceptions of candidates. In F. Biocca (Ed.), *Television and political advertising* (vol. 1, pp. 245–62). Hillsdale, NJ: Erlbaum.

Becker, L. B., & Doolittle, J. C. (1975). How repetition affects evaluations of and information seeking about candidates. *Journalism Quarterly, 52*, 611–17.

Benoit, P. J. (1997). *Telling the success story: Acclaiming and disclaiming discourse.* Albany: State University of New York Press.

Benoit, W. L. (1995a). *Accounts, excuses, and apologies: A theory of image restoration strategies.* Albany: State University of New York Press.

Benoit, W. L. (1995b). Sears' repair of its auto service image: Image restoration discourse in the corporate sector. *Communication Studies, 46*, 89–109.

Benoit, W. L. (1997a). Hugh Grant's image restoration discourse: An actor apologizes. *Communication Quarterly, 45*, 251–67.

Benoit, W. L. (1997b). Image restoration discourse and crisis communication. *Public Relations Review, 23*, 177–86.

Benoit, W. L. (1998). Merchants of death: Persuasive defenses by the tobacco industry. In J. F. Klumpp (Ed.), *Argument in a time of change: Definition, frameworks, and critiques* (pp. 220–25). Annandale, VA: National Communication Association.

Benoit, W. L., & Anderson, K. K. (1996). Blending politics and entertainment: Dan Quayle versus Murphy Brown. *Southern Communication Journal, 62,* 73–85.

Benoit, W. L., Blaney, J. R., & Pier, P. M. (1996). *Attack, defense, and acclaiming in nominating convention keynote speeches.* Paper presented at the Speech Communication Association Convention, San Diego, CA.

Benoit, W. L., Blaney, J. R., & Pier, P. M. (1998). *Functions of campaign '96: Acclaiming, attacking, and defending discourse.* Westport, CT: Praeger.

Benoit, W. L., & Brinson, S. L. (1994). AT&T: Apologies are not enough. *Communication Quarterly, 42,* 75–88.

Benoit, W. L., & Brinson, S. L. (in press). Queen Elizabeth's image repair discourse: Insensitive royal or compassionate Queen? *Public Relations Review.*

Benoit, W. L., & Czerwinski, A. (1997). A critical analysis of USAir's image repair discourse. *Business Communication Quarterly, 60,* 38–57.

Benoit, W. L., & Dorries, B. (1996). *Dateline NBC's* persuasive attack on Wal-Mart. *Communication Quarterly, 44,* 463–77.

Benoit, W. L., Gullifor, P., & Panici, D. A. (1991). President Reagan's defense discourse on the Iran-Contra affair. *Communication Studies, 42,* 272–94.

Benoit, W. L., & Hanczor, R. (1994). The Tonya Harding controversy: An analysis of image repair strategies. *Communication Quarterly, 42,* 416–33.

Benoit, W. L., & Harthcock, A. (1998). *Functions of the great debates: Acclaims, attacks, and defenses in the 1960 presidential debates.* Unpublished manuscript.

Benoit, W. L., & Nill, D. (1998). Oliver Stone's defense of *JFK. Communication Quarterly, 46,* 127–43.

Benoit, W. L., & Nill, D. M. (in press). A critical analysis of Judge Clarence Thomas's statement before the Senate Judiciary Committee. *Communication Studies.*

Benoit, W. L., Pier, P. M., & Blaney, J. R. (1997). A functional analysis of presidential television spots: Acclaiming, attacking, and defending. *Communication Quarterly, 45,* 1–20.

Benoit, W. L., & Wells, W. T. (1996). *Candidates in conflict: Persuasive attack and defense in the 1992 presidential debates.* Tuscaloosa: University of Alabama Press.

Benoit, W. L., & Wells, W. T. (1998). An analysis of three image restoration discourses on Whitewater. *Journal of Public Advocacy, 3,* 21–37.

Benoit, W. L., Wells, W. T., Pier, P. M., & Blaney, J. R. (in press). Acclaiming, attacking, and defending in nominating convention acceptance addresses. *Quarterly Journal of Speech.*

Benze, J. G., & Declercq, E. R. (1985). Content of television political spot ads for female candidates. *Journalism Quarterly, 62,* 278–83, 288.

Blaney, J. R., & Benoit, W. L. (1997). The persuasive defense of Jesus in the Gospel according to John. *Journal of Communication and Religion, 20,* 25–30.

Bowers, R. A. (1972). Issue and personality information in newspaper political advertising. *Journalism Quarterly, 49,* 446–52.

Boynton, G. R., & Nelson, J. S. (1997). Making sound arguments: Would a claim by any other sound mean the same or argue as sweet? In J. F. Klumpp

(Ed.), *Argument in a time of change: Definitions, frameworks, and critiques* (pp. 12–17). Annandale, VA: National Communication Association.

Brinson, S. L., & Benoit, W. L. (1996). Dow Corning's image repair strategies in the breast implant crisis. *Communication Quarterly, 44,* 29–41.

Brinson, S. L., & Benoit, W. L. (in press). The tarnished star: Restoring Texaco's damaged public image. *Management Communication Quarterly.*

Burke, K. (1970). *Rhetoric of religion.* Berkeley: University of California Press.

Christ, W. G., Thorson, E., & Caywood, C. (1994). Do attitudes toward political advertising affect information processing of televised political commercials? *Journal of Broadcasting & Electronic Media, 38,* 251–70.

Clines, F. X. (1996, June 3). Experience has colored his lessons with regret. *New York Times,* p. A12.

Cronkhite, G., Liska, J., & Schrader, D. (1991). Toward an integration of textual and response analysis applied to the 1988 presidential campaign. In F. Biocca (Ed.), *Television and political advertising* (vol. 2, pp. 163–84). Hillsdale, NJ: Erlbaum.

Cundy, D. T. (1986). Political commercials and candidate image: The effect can be substantial. In L. L. Kaid, D. Nimmo, & K. R. Sanders (Eds.), *New perspectives on political advertising* (pp. 210–34). Carbondale: Southern Illinois Press.

Descutner, D., Burnier, D., Mickunas, A., & Letteri, R. (1991). Bad signs and cryptic codes in a postmodern world: A semiotic analysis of the Dukakis advertising. In F. Biocca (Ed.), *Television and political advertising* (vol. 2, pp. 93–114). Hillsdale, NJ: Erlbaum.

Devlin, L. P. (1977). Contrasts in presidential campaign commercials of 1972. *Central States Speech Journal, 28,* 238–49.

Devlin, L. P. (1982). Contrasts in presidential campaign commercials of 1980. *Political Communication Review, 7,* 1–38.

Devlin, L. P. (1986). An analysis of presidential television commercials, 1952–1984. In L. L. Kaid, D. Nimmo, & K. R. Sanders (Eds.), *New perspectives on political advertising* (pp. 21–54). Carbondale: Southern Illinois Press.

Devlin, L. P. (1987a). Campaign commercials. In L. P. Devlin (Ed.), *Political persuasion in presidential campaigns* (pp. 208–16). New Brunswick, NJ: Transaction Books.

Devlin, L. P. (1987b). Contrasts in presidential campaign commercials of 1984. *Political Communication Review, 12,* 25–55.

Devlin, L. P. (1989). Contrasts in presidential campaign commercials of 1988. *American Behavioral Scientist, 32,* 389–414.

Devlin, L. P. (1993). Contrasts in presidential campaign commercials of 1992. *American Behavioral Scientist, 37,* 272–90.

Devlin, L. P. (1994). Television advertising in the 1992 New Hampshire presidential primary election. *Political Communication, 11,* 81–99.

Devlin, L. P. (1997). Contrasts in presidential campaign commercials of 1996. *American Behavioral Scientist, 40,* 1058–84.

Diamond, E., & Bates, S. (1992). *The spot: The rise of political advertising on television* (3rd ed.). Cambridge, MA: MIT Press.

Donohue, T. R. (1973). Viewer perceptions of color and black-and-white paid political advertising. *Journalism Quarterly, 50,* 660–65.

Faber, R. J., & Storey, M. C. (1984). Recall of information from political advertising. *Journal of Advertising, 13,* 39–44.

Faber, R. J., Tims, A. R., & Schmitt, K. G. (1993). Negative political advertising and voting intent: The role of involvement and alternative information sources. *Journal of Advertising, 22,* 67–76.

Fisher, W. R. (1970). A motive view of communication. *Quarterly Journal of Speech, 56,* 131–39.

Fleiss, J. L. (1981). *Statistical methods for ratios and proportions.* New York: Wiley.

Foote, J. S. (1991). Implications of presidential communication for electoral success. In L. L. Kaid, J. Gerstle, & K. R. Sanders (Eds.), *Mediated politics in two cultures: Presidential campaigning in the United States and France* (pp. 261–70). New York: Praeger.

Garramone, G. M. (1984). Voter responses to negative political ads. *Journalism Quarterly, 61,* 250–69.

Garramone, G. M. (1985). Effects of negative political advertising: The roles of sponsor and rebuttal. *Journal of Broadcasting and Electronic Media, 29,* 147–59.

Garramone, G. M., Atkin, C. K., Pinkleton, B. E., & Cole, R. T. (1990). Effects of negative political advertising on the political process. *Journal of Broadcasting and Electronic Media, 34,* 299–311.

Garramone, G. M., & Smith, S. J. (1984). Reactions to political advertising: Clarifying sponsor effects. *Journalism Quarterly, 51,* 771–75.

Geiger, S. F., & Reeves, B. (1991). The effects of visual structure and content emphasis on the evaluation and memory for political candidates. In F. Biocca (Ed.), *Television and political advertising* (vol. 1, pp. 125–43). Hillsdale, NJ: Erlbaum.

Geer, J. G. (1998). Campaigns, party competition, and political advertising. In J. G. Geer (Ed.), *Politicians and party politics* (pp. 186–217). Baltimore, MD: Johns Hopkins University Press.

Ghorpade, S. (1986). Agenda setting: A test of advertising's neglected function. *Journal of Advertising Research, 26,* 23–27.

Gold, E. R. (1978). Political *apologia*: The ritual of self-defense. *Communication Monographs, 46,* 306–16.

Griffin, M., & Kagan, S. (1996). Picturing culture in political spots: 1992 campaigns in Israel and the United States. *Political Communication, 13,* 43–61.

Gronbeck, B. E. (1978). The functions of presidential campaigning. *Communication Monographs, 45,* 268–80.

Gronbeck, B. E. (1992). Negative narratives in 1988 presidential campaign ads. *Quarterly Journal of Speech, 78,* 333–46.

Hallin, D. (1992). Sound bite news: Television coverage of elections, 1968–1988. *Journal of Communication, 42,* 5–24.

Hill, R. P. (1989). An exploration of voter responses to political advertisements. *Journal of Advertising, 18,* 14–22.

Hitchon, J. C., & Chang, C. (1995). Effects of gender schematic processing on the reception of political commercials for men and women candidates. *Communication Research, 22,* 430–58.

Hofstetter, C. R., & Zukin, C. (1979). TV network news and advertising in the Nixon and McGovern campaigns. *Journalism Quarterly, 56,* 106–15, 152.

Holtz-Bacha, C., & Kaid, L. L. (1995). A comparative perspective on political advertising. In L. L. Kaid & C. Holtz-Bacha (Eds.), *Political advertising in western democracies: Parties and candidates on television* (pp. 8–18). Thousand Oaks, CA: Sage.

Holtz-Bacha, C., Kaid, L. L., & Johnston, A. (1994). Political television advertising in western democracies: A comparison of campaign broadcasts in the Unites States, Germany, and France. *Political Communication, 11,* 67–80.

Hughes, E. M. B. G. (1994). *The logical choice: How political commercials use logic to win votes.* Lanham, MD: University Press of America.

Humke, R. G., Schmitt, R. L., & Grupp, S. E. (1975). Candidates, issues and party in newspaper political advertisements. *Journalism Quarterly, 52,* 499–504.

Iyengar, S., & Kinder, D. R. (1988). *News that matters: Television and American opinion.* Chicago: University of Chicago Press.

Jackson, J. S., & Crotty, W. (1996). *The politics of presidential selection.* New York: HarperCollins.

James, K. E., & Hensel, P. J. (1991). Negative advertising: The malicious strain of comparative advertising. *Journal of Advertising, 20,* 53–69.

Jamieson, K. H. (1989). Context and the creation of meaning in the advertising of the 1988 presidential campaign. *American Behavioral Scientist, 32,* 415–24.

Jamieson, K. H. (1992a). *Dirty politics: Deception, distraction, and democracy.* New York: Oxford University Press.

Jamieson, K. H. (1992). *Packaging the presidency: A history and criticism of presidential campaign advertising* (2nd ed.). New York: Oxford University Press.

Jamieson, K. H. (1996). *Packaging the presidency: A history and criticism of presidential campaign advertising* (3rd ed.). New York: Oxford University Press.

Johnson-Cartee, K. S., & Copeland, G. (1989). Southern voters' reactions to negative political ads in the 1986 election. *Journalism Quarterly, 66,* 888–93, 986.

Johnson-Cartee, K. S., & Copeland, G. (1993). *Negative political advertising: Coming of age.* Hillsdale, NJ: Erlbaum.

Johnson-Cartee, K. S., & Copeland, G. (1997). *Manipulation of the American voter: Political campaign commercials.* Westport, CT: Praeger.

Johnston, A. (1991). Political broadcasts: An analysis of form, content, and style in presidential communication. In L. L. Kaid, J. Gerstle, & K. R. Sanders (Eds.), *Mediated politics in two cultures: Presidential campaigning in the United States and France* (pp. 59–72). New York: Praeger.

Johnston, A., & White, A. B. (1994). Communication styles and female candidates: A study of the political advertising during the 1986 Senate elections. *Journalism Quarterly, 71,* 321–20.

Johnston, D. D. (1989). Image and issue political information: Message content or interpretation? *Journalism Quarterly, 66,* 379–82.

Joslyn, R. (1986). Political advertising and the meaning of elections. In L. L. Kaid, D. Nimmo, & K. R. Sanders (Eds.), *New perspectives on political advertising* (pp. 139–83). Carbondale: Southern Illinois Press.

Joslyn, R. A. (1980). The content of political spot ads. *Journalism Quarterly, 57,* 92–98.

Joslyn, R. A. (1981). The impact of campaign spot advertising on voting defections. *Human Communication Research, 7,* 347–60.

Just, M., Crigler, A., & Wallach, L. (1990). Thirty seconds or thirty minutes: What viewers learn from spot advertisements and candidate debates. *Journal of Communication, 40,* 120–32.

Kaid, L. L. (1991). The effects of television broadcasts on perceptions of presidential candidates in the United States and France. In L. L. Kaid, J. Gerstle, & K. R. Sanders (Eds.), *Mediated politics in two cultures: Presidential campaigning in the United States and France* (pp. 247–60). New York: Praeger.

Kaid, L. L. (1994). Political advertising in the 1992 campaign. In R. E. Denton (Ed.), *The 1992 presidential campaign: A communication perspective* (pp. 111–27). Westport, CT: Praeger.

Kaid, L. L. (1996). Technology and political advertising: The application of ethical standards to the 1992 spots. *Communication Research Reports, 13,* 129–37.

Kaid, L. L. (1997). Effects of the television spots on images of Dole and Clinton. *American Behavioral Scientist, 40,* 1085–94.

Kaid, L. L., & Ballotti, J. (1991). *Television advertising in presidential primaries and caucuses.* Paper presented at the annual conference of the Speech Communication Association, Atlanta, GA.

Kaid, L. L., & Boydson, J. (1987). An experimental study of the effectiveness of negative political advertisements. *Communication Quarterly, 35,* 193–201.

Kaid, L. L., & Davidson, D. K. (1986). Elements of video style: Candidate presentation through television advertising. In L. L. Kaid, D. Nimmo, & K. R. Sanders (Eds.), *New perspectives on political advertising* (pp. 184–209). Carbondale: Southern Illinois Press.

Kaid, L. L., & Holtz-Bacha, C. (1995a). An introduction to parties and candidates on television. In L. L. Kaid & C. Holtz-Bacha (Eds.), *Political advertising in western democracies: Parties and candidates on television* (pp. 1–7). Thousand Oaks, CA: Sage.

Kaid, L. L., & Holtz-Bacha, C. (1995b). Political advertising across cultures: Comparing content, styles, and effects. In L. L. Kaid & C. Holtz-Bacha (Eds.), *Political advertising in western democracies: Parties and candidates on television* (pp. 206–27). Thousand Oaks, CA: Sage.

Kaid, L. L., & Johnston, A. (1991). Negative versus positive television advertising in U.S. presidential campaigns, 1960–1988. *Journal of Communication, 41,* 53–64.

Kaid, L. L., Leland, C. M., & Whitney, S. (1992). The impact of televised political ads: Evoking viewer responses in the 1988 presidential campaign. *Southern Communication Journal, 57,* 285–95.

Kaid, L. L., Nimmo, D., & Sanders, K. R. (Eds.) (1986). *New perspectives on political advertising.* Carbondale: Southern Illinois Press.

Kaid, L. L., & Sanders, K. R. (1978). Political television commercials: An experimental study of type and length. *Communication Research, 5,* 57–70.

Kaid, L. L., & Tedesco, J. C. (1999). Presidential candidate presentation: Videostyle in the 1996 presidential spots. In L. L. Kaid & D. G. Bystrom (Eds.), *The electronic election: Perspectives on the 1996 campaign communication* (pp. 209–21). Mahwah, NJ: Lawrence Erlbaum Associates.

Kennedy, K. A., & Benoit, W. L. (1997). The Newt Gingrich book deal controversy: Self-defense rhetoric. *Southern Communication Journal, 62,* 197–216.

Kern, M. (1989). *30 second politics: Political advertising in the eighties.* New York: Praeger.

Lang, A. (1991). Emotion, formal features, and memory for televised political advertisements. In F. Biocca (Ed.), *Television and political advertising* (vol. 1, pp. 221–43). Hillsdale, NJ: Erlbaum.

Larson, C. U. (1982). Media metaphors: Two models for rhetorically criticizing the political television spot advertisement. *Central States Speech Journal, 33,* 533–46.

Latimer, M. K. (1984). Policy issues and personal images in political advertising in a state election. *Journalism Quarterly, 61,* 776–84, 852.

Latimer, M. K. (1989). Legislators' advertising messages in seven state campaigns in 1986. *Journalism Quarterly, 66,* 338–48, 527.

Levine, M. A. (1995). *Presidential campaigns and elections: Issues and images in the media age.* Itasca, IL: Peacock Publishers.

Loden, A. D. (1989). Political advertising bibliography. *Political Communication Review, 14,* 19–46.

Martinez, M. D., & Delegal, T. (1990). The irrelevance of negative campaigns to political trust: Experimental and survey results. *Political Communication and Persuasion, 7,* 25–40.

McClure, R. D., & Patterson, T. E. (1974). Television news and political advertising: The impact of exposure on voter beliefs. *Communication Research, 1,* 3–21.

Meadow, R. G., & Sigelman, L. (1982). Some effects and non-effects of campaign commercials: An experimental study. *Political Behavior, 4,* 163–75.

Merritt, S. (1984). Negative political advertising: Some empirical findings. *Journal of Advertising, 13,* 27–38.

Mulder, R. (1979). The effects of televised political ads in the 1975 Chicago mayoral election. *Journalism Quarterly, 56,* 335–41.

Nelson, J. S., & Boynton, G. R. (1997). *Video rhetorics: Televised advertising in American politics.* Urbana: University of Illinois Press.

Newhagen, J. E., & Reeves, B. (1991). Emotion and memory responses for negative political advertising: A study of television commercials used in the 1988 presidential election. In F. Biocca (Ed.), *Television and political advertising* (vol. 1, pp. 197–220). Hillsdale, NJ: Erlbaum.

Nie, N. H., Verba, S., & Petrocik, J. R. (1979). *The changing American voter,* enlarged ed. Cambridge, MA: Harvard University Press.

Nowlan, J. D., & Moutray, M. J. (1984). Broadcast advertising and party endorsements in a statewide primary. *Journal of Broadcasting, 28,* 361–63.

Palda, K. S. (1973). Does advertising influence votes? An analysis of the 1966 and 1970 Quebec elections. *Canadian Journal of Political Science, 6,* 638–55.

Patterson, T. E. (1980). *The mass media election: How Americans choose their president.* New York: Praeger.

Patterson, T. E., & McClure, R. D. (1973). Political advertising on television: Spot commercials in the 1972 presidential election. *Maxwell Review,* 57–69.

Patterson, T. E., & McClure, R. D. (1976). *The unseeing eye: The myth of television power in national politics.* New York: Putnam.

Payne, J. G., & Baukus, R. A. (1988). Trend analysis of the 1984 GOP senatorial spots. *Political Communication and Persuasion, 5,* 161–77.

Payne, J. G., Marlier, J., & Baukus, R. A. (1989). Polispots in the 1988 presidential primaries: Separating the nominees from the rest of the guys. *American Behavioral Scientist, 32,* 365–81.

Pfau, M., Diedrich, T., Larson, K. M., & van Winkle, K. M. (1993). Relational and competence perceptions of presidential candidates during primary election campaigns. *Journal of Broadcasting & Electronic Media, 37,* 275–92.

Pfau, M., & Kenski, H. C. (1990). *Attack politics: Strategy and defense.* New York: Praeger.

Popkin, S. L. (1994). *The reasoning voter: Communication and persuasion in presidential campaigns.* Chicago: University of Chicago Press.

Prisuta, R. H. (1972). Broadcast advertising by candidates for the Michigan legislature: 1970. *Journal of Broadcasting, 16,* 453–59.

Roberts, M., & McCombs, M. (1994). Agenda setting and political advertising: Origins of the news agenda. *Political Communication, 11,* 249–62.

Roddy, B. L., & Garramone, G. M. (1988). Appeals and strategies of negative political advertising. *Journal of Broadcasting & Electronic Media, 32,* 415–27.

Rose, E. D., & Fuchs, D. (1968). Reagan vs. Brown: A TV image playback. *Journal of Broadcasting, 12,* 247–60.

Rudd, R. (1986). Issues as image in political campaign commercials. *Western Journal of Speech Communication, 50,* 102–18.

Rudd, R. (1989). Effects of issue specificity, ambiguity on evaluations of candidate image. *Journalism Quarterly, 66,* 675–82, 691.

Ryan, H. R. (1982). *Kategoria* and *apologia*: On their rhetorical criticism as a speech set. *Quarterly Journal of Speech, 68,* 256–61.

Schlenker, B. R. (1980). *Impression management: The self-concept, social identity, and interpersonal relations.* Monterey, CA: Brooks/Cole.

Schleuder, J., McCombs, M., & Wanta, W. (1991). Inside the agenda-setting process: How political advertising and TV news prime viewers to think about issues and candidates. In F. Biocca (Ed.), *Television and political advertising* (vol. 1, pp. 265–309). Hillsdale, NJ: Erlbaum.

Scott, M. H., & Lyman, S. M. (1968). Accounts. *American Sociological Review, 33,* 46–62.

Shapiro, M. A., & Rieger, R. H. (1992). Comparing positive and negative political advertising on radio. *Journalism Quarterly, 69,* 135–45.

Shyles, L. (1983). Defining the issues of a presidential election from televised political spot advertisements. *Journal of Broadcasting, 27,* 333–43.

Shyles, L. (1984). The relationships of images, issues, and presentational methods in televised spot advertisements for 1980's American presidential primaries. *Journal of Broadcasting, 28,* 405–21.

Shyles, L. (1986). The televised political spot advertisement: Its structure, content, and role in the political system. In L. L. Kaid, D. Nimmo, & K. R. Sanders (Eds.), *New perspectives on political advertising* (pp. 107–38). Carbondale: Southern Illinois Press.

Shyles, L. (1991). Issue content and legitimacy in 1988 televised political advertising: Hubris and synecdoche in promoting presidential candidates. In F. Biocca (Ed.), *Television and political advertising* (vol. 2, pp. 133–62). Hillsdale, NJ: Erlbaum.

Smith, L. D., & Johnston, A. (1991). Burke's sociological criticism applied to political advertising: An anecdotal taxonomy of presidential commercials. In F. Biocca (Ed.), *Television and political advertising* (vol. 2, pp. 115–31). Hillsdale, NJ: Erlbaum.

Splaine, J. (1995). *The road to the White House since television.* Washington, DC: C-SPAN.

Steele, C. A., & Barnhurst, K. G. (1996). The journalism of opinion: Network news coverage of U.S. presidential campaigns, 1968–1988. *Critical Studies in Mass Communication, 13,* 187–209.

Stewart, C. J. (1975). Voter perception of mudslinging in political communication. *Central States Speech Journal, 26,* 279–86.

Thorson, E., Christ, W. G., & Caywood, C. (1991). Effects of issue-image strategies, attack and support appeals, music, and visual content in political commercials. *Journal of Broadcasting and Electronic Media, 35,* 465–86.

Tinkham, S. F., & Weaver-Lariscy, R. A. (1995). *Political Communication, 12,* 291–304.

Trent, J. D., & Trent, J. S. (1995). The incumbent and his challengers: The problem of adapting to prevailing conditions. In K. E. Kendall (Ed.), *Presidential campaign discourse: Strategic communication problems* (pp. 69–93). Albany: State University of New York Press.

Trent, J. S., & Friedenberg, R. V. (1995). *Political campaign communication: Principles and practices* (3rd ed.). Westport, CT: Praeger.

Trent, J. S., & Trent, J. D. (1974). The rhetoric of the challenger: George Stanley McGovern. *Central States Speech Journal, 25,* 11–18.

Tucker, D. E. (1959). Broadcasting in the 1956 Oregon senatorial campaign. *Journal of Broadcasting, 3,* 225–43.

Wanat, J. (1974). Political broadcast advertising and primary election voting. *Journal of Broadcasting, 18,* 413–22.

Ware, B. L., & Linkugel, W. A. (1973). They spoke in defense of themselves: On the generic criticism of *apologia. Quarterly Journal of Speech, 59,* 273–83.

Weaver-Lariscy, R. A., & Tinkham, S. F. (1987). The influence of media expenditure and allocations strategies in congressional advertising campaigns. *Journal of Advertising, 16,* 13–21.

Wells, W. T. (in progress). *Attacking, acclaiming, and defending in the 1976–1984 presidential debates.* Ph.D. Dissertation, University of Missouri, Columbia.

Weisberg, H. F., & Kimball, D. C. (1993). *The 1992 presidential election: Party identification and beyond.* Paper presented at the American Political Science Association, Washington, DC (quoted in M. A. Levine, 1995. *Presidential campaigns and elections: Issues and images in the media age.* Itasca, IL: Peacock Publishers).

West, D. M. (1993). *Air wars: Television advertising in election campaigns, 1952–1992.* Washington, DC: Congressional Quarterly.

West, D. M. (1997). *Air wars: Television advertising in election campaigns, 1952–1996* (2nd ed.). Washington, DC: Congressional Quarterly.

West, D. M., Kern, M., Alger, D., & Goggin, J. M. (1995). Ad buys in presidential campaigns: The strategies of electoral appeal. *Political Communication, 12,* 275–90.

Name Index

Subject Index

About the Author

WILLIAM L. BENOIT is Professor of Communication at the University of Missouri. Among his earlier publications are *Accounts, Excuses, and Apologies: A Theory of Image Restoration Strategies* (1995), *Candidates in Conflict: Persuasive Attack and Defense in the 1992 Presidential Debates* (1996, with William T. Wells), and his first Praeger book, *Campaign '96: A Functional Analysis of Acclaiming, Attacking, and Defending* (1998, with Joseph R. Blaney and P. M. Pier).

ISBN 0-275-96645-3

90000>

EAN

9 780275 966454

HARDCOVER BAR CODE